MARK GRIFFITHS & JOANNE FOSTER

THE LIGHTBRINGERS

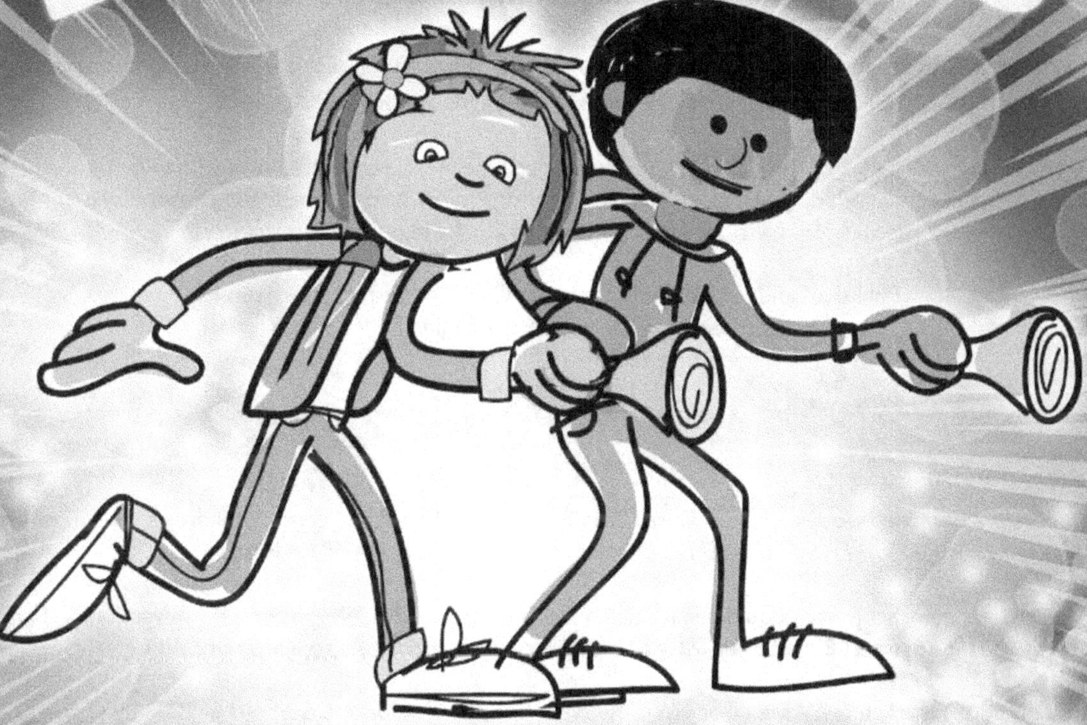

FREEDOM IN CHRIST FOR CHILDREN

CHURCH EDITION LEADER'S GUIDE

The Lightbringers Church Edition Leader's Guide
British English Version
(also available: American English Version)

Copyright © 2019 Freedom In Christ Ministries International

The right of Mark Griffiths and Joanne Foster to be identified as the authors of this work has been asserted by them in accordance with the Copyright, Designs and Patents Act 1988.

All rights reserved. No part of this publication may be reproduced or transmitted in any form or by any means, electronic or mechanical, including photocopy, recording or any information storage and retrieval system, without permission in writing from Freedom in Christ Ministries International.

Published and printed by Freedom In Christ Ministries International
4 Beacontree Plaza, Gillette Way, Reading RG2 0BS, UK.

ISBN 978 1 913082 05 5

First edition 2019

"*The Lightbringers* Trail: *Steps To Freedom In Christ*" has been adapted from the original children's version of *The Steps To Freedom In Christ* by kind permission of Dr. Neil T. Anderson.

Unless otherwise stated, Scripture quotations are taken from the Holy Bible, New International Version, © 1973, 1978, 1984 by the International Bible Society. Used by permission of Hodder & Stoughton Ltd. All rights reserved.

Scripture quotations marked NCV are taken from the New Century Version®. Copyright © 2005 by Thomas Nelson. Used by permission. All rights reserved.

Scripture quotations marked NLT are taken from the Holy Bible, New Living Translation, copyright © 1996, 2004, 2015 by Tyndale House Foundation. Used by permission of Tyndale House Publishers, Inc., Carol Stream, Illinois 60188. All rights reserved.

A catalogue record for this book is available from the British Library.

What Leaders Say

"What a brilliant resource for any church wanting to release a generation to live their lives for Jesus today. Whether you have ones or hundreds of children in your church, Lightbringers will enable them to grow as disciples and continue to be in awe and wonder at the love father God has for them. I am very excited to see the impact this will have with my own children as well as those I work with."
Rick Otto, Head of Kids & Family Ministry for New Wine, UK

"*The Lightbringers* Curriculum is a great resource to help parents and church leaders to bring life and freedom to kids' lives and that is a blessing to any family or Church. It is comprehensive and interactive. Well done team!"
Tammy Tolman, speaker and author, Sydney, Australia

"As an educator who supervises and trains elementary teachers and works extensively with children in both church, and public and private schools settings, I highly endorse and am excited to use *The Lightbringers* discipleship course. *The Lightbringers* is a much-needed resource for churches which provides children with an opportunity to move from simply knowing about Jesus to growing as His disciples. The lessons are presented in an interactive, age-appropriate, and engaging way that equip children to live their lives as followers of Jesus to the full."
Kathleen Matson, PhD, Trainer of elementary teachers, University Supervisor, Adjunct Professor George Mason University, Church deacon and lay leader, Virginia, USA

"Fantastic material, sensitively and appropriately pitched, so that children and young people will encounter Jesus' power to save and heal. Raising emotionally healthy children is one of, if not the greatest, priority for every parent and every church. This will help you do it!"
Paul Harcourt, National Leader, New Wine England, UK

"Parents, educators, children's leaders, and pastors rejoice! There is no longer a void in quality children's curriculum that instills the essentials of identity in Christ and freedom in Christ. *The Lightbringers* curriculum is the best biblically-based, faith-equipping, childhood resource bar none. It hits the mark with content, construct, and user-friendliness. Teachers, parents and kids will all love this resource."
Chris Campbell M.A.B.S.; M.A.P.C. Founder of Resolutions Counseling Inc.; Director of Generation Freedom and FiCM U.S. Staff, USA.

"What a powerful resource to put in the hands of parents and children's workers! *The Lightbringers* course enables children to be rooted in crucial foundations of how to live life with Christ to the full. The creation of this course enables children to be equipped along the same journey as adults, but in a way that makes sense to them. *The Lightbringers* course is also so flexible that it empowers parents to do it with their children at home, at their own pace. This is a brilliant resource and an important step forward in equipping multiple generations to walk in freedom and discipleship together."
Rachel Turner, Parenting for Faith, UK

"This is brilliant stuff. Mark and Jo have done the seeming impossible with this work which offers a tool to bridge the cultural gap between generations, and promises to effectively grow a generation hungry to live and minister in the power of the Holy Spirit. We commend this resource to you, secure in the knowledge that many churches in New Zealand are crying out for this very material."
Lydia Read, Senior Pastor, Hope Vineyard, Palmerston North, New Zealand

"Mark Griffiths is back with another groundbreaking and life-changing project for kids. Along with Jo Foster, they have created a resource that will help 5-to-11-year-olds know who they are in Jesus and also equip them as they grow into young adults in their faith. Throw in a bunch of great new songs, online resources, downloads and teaching videos, and this is a world-class resource that you as a family or church need to access. As a father of three, I know how vital and important it is to ensure that our children not only know Jesus as their friend and saviour, but to also grow in their walk with Him and to be fruitful disciples in this busy crazy world we live in. I can't recommend this resource more highly. Go get it!"
Simon Parry, Kids Songwriter and Founder of Allstars Kids Club, UK

"In my parish ministry, "Freedom in Christ" continues to be a powerful tool to help new Christians bear fruit. The key truths and the way they are presented have produced a deep and lasting impact on Christians who were stuck in their growth. The new ministry tool for children called *The Lightbringers* looks great! I'm looking forward to it being translated into Spanish so I can start using it with the children of my parish."
Modesto Álvarez Calvo, Catholic Parish priest in Madrid, Spain

"Leading children to a place where they genuinely know God is one of the major needs in the church today. My own research has shown that by the time most church kids reach their teenage years they still do not know how to pray, how to read their Bible or how to face temptation. This is the problem that this new curriculum seeks to address. I am a great fan of Mark Griffiths' writings. I have seen his earlier curriculums touch the lives of thousands of kids all over the globe. Now I am excited as I have the opportunity to preview his latest work where he has teamed up with Joanne Foster, a gifted writer and presenter, to produce this new curriculum to help lead children from age 5 to 11, to become disciples of Christ. It has awesome content, is easy to follow and will fill what has been a huge gap in kids ministry up to this time."
Ps. David Goodwin, Director of Kidsreach International, UK

"What an excellent job the Freedom in Christ team has done in putting this solid family and child-friendly material together. It is full of engaging, interactive truth for those who teach in the church setting, and also for children and their parents at home. It is definitely top shelf material for anyone desiring to lay a solid foundation in their children."
James Whittaker, Pastor of Family and Student Ministries, Fellowship Bible Church, West Virginia, USA

"Lightbringers is a fantastic new resource to help children know their identity in Christ and how to view the rest of the world through that lens. It brings together exciting activities, engrossing stories and up-to-date, catchy music which children are sure to love. With practical information and a range of tools for leaders, this resource would be a blessing to any children's group leader who wants to walk with them on their journey of faith."
Rachel Bunting, Bishop's Officer for Family Ministry, Swansea and Brecon Diocese, UK

Contents

Welcome	6
Quick Start Guide	7
The Lightbringers Approach To Discipling Children	9
Leading *The Lightbringers* Sessions	19
Session 1: I Am Special, Safe, And Accepted	35
Session 2: I Am A New Creation	53
Session 3: I Can Trust Father God	71
Session 4: I Can Choose To See Things As God Says They Really Are	91
Session 5: I Can Make Good Choices With God's Help	111
Session 6: I Can Choose To Have Good Thoughts That Come From God	129
Session 7: I Am Protected Because God Is Stronger Than Anything	147
Session 8: I Can Have Peace Because God Will Help Me Whatever I'm Feeling	169
Session 9: I Can Forgive Others	187
Session 10: I Can Live Every Day Walking In God's Truths	207
The Lightbringers Trail: *The Steps To Freedom In Christ* For Children	227
Commissioning As Lightbringers	255
Extra Activities	257
Impact Your Community And Grow Your Church	263
Credits	274

Welcome To *The Lightbringers* Church Edition!

The Lightbringers is a powerful resource for churches and parents to use with 5-to-11-year-olds. It is designed to equip them to become fruitful disciples who stay connected to Jesus into their adult lives. They will understand:
- Who they are in Jesus
- What they have in Jesus
- How to become fruitful disciples who follow Jesus closely.

It consists of ten action-packed sessions (plus *Steps To Freedom In Christ* ministry session) for use in:
- Churches
- Bible clubs
- Families

It is based on the best-selling *Freedom In Christ Course* by Dr Neil T. Anderson and Steve Goss. It offers:
- Flexibility to be run on its own or alongside The *Freedom In Christ Course* so that parents and children get the same messages at the same time
- Two new stories: one for 5-to-8-Year-Olds and the other for 9-to-11-Year-Olds
- Two new age-appropriate versions of *The Steps To Freedom In Christ*, a gentle prayer/repentance tool by Dr Neil T. Anderson

As well as this comprehensive Leader's Guide with activities, stories and guidelines, *The Lightbringers* Church Edition includes:
- Downloadable activity sheets for participants with notes, activities and lots of fun stuff
- Downloadable versions of *The Steps To Freedom In Christ* for children
- Specially filmed videos telling the stories for each session
- PowerPoint presentations with specially-commissioned illustrations of the Bible and application stories, allowing you to tell them yourself, if you prefer
- Eleven fantastic new songs written and recorded by Wayne and Esther Tester in Nashville
- Lyric videos for the songs to make it easy for children to sing along

For details of how to purchase the downloadable resources (and to claim the significant discount available to you as a purchaser of this Leader's Guide) see the following page.

There is also an online-only Family Version of *The Lightbringers* designed for use at home. It is great for families whose churches don't run *The Lightbringers* or who want to reinforce the teaching (and see it for themselves) as their children go through it in a church setting.

Quick Start Guide

1. Access The Lightbringers Online Resources – Save 25%

To run *The Lightbringers* in your church you need this Leader's Guide and the accompanying downloadable materials. These include:

- Excellent video presentations of the two stories featured in each session to download or stream (not available on DVD).
- PowerPoint presentations for each session with the Bible verse and illustrations for the Bible and application stories.
- Eleven specially written songs. Downloads include:
    - MP3 audio versions.
    - Lyric videos for each song so that your group can easily sing along.
- A comprehensive activity sheet for each session (and each age group) that you can print out for each participant.
- Other helpful resources such as suggested parental permission form and course completion certificate to print out for each child.

The downloads are yours to keep for ever, so you can use them for as long as you like with as many children as you like within your church/organization at no further cost! Purchase of this Leader's Guide qualifies you for a 25% discount on the Lightbringers Online Resources – equivalent to the cost of the Leader's Guide!

Go to www.FreedomInChrist.org/Lightbringers and quote your code:

```
LFBL23A
```

2. Join *The Lightbringers* Community

Our Facebook group for Lightbringers leaders provides a place to ask questions of *The Lightbringers* team at Freedom In Christ and to compare notes with other children's leaders running the course. We also really appreciate your suggestions for improvement. We do our best to respond quickly to any questions you may have as you run *The Lightbringers*.

Join at **www.facebook.com/groups/LightbringersLeaders/**

The Lightbringers Family Edition

The Lightbringers Family Edition is an online-only version of this resource that is licensed solely for use in homes. It is available at a family-friendly price and includes:

- Access to streamed versions of the story videos (cannot be downloaded)
- Access to streamed versions of three of the specially written songs
- An activity sheet for each session to print out

It can be purchased at www.freedominchrist.org/families

It's ideal for parents whose children are going through *The Lightbringers* in your church and who want to reinforce the teaching at home, or for those whose church does not run *The Lightbringers*.

Meet The Authors And Presenters

Mark Griffiths is part of St. Padarn's Institute, the training arm of the Church in Wales, where he is responsible for the training of new ministers and oversees the development of ministry to children, young people, and families. He has ministered nationally and internationally for several decades. *The Lightbringers* is his tenth book. He has led and been involved in leading growing churches in various denominations and was Head of Children and Family Ministry for New Wine England for 13 years. His PhD is in church growth and child evangelism. Mark is also a member of the Scripture Union National Council. He is married to Rhian and they have three children, Nia, Owen, and Elliot.

Joanne Foster is the children's pastor for St. Saviour's Church in Guildford, UK. She has been involved in children's and family ministry for over 15 years, creating programmes, running schools teams and leading kids and holiday clubs for churches and a large annual Christian festival. Jo also runs seminars for churches and leaders to be inspired and better equipped in transitioning kids from children to youth. She is married to Steve and they have three children, Tom, JJ, and Sam.

Other useful resources by Mark Griffiths include:
- *Fusion* – a year's worth of curriculum for 5-11's
- *Detonate* – a year's worth of curriculum for 5-11's
- *Impact* – a year's worth of curriculum for 5-11's
- *Don't Tell Cute Stories – Change Lives* (The 'how to' guide for children's workers)
- *One Generation from Extinction* – A strategy to re-evangelize the world
- *Hanging on Every Word* – 48 Stories for telling
- *Changing Lives*

The Lightbringers Approach To Discipling Children

What is Freedom In Christ?

The *Freedom In Christ Course* is a resource that helps churches make fruitful disciples (as opposed to mere converts). It has a proven track record. It's been translated into over 30 languages and used by hundreds of thousands of people.

There are versions of the course specifically for Christians in their 20s and 30s, and for teens (there is further information on pages 265-267). Now this effective and powerful resource is at last available for children in the shape of *The Lightbringers*. So you can teach this message in your church across every generation at the same time!

The comment we hear most often from adults who have been through Freedom In Christ is, "Why didn't anyone tell me this 30 or 40 years ago?" What earth shattering new piece of information have they learned from the course? Simply, what happened to them at the moment they chose to make Jesus Christ their Saviour and Lord. Just the straightforward gospel message. Yes, they have already grasped *some* of it, but key elements that the Apostle Paul might have called "basic principles" seem entirely new. It's perfectly possible to grow up in church and never really understand who you are in Jesus.

We like to characterize these "basic principles" as Truth, Turning and Transformation.

Truth is about learning to see the world as God says it is, learning to see yourself as the amazing person that God says you are, and learning to see God as He is.

Turning has to do with understanding why sin is so damaging to us. Sin does not only alienate us from our Heavenly Father but it opens a big wide door for our enemy, the devil, to influence us negatively. So we make the choice to deal with it.

Transformation comes when we train ourselves constantly to see things as God says they actually are, rather than how the world, the flesh, the devil, and our own past experiences tell us to see them.

This course is designed to help children take hold of these basic principles from God's Word at a deep level at an early stage in their lives. So that believing in Jesus makes real sense to them. So that they become fruitful followers of Jesus. So that they persevere as Christians into adult life rather than turning away as soon as the influence of their parents wanes.

Freedom In Christ For Children

The vast majority of Christians alive on the planet today made decisions to become followers of Jesus before their 14th birthday. This should always be the target, as prevention is always better than cure. Maybe a story will help communicate this:

Amy Carmichael was a missionary in the 19th century. One night she had a dream. In her dream she found herself on the edge of a cliff. Far below she could see the waves hammering onto the rocks. As she stood there she saw people rushing towards the edge. She ran back and forth trying to stop them falling off the cliff. She managed to rescue many, but couldn't get to them all. Then, she noticed that not far from the cliff's edge there were people sitting on picnic blankets making daisy chains. In her dream Amy shouted to them to summon help, but they didn't move. They continued making daisy chains. Amy was still running back and forth when she awoke.

She asked God what it meant, and then she understood. The people were walking and toppling over the cliff towards hell and she was rescuing them. Those who sat and made daisy chains represented the Church of her day, apathetic and ineffective, content in its own pastimes and having no interest in the lost world outside. Amy committed her life to patrol the edge of that cliff and rescue as many as she could. She opened many orphanages in India and rescued hundreds of children from idolatry.

But the Church today is not the same as the Church in Amy's day. We have, for the most part, conquered apathy and complacency. Our biggest enemy today is not indifference; our biggest enemy today is activity! We are all busy doing something. It would appear that we are no longer making daisy chains, but neither have we taken the step of standing on the cliff edge. Instead, we set up rescue shelters at the bottom of the cliff. When people fall off the cliffs we then try and help them. There is nothing wrong with helping people in trouble, but isn't prevention always better than cure?

The Freedom In Christ approach is to help individuals stand as disciples who know who they are in Christ so that they are far less likely to 'fall apart' when tough times come. The *Freedom In Christ Course* is highly effective in doing this. *The Lightbringers* will do the same for children. It is surely better to help boys and girls know their true identity in Christ and live in freedom, than to repair men and women later on in their lives.

The Lightbringers is a resource that enables and empowers parents and children's workers to stand at the top of the cliff with arms wide. It is about building strong children who recognize who they are in Christ and know the truth that they have a destiny that God set apart for them, even before He began to put the universe together.

The Bible leaves us in no doubt that the devil comes to kill, steal and destroy; to kill innocence, to steal destiny, and to destroy lives. For believers, it is a flawed strategy to watch the devil do these things and then, some years later, try to repair the damage. In order to reach children before they hit the rocks we must stand at the edge of the cliff.

There is another dimension; most church leaders and many parents will tell you of the sadness of a child who seemingly followed Jesus for many years only to drop out as they entered their teenage years. Why do so many not make it as adult disciples? The reasons are numerous and complex, but at the top of the list is our understanding of what a disciple of Jesus actually is.

Traditional discipleship teaching can sound like this: "Do this every day"; "Don't do that anymore"; "Successful Christians behave like this". So, they end up simply acting like Christians. Some manage to do and say the right things but don't necessarily live fruitful lives. Others constantly require help with the same old issues. Some just drift away. In short, we have taught them to 'act like Christians' rather than to develop a real personal walk and relationship with the resurrected Jesus. They, in effect, develop a superficial spirituality and learn to become one thing at church and another at school and to their friends.

Read any of Paul's letters to the churches and you'll usually get about half way through before you find instructions on how to behave. First, he concentrates on what's already been done; who we are – the "riches" we have in Christ (e.g. Ephesians 1:18) – because it's not what we do that determines who we are; it's who we are that determines what we do.

Therefore, *The Lightbringers* Course for children does what the adult course does in helping people know who they are in Jesus. It also helps them identify and deal with lies, unresolved issues, and unconfessed sin. But, it also works at creating opportunity for genuine encounter with Jesus and building spiritual understanding into the life of the child. This means we are not having to work in years to come to repair them. Because we will have given them the spiritual understanding that, having done all else, they can stand – bold, courageous, and resolute against every fiery dart.

We firmly believe that this will help train and equip children to be strong followers of Jesus and stem the exodus of children from our churches as they enter their teenage years.

What's Different To The Adult Version?

The Lightbringers is *The Freedom In Christ Course* specifically adapted for children. The message has not changed. If you are familiar with the other Freedom In Christ resources, then the content will be familiar and many of the illustrations have been incorporated. However, the form and style of presentation had to be radically different. Taking the adult course and simplifying the language would not have worked. This is not only a younger generation, but rather a completely different culture. Our usual methods of rational, systematic, and logical presentation of facts does not directly translate.

The world has changed, making a radical rethink necessary. Communicating with this rising generation necessitates a deeper understanding of how children learn today, and therefore how we can interface with them. Modern communicators somehow believe that it is about communicating facts and imparting nuggets of information. No, it is rather about crafting an *experience*. This is about the joy and pain, wonder and angst, uncertainty and delight of journeying. It is about taking a child (or a group of children) on a spiritual journey and, like any memorable journey, all of those who journey are likely to be changed by it (children and communicator alike). Therefore, the goal is to take them on a spiritual journey that becomes transformative as they encounter and re-encounter the Living God.

The Lightbringers was piloted in a number of different churches and groups. The original pilot was presented to 150+ primary school aged children each Friday evening for 10 weeks. It works equally well with large or small groups of children. There is also a Family Version that can be led by a parent/carer one-to-one at home.

At the end of *The Lightbringers* comes a separate ministry session called *The Steps To Freedom In Christ*. This needs a different approach and is best done one-to-one or in small groups.

The suggested time for each session is one hour and 45 minutes. This could be easily reduced to one hour for use at home, in a small group, or Sunday Kids Club. Examples of each time format will be shown. But remember, the format is your slave, not your master. If you want more prayer and less games, go ahead. If you want an extra game and one less song, feel free.

Communicating Effectively

When we communicate:
- 15% of our message is to do with content;
- 25% of our message is to do with tone;
- 60% of our message is to do with who we are.

Any communicator whose heart is not in it will mess up the delivery, even if they deliver every word of the stories perfectly, with dazzling enunciation, razor-sharp wit, and a range of regional accents. Be credible by ensuring that you carry yourself with integrity and are completely connected to Jesus. The communicator needs to have a heart free of baggage and a sweet spirit – not always easy to maintain – but essential. Who we are comes across clearly. It is therefore recommended that the leader/parent go through the adult version of Freedom In Christ including *The Steps To Freedom In Christ* before leading this course.

Using The Stories

There are two stories in the resource, one aimed primarily at older children and the other primarily at younger children. Take time to look at them both and use the one you think is best suited to your group.

The Lightbringers is the story for older children and describes the journey of a young girl called Sophie as she finds out that the world is not as she thought. As she learns who she is, who she has been created to be, and her spiritual authority in Christ, the children will journey with her and her friend, Thomas, learning what they learn.

The Adventures Of Lilly Pepper is the story for younger children. Children will journey with Lilly as she uncovers the truth of her new identity in Jesus and how to stand in His strength.

We have provided videos of the stories but, if you prefer to tell the stories yourself, they are written out in full. PowerPoint presentations with illustrations are included in the downloadable resources.

As you lead, remember that, for younger children especially, the communicator is everything; the messenger is part of the message and in many ways, most of the message. The personal credibility of the communicator cannot be underestimated. You are the key to this transformative journey.

Should We Teach Children About Evil?

One of the main themes in the story for older children in *The Lightbringers* is the truth that in Jesus we have authority over evil. By introducing characters called "The Gloom" who are under the control of "wolf creatures", the story is able to communicate this truth in an age-appropriate manner. The Gloom and the wolf creatures appear, at first sight, to be powerful and scary but are ultimately defeated by Sophie and Thomas as they learn to operate in the power and authority they have in Jesus.

We thought long and hard about the appropriateness of a story set in a graveyard with evil characters. We concluded that, in an age where evil is often glorified in the media our children routinely encounter, it is absolutely appropriate to provide a tool to equip children's workers and parents to help children know the very real power and authority they have in Jesus. "We are not unaware of his schemes," said the Apostle Paul in 2 Corinthians 2:11. Our children need to know how to recognize and deal with the enemy's schemes against them. If they are not to become spiritual casualties, they need to learn to see the world as God says it is in His Word. Yes, there is an enemy who wants to "steal and kill and destroy" (John 10:10) but we are seated with Christ at the right hand of the Father "far above" all rule and authority, power and dominion (Ephesians 1:20-21, 2:6).

Steve Goss, International Director of Freedom In Christ, tells of occasions when his young children felt scared at night, sensing some kind of evil presence in their bedrooms. Maybe this was simply the product of an overactive imagination, or maybe it was the enemy trying to scare them and gain influence in their lives. He and his wife would read them 1 John 5:18 which says, "We know that anyone born of God does not continue to sin; the One who was born of God keeps them safe, and the evil one cannot harm them". Then, they would encourage them to ask God if there were any issues they needed to deal with in their lives. Next, they would get them to say out loud something along the lines of, "I am a child of God and everything evil must go away." Without fail, they then went peacefully off to sleep. Understanding this at an early age equipped them well for their teenage years and now, as adults, they are both going on well as disciples of Jesus.

Does teaching children this kind of truth scare them? Well, what on earth is scary about knowing that you are completely safe in Jesus? Or, that in Him you have far more power and authority than any evil presence in your room (whatever its cause). It's surely far more unsettling if your parents seem frightened of this kind of thing and never talk about it, or if they tell you that the 'presence' isn't real when it feels *very* real to you.

Isn't it better to teach our children – in an age-appropriate way of course – what the world is really like and equip them to live in it as victorious children of God? We have come across adult Christians who still wake up scared night after night with the sense of an evil presence harassing them and don't know what to do about it. How much heartache would have been prevented if their parents had known how to help them deal with this kind of thing at a young age.

That said, we urge you to read or watch *The Lightbringers* story in its entirety before you start the course so that you can make sure that you are completely comfortable with it. If you are not, then simply use the other story, *The Adventures Of Lilly Pepper*, as you take your group through the course.

The Steps To Freedom In Christ

The Steps To Freedom In Christ is the main ministry component of *The Lightbringers* and is an essential part of the course that needs to be scheduled, in addition to the ten teaching sessions. The title of this essential additional session is "*The Lightbringers* Trail," in order to give children the sense of a fun journey.

It is a prayer/repentance process during which children will be encouraged to take responsibility for their life and growth by asking the Holy Spirit to show them any area in their life where something needs to be resolved. They then choose to confess and repent of everything He shows them, thus removing any grounds the enemy may have had in their life. It is based on James 4:7, "Submit to God. Resist the devil and he will flee from you." It is very simple and gentle but amazingly effective!

Each Step starts with a prayer of repentance asking the Holy Spirit to bring to mind the specific areas that apply to them. Then there are particular instances listed (usually with check boxes) and a short written prayer of renunciation used to deal with specific areas they want to renounce. Some sections also include declarations of truth from the Bible in which children affirm their choice to believe what God says is true. Of course, we don't generally use words such as "repent" and "renounce" with young children. We find ways of explaining these concepts that they will readily understand, using phrases such as "turn away from" and "say no to".

We have supplied two versions of *The Steps To Freedom In Christ*, one aimed at younger children and the other at older children. Both are written in child-friendly language. Don't just select the version you will use based on age, however, but use your knowledge of the level of understanding of the children you are working with to make the appropriate choice for them.

There are guidelines on how to lead this session on page 30.

Do It Yourself First!

When you travel by air, the flight attendant will dutifully point out the safety features of the aircraft and tell you what to do in the event of an emergency. Have you noticed that they make a point of telling passengers travelling with children to put their own oxygen mask on first before they attempt to help their children? A panic-struck parent gasping for air is in no position to help their child. Even though the air is thin, the child is in no immediate danger. They can wait until the parent has got themselves ready. The same follows for helping our children spiritually. They need us to be strong and confident in Jesus. We cannot impart to them what we don't possess ourselves.

If you are trying to help children take hold of their freedom in Christ so that they can become fruitful disciples, we strongly recommend that you should have already gone through Freedom In Christ's main teaching yourself first. Your group will get the most out of this course if you yourself have personal experience with what you are teaching. As well as making you familiar with the process and ensuring that there is nothing holding you back in your own walk with God, it will also make you an example to follow. The joy of knowing your own identity and freedom in Christ will be something children will recognize and want to have for themselves.

Ideally you will have gone through the main *Freedom In Christ Course* and the *Steps To Freedom In Christ* yourself before you teach this course. If you can't get to a course, a good alternative would be to read the *Discipleship Series* of four small books by Steve Goss (page 270).

Adopt An Attitude Of Grace

All of us have experienced things or done things that cause us guilt and shame, even young children. We need to hear the great news that Jesus died to take away our guilt and shame so that we don't need to hold on to it any longer. If a child tells you something that shocks or angers you, be careful to come to them as Jesus does – with love and acceptance and no condemnation whatsoever. If your attitude is wrong and you say something like, "What's wrong with you?", children will understandably become defensive and clam up.

It's important that children are able to trust you enough to share any mental thoughts they may have which are in direct opposition to what you are attempting to do in the Steps. One young boy plucked up the courage to share that he had continual thoughts in his head saying, "I'm no good." The frustrated parents of this adopted child had all but thrown in the towel trying to control his behaviour. The message that he was getting internally and externally was that he was no good, hopeless, and helpless. The power of Satan is in the lie. As soon as the lie is exposed, you can explain the truth from God's Word – for example, they can do all things through Christ, they are special and dearly loved by God – and the lie is broken.

Safeguarding And Consent

Assuming you are running *The Lightbringers* in the context of a local church, make sure that the church leaders are aware of what it is, when and where it is taking place, and that you do it in accordance with whatever guidelines and processes have already been established by the church. It is also imperative that you and all leaders are well acquainted with the child protection procedures that should already have been set up by your church. It is possible that, during the course, a child might disclose something that needs to be reported. You need to know in advance what to do in that event.

We strongly recommend that you inform parents about the Steps to Freedom session and obtain their consent before you take their child through *The Steps To Freedom In Christ*. You can download a sample consent form and letter to parents/guardians.

Are They Sitting Comfortably?

Curiously, this is not just an expression. Some children would love to listen to you but can't! Several years ago, I visited a project run out of a community centre in one of the lower socioeconomic parts of Sydney, Australia. For the first few months, the leaders could not get the children to listen. They were truly wild. These children didn't just write on the bathroom doors, they set fire to them. The change came one evening when a leader began to chat with the children and realized that many of them hadn't eaten a proper meal for several days and would probably go several more days before they got fed again. The leader realized that the children couldn't sit still because they were hungry.

Abraham Maslow proposed a theory in a 1943 paper called, "A Theory of Human Motivation." It suggests that we all have basic needs and we are looking for those needs to be met in an order of importance. The base needs are physiological needs: Am I warm, clothed, housed etc.? They are the needs highlighted above in my story from Sydney. But the second tier of needs are to do with safety and protection. They ask, "Am I secure?" People who feel secure are good listeners.

It's worth thinking through the questions, "Are your listeners sitting comfortably? What can you do to make them feel comfortable?"

That Sydney project now feeds dozens of hungry children copious amounts of pasta at the start of every session. The result is well-fed children who are ready to listen. It will prove invaluable to spend the time to discover what the extra need is. Maybe you simply need to spend time with them; time making them feel secure. It's worth exploring; don't take anything for granted in our 21st century world.

It Has To Be Fun!

If you create a school environment and behave like the school teacher, don't be surprised if most children opt out very early on. It has to be fun. That's why we have provided you with lots of games and fun items. The whole session is worship, not just the teaching elements or the songs, all is an offering to God- even if it does involve a surprising number of messy games. Therefore, we advocate starting with free-play; let them wander in and have fun with each other for the first 20 minutes – bouncy castles, computer games, soft balls for football etc. Be creative.

The Key Is Involvement

Get them involved. They have to do stuff! You need to give them opportunity to see that God actually shows up. He really does break into time and space and do stuff. Really… if He doesn't, what's the point? This is not about a God who created and then walked away from His creation. He wants to be involved.

A. W. Tozer told us:

> Between the person who knows about God and the person who has encountered God there is a difference as wide as the sea. We are today overrun with people who know about God, they have read about God, they have an opinion about God, their voices grate through our churches, our synods, our world. But where are those who have encountered? Where is the voice of the one who has gazed on the wonder of God? The church waits for that voice. The church is desperate for that voice. Yet to gaze there is a privilege open to every believer.

Every believer. No exceptions. That means children can gaze there too. An army of children who have gazed on the wonder of God. Who have truly encountered Jesus. They will be the generation that changes the world.

The Lightbringers Approach To Discipling Children

Leading *The* Lightbringers Sessions

Summary Of Sessions

Part A — Key Truths

Jesus said that we will know the truth and the truth will set us free! In the first three sessions we look at some of the key truths we need to know to understand what it means to be a Christian.

Session 1: I Am Special, Safe, And Accepted

When Adam and Eve were created, they had life in all its fullness. God met all their needs. They were perfectly accepted, safe, and significant. When they chose to sin, they lost their relationship with God. The result for us is that we are born with a huge need for acceptance, security, and significance. Jesus came to give us back that life we lost. Our new identity in Jesus means we have the acceptance, security, and significance that Adam and Eve lost.

Session 2: I Am A New Creation

The Bible makes it clear that, because of what Jesus has done for us, we are new creations in Christ. Knowing that we are children of God who can come boldly into God's presence changes everything.

Session 3: I Can Trust Father God

Everyone lives by faith, even those who are not Christians. It's who or what we put our faith in that determines whether or not it will be effective. As Christians, it's essential that what we believe is in agreement with what God has revealed in His Word.

Part B — The World, The Flesh, And The Devil

Every day we struggle against three things that conspire to push us away from truth. Understanding how the world, the flesh, and the devil work will enable us to renew our minds and stand firm.

Session 4: I Can Choose To See Things As God Says They Really Are

Depending on where they were brought up, children will have learned to look at the world in a particular way that seems right to them. But is it? We need to teach children to stop looking at the world in that way and start seeing it from God's perspective.

Session 5: I Can Make Good Choices With God's Help

Christians have a new heart and a new spirit, but we still struggle with many of the unhelpful ways of thinking and behaving to which we've grown accustomed. This session shows children that we can choose to live as God wants us to, being led by the Holy Spirit.

Session 6: I Can Choose To Have Good Thoughts That Come From God

Becoming a Christian does not instantly change the way we have learned to think, but we can demolish strongholds — by which we mean strong, embedded thought patterns — by choosing actively to renew our minds according to the truth of God's Word.

Session 7: I Am Protected Because God Is Stronger Than Anything
It's important to understand that we are in a spiritual battle, which makes dismantling strongholds less straightforward than if it were simply a question of learning to think differently. Every day children face a battle for their minds – often our very education system undermines a Biblical worldview. However, understanding this, knowing that we have a spiritual enemy, and recognizing that we have an amazing position in Christ will equip us to win.

Part C — Breaking The Hold Of The Past

God does not change our past but by His grace He enables us to walk free of it. In this section of the course we look at how we can take hold of what Christ has done for us in order to do just that. *The Steps To Freedom In Christ* at the end of the course will complete this process.

Session 8: I Can Have Peace Because God Will Help Me Whatever I'm Feeling
There are feelings and then there is the truth. They are not always related. In this session we will look at how, the more we commit ourselves to the truth and choose to believe that what God says is true, the less our feelings will run away with us.

Session 9: I Can Forgive Others
Learning to forgive from the heart sets us free from our past and heals our emotional pain. It's not easy but it is essential. This session will take some time exploring this and giving children opportunity to truly forgive. *The Lightbringers* Trail (*The Steps To Freedom In Christ* for Children) is to follow this session.

The Lightbringers Trail: *The Steps To Freedom In Christ* For Children
This is the main "ministry" component of the course. You will have the opportunity to lead children through the gentle age-appropriate *Steps To Freedom In Christ*. They will go step-by-step (hence the idea of a "trail") through prayers inviting God to show them stuff they need to deal with, say sorry, and turn their back on it. It's about submitting to God and resisting the devil (James 4:7), reconnecting with God's love, and assuming responsibility for their walk with Him. This should be done after Session 9 or 10.

Part D — Growing As Disciples

We now need to turn our attention to developing mature disciples. This section, with a final teaching session, will look at how children can stand firm and become more and more like Jesus in character.

Session 10: I Can Live Every Day Walking In God's Truths
Growth in maturity depends on the extent to which children continue to renew their minds and learn to distinguish good from evil. We aim to equip them to do just that.

The Lightbringers Commission
This is to mark the children's completion of the course by giving them an opportunity to tell God they want to follow Him for the rest of their lives, and then commission them as Lightbringers. This is the end of *The Lightbringers* course but just the start for them as they walk in their new identity and the freedom they have in Christ.

Session Timing Options

The table below shows two possible sets of activities and timing for each main session, depending on the time available to you and on the age and temperament of your group (younger children may not cope with the full-length session.)

The longer time plan is also included in the notes at the start of each session and sometimes varies slightly from what is below. The shorter version shows you which elements can be left out if time is short.

In the next section we outline the various elements in each session and have included some examples. But feel free to be creative – there are many games and activities in the following pages and you don't have to use them in the places we suggest.

But do keep a careful eye on time and ensure especially that you leave plenty of time for the Teaching Time section.

Longer Version (105 mins.)

Getting Started (30 minutes)
Free Play – 20 minutes
Welcome – 5 minutes
Announcements And Ground Rules – 5 minutes

Worship (20 minutes)
Prayer – 5 minutes
Game – 5 minutes
Praise and Worship – 10 minutes

Word (45 minutes)
Bible Verse – 5 minutes
Interview – 5 minutes
Teaching Time – 20 minutes
- Reflective Worship
- Explore The Bible
- Illustration

Story Time – 15 minutes

Response (10 minutes)
Prayer – 5 minutes
Next Week – 5 minutes

Total time: 1 hour 45 minutes

Shorter Version (60 mins.)

Getting Started (10 minutes)
Welcome – 5 minutes
Announcements And Ground Rules – 5 minutes

Worship (10 minutes)
Prayer – 5 minutes
Praise – 5 minutes

Word (30 minutes)
Bible Verse – 5 minutes
Teaching Time – 10 minutes
- Reflective Worship
- Explore The Bible
- Illustration

Story Time – 15 minutes

Response (10 minutes)
Prayer – 5 minutes
Next Week – 5 minutes

Total time: 1 hour

COMMENT: All the elements need to follow on from each other quite rapidly.

Elements In Each Session

In this section we outline the different elements that you will find in each of the main ten sessions of the course with some guidelines, hints, and tips. You do not have to include every element every time. The previous page gives some guidelines on which elements to leave out if time is short.

Getting Started

Free Play (20 minutes)

If you will not have fun with them, they will not listen to you. If they do not like you, they will not listen to you. If you will not listen to them, they will not listen to you. Spend the first 20 minutes playing with them, having fun, and listening to the stories of their week.

Welcome (5 minutes)

This is a chance to welcome the children but also an opportunity to have fun with them. I prefer to lead the course with others at the front, e.g. the score person, team leaders, your trainee leader. This allows comical banter between the two.

Announcements And Ground Rules (5 minutes)

Announcements:
Summer camps, holiday clubs, competitions, birthdays, special events, etc. can be mentioned here. If you are going to do birthdays be consistent – don't do birthdays one week and then miss two weeks; some children will miss out and feel hurt.

Ground Rules:
Just like games have boundaries and rules so you can play and have fun, so clear guidelines are needed so the children know what is or isn't acceptable in the context of this gathering. Only two simple rules are necessary:
1. Nobody leaves their seat. If they need to go to the bathroom then they need to put their hand up and ask permission from a leader.
2. When you ask for quiet, everyone sits down, focuses on the front, and makes no sound.

These two simple rules will help keep everything in order. Children feel safer and more secure in a disciplined atmosphere. There must be a method of applying these rules. You could try the two-fold system:
- If a team is particularly good – i.e. they sit well, they listen well, they cheer the loudest, they win a game – then they get to roll the dice. The score from the dice is added to their overall score. The team with the most points get the biggest prizes. The other teams also receive prizes, but lesser prizes; for example, the winning team might receive a box of chocolates, the other teams a bar of chocolate.
- If a child talks after the whistle or is not sitting and facing the front, then they instantly lose six points off their score.

THE LIGHTBRINGERS

TIP: You don't have to bring prizes every week. You can keep a running score for each team and inform them that they are working towards the best score for the end of the course, when the team that comes first will receive the largest prize, and the other two teams will receive smaller prizes. Also, the age-old tactic of rewarding those who attend the most with attendance prizes at the end of the course will ensure that you don't hit the sporadic attendance common to many children's clubs.

Worship

Prayer (5 minutes)

In two sections:
- **Giving Thanks:** Children who have prayed for something the week before (or several weeks before) and whose prayers have been answered can be asked to come and tell the others how God answered their prayer.
- **Bringing Needs:** Some of the children will want to pray for certain things. Allow them to come and share what they are praying for and ask God together to answer prayer.

Remember, when children have prayers answered they need to be invited to the front to give God thanks. See Extra Activities on page 259 for more ideas on prayer.

Game Choose one from the ones suggested (5 minutes)

It's best to change the games from week to week. You may find the following tips useful:
- In order to play a game, they need to answer a question on last week's session.
- Choose one person from each team and then allow that person to choose the rest of the team.
- Give points for the teams that cheer people the loudest!
- Play music while the game runs – fast music, played live if possible.
- The first team to complete the game must sit down.

There are a couple of games suggested for each session and some further ideas in the Extra Activities section on page 260.

Praise (10 minutes)

This slot allows for a time of praise with several songs being used together. Encourage banners, streamers, dancing, etc. Allow some of the children to form a praise group that stands with a microphone to lead the others. *The Lightbringers* comes with some incredible new songs (in the downloadable resources). There's one song specially written to go along with the theme of each session. However you can use them throughout the course as you feel is appropriate. The lyrics are included in the plan for each session. There is further information on using the songs a little later in this section. A quieter time of reflective worship will be included later as part of the Word section.

Word

Bible Verse To Memorize (5 minutes)

Each session has a Bible verse. It would be helpful to have the children learn it off by heart. However, remember that being able to recite a verse is not as important as understanding it. Being able to quote "The Lord is my shepherd" may win a child a prize, but will change their lives only if they understand it for themselves.

The Bible verse from the start of the teaching time features on the downloadable PowerPoint presentation. It is good to refer to the verse frequently.

We have provided a specially drawn picture (which is on a slide in the downloadable PowerPoint presentation and usually also printed in this book at the start of each session) that you can use to talk about the verse.

There are many ways to teach a Bible verse, and a few ideas are highlighted below, but there are literally hundreds. Be creative!

- Write the Bible verse on balloons and burst the balloon as the verse is read.
- Make the verse into a jigsaw puzzle.
- Write the verse on an object which communicates its message
- "You are a light to my path" could be written on a lamp or a drawing of a bulb.
- "The Lord is my shepherd" could be written on five cut-out sheep.

Using the PowerPoint presentations: In these notes, we have generally provided an image of each PowerPoint slide so that you can know what to expect next.

▶ This symbol indicates when you should move the presentation on to the next slide.

Interview (5 minutes)

Invite one of the leaders or one of the children to come and tell the group what Jesus has done for them; how He's helped them in work/school; how He cares for them; how they first made their decision to become a Christian. If the person is very nervous, interview them. If they are more confident, allow them to speak freely – taking notice of the timing allowed for this section.

Teaching Time (20 minutes total: Reflective Worship (10 minutes) + Explore the Bible (5 minutes) + Illustration (5 minutes))

Most of the rest of the session falls under the heading of "Teaching Time". This will include Bible lessons, illustrations, and a story. Take a couple of minutes to explain the ground rules.

Tell the children that they are now moving into Teaching Time and this means everyone being still, silent, and facing the front. There are some special ground rules for this section for those running the course with a large group:

- The leader will raise their hand to indicate it is time to be quiet and listen.
- The way you let the leader know you are listening is by facing the front, not talking, and raising your hand.

1. Reflective Worship (10 minutes)

A quieter time of worship songs can be introduced. Encourage the children who know the words to close their eyes and begin to think about King Jesus. Take your time here, it is important to introduce them to worship.

Instruct the children that praise is generally loud and lively, a time where we have fun singing to God. Worship is where we come closer to God, to think about God more. Worship comes from our hearts and our minds. It involves all our emotions. The definitions of praise and worship may be much broader and more theological than this, but a bite-size theological portion is more easily swallowed by children.

Blow the whistle at the end of worship and inform the children again that this is Teaching Time (the whistle can be put away now, it will no longer be needed).

2. Explore The Bible (5 minutes)

There are various ideas to help with the presentation of the Bible lesson:

- Dress some of the children up as characters in the story.
- If you are presenting the story in narrative form, then tell the story as Hollywood would, don't just read the account.
- There is a PowerPoint picture for each lesson (in the downloadable resources).

3. Illustration (5 minutes)

Illustrations can take many forms.

Object Lessons:
An object can be used to communicate a truth. For example:

Objects Needed: A light bulb and a sheet of paper.
People are always complaining that we are wasting things: turn off the light, you are wasting electricity; use the back of that piece of paper, don't waste paper; don't leave the tap running, you are wasting water…

All these things are important and we should not waste things. But I heard a story once of someone who wasted something even more important. It was an old lady and she said one of the saddest things I have ever heard. She said that God had told her when she was young that she should be a missionary for Him and go to a faraway country. The old lady said that she hadn't gone because she had found something else to do and now she feels that she has wasted her life.

It's not good to waste money or electricity or paper or water but it is the saddest thing in the world to waste a life. Being a Christian may be tough sometimes, but if we obey God we will not waste our lives.

Video Clips
With a video camera go to the streets and get a teen to interview passers-by. Passers-by can be asked: if they believe in God; if they own a Bible; what they understand by the word 'trust'.

Commercial Movie Clips
Video clips can also be used to communicate.

Personal Testimony
Things which happen to us often illustrate important truths. Here's an example:

I had to go on a journey once to a place a long way away. I got on a train very early in the morning and was on my way. We hadn't travelled very far when it started to snow. It kept on snowing and didn't look as if it was ever going to stop snowing. When I was half-way there I had to change trains. When I got off my train the whole world had gone white. The snow kept on falling and most of the trains were cancelled. There were just a few trains left running, one was going back towards my home and another was going in the direction I was heading but not exactly the right way.

I had to make a decision. It would have been the easiest thing in the world to get back on the other train and go home. But I didn't. I got on the other train. You see I had friends waiting for me, and I didn't want to let them down. I got on the other train.

God is desperate for us to finish the journey we started with Him. He doesn't want us to turn back; He wants us to keep going.

The train took me to somewhere near where I wanted to go and then I had to get in a taxi and travel the last 40 miles. The taxi couldn't get me all the way, so in the freezing cold and well after midnight, I had to walk the last bit. And then to my horror I discovered the person I was going to stay with wasn't there. He hadn't been able to get home because of the snow. I had to phone someone else and only eventually found someone to stay with. But I had got there. I didn't turn back. I finished the journey. I reached the destination.

God didn't tell us it would be easy serving Him, in fact He promised that it would be hard at times. But we need to keep going, if we start something we need to see it through to the end.

Testimonies From Others
Not only are stories about our own lives useful, things which happen to others can also be an excellent communication tool:

Once during the American Revolutionary War, an accident happened as several of the American troops were travelling along a muddy path. A wagon they were using had overturned and was blocking the road. The Captain of the troops lined up several of the men and was shouting at them to push and push and push to try and turn the wagon back over.

When the wagon wouldn't budge the Captain got even more annoyed and shouted louder at his men to push. After some time, a man on horseback arrived at the place where the wagon had turned over and asked:

"Captain, why don't you help these men rather than just shout at them?"

The Captain was amazed at the request.

"I am their Captain," he replied, "I should not dirty my uniform in such a manner."

With that the man got off his horse. His uniform was already dirty. He walked over to the men and said:

"I will help! Let's push again."

Now with the help of this stranger the wagon was pushed upright.

The Captain was glad that the wagon was restored but annoyed that this stranger should interfere. As the stranger got back onto his horse, the Captain demanded:

"Who are you, sir? What gives you the right to interfere in my affairs?"

The man now on horseback smiled. "I am General George Washington and I interfere because you are in my army and from now on, Captain, you will lead by example."

The Captain didn't know how to answer. So he simply said: "Yes sir!" That day the Captain learned the importance of leading by example. Do we give a good example for others to follow or not?

Anything that will help to present the overall lesson can be placed here.

Story Time (15 minutes)

We've provided two stories:. *The Adventures Of Lilly Pepper* is aimed at children aged 5 to 8 years and *The Lightbringers* is aimed at children aged 9 to 11 years. They are both modern day parables which roll all the themes presented so far into one neat narrative package.

Note that the ages given are just a guide. You might decide to use *The Lightbringers* with younger children if you think their understanding is advanced enough. Similarly, you might decide that it is not suitable for your group of older children, in which case they will be fine with *The Adventures Of Lilly Pepper*. You might also decide to do this if you judge it to be a little too scary (see page 14). Please read it through yourself first and decide whether or not it is suitable for your children/group. If you decide it is not, that's fine – use the story of the wonderful Lilly Pepper instead. However, make your decision prayerfully and with a clear understanding of the children you are ministering to and their backgrounds. We believe it is important for children to know the power and authority they have in Jesus and *The Lightbringers* communicates this well.

You can either read the story yourself (the full script for each is provided and you can download PowerPoint presentations with illustrations) or you can show the downloadable videos in which

Mark Griffiths and Jo Foster read them. We have included the approximate time you will need to show each episode of the videos in the time plan for each session.

If you are reading yourself and using the PowerPoint presentation, the ▶ symbol in the script means that it's time to move the presentation on.

For help with presenting yourself, see *Hanging On Every Word* by Mark Griffiths (Monarch, 2014).

Do not try and explain the story or say, "This means, boys and girls…" The story will communicate in its own right. It's a good story!

Using The Videos: You can either download the videos or stream them. If you stream them, you can benefit from the closed caption subtitles by pressing the "CC" icon at the bottom right of the screen.

Response

Prayer/Response (5 minutes)

It's always good to ask for a response. For example, ask the children who felt the lesson applied to them to stand. If it required forgiveness, pray a prayer of forgiveness together. Let the children respond by repeating the prayer after you. Sometimes you may need to give the children space to listen and encounter God themselves. Other times it may be that you pray for them. Each lesson gives you some suggestions – just be sensitive to the Holy Spirit.

Activity Sheets

Specially designed activity sheets for each age group can be downloaded for all the sessions, including *The Steps To Freedom In Christ*. These can be used at the end of each session if you have spare time or if you want to do small group work with the children during the session. They can also be used as take-home sheets so that parents can see what their child has been learning and get involved! Each activity sheet has key notes, Bible verses, fun activities, space for journaling and a challenge that they can do over the week. If children complete the challenge you could give them a small reward the following week.

Next Week (5 minutes)

Highlight next week's session. Keep it exciting: "Next week everyone who comes will get a _____", "Next week we'll hear the next part of this exciting story", etc.

Leading *The Steps To Freedom In Christ*

The ideal time to schedule your Steps session is between Sessions 9 and 10. It can also be run at the end of the course after Session 10. There are two ways you can approach this: in small groups; or one-to-one.

Small Groups

In a small group scenario, it's important to understand that children are not being asked to tell anyone else their "stuff". This is not some kind of group confessional. Although other people are in the room with them, the idea is to create a space where each person can talk to God, just Him and them. So, the group will say together the prayers that start each section of *The Steps To Freedom In Christ* and then be given time on their own to pray and work through the checklists. One way of facilitating this is to play some gentle instrumental music during the times of prayer so that they can speak out their prayers quietly without anyone else hearing. (Note that music with lyrics tends to be distracting). You will need to have a few helpers around for those with questions or who are in need of help.

The main advantage of small groups is that it is relatively quick and less resource-intensive to "process" everyone. The main disadvantage is the challenge to monitor well how each individual is doing. Inevitably, some will struggle to concentrate.

You will need a longer time than a shorter session allows. A special additional Saturday morning or afternoon session would work well if you are taking your children through it as a group.

Make sure you plan the date well in advance so that you can inform parents and get consent forms returned before the day.

One-To-One

When people are led through the Steps by someone else (ideally with a prayer partner present too), they speak the prayers out loud in front of that person and tend to go much deeper, even though the process is still very much between them and God. They are also helped to identify lies they have come to believe and can then work through so that they are "transformed through the renewing of their mind" (Romans 12:2). For that reason, this is the preferred method.

The ideal scenario for young children is to be led through the Steps by their Christian parents who have themselves been through the adult teaching and Steps. It very much depends on individual circumstances whether or not this is appropriate. It won't work in a dysfunctional home or with parents who aren't going on with God themselves. If a whole church is going through Freedom In Christ at the same time, this can be excellent, especially if the parents use the Family Edition of this course (see page 8). If most of the children in your group have Christian parents who have themselves gone through Freedom In Christ, you could suggest that the parents do this with the children. You will, of course, need to make appropriate arrangements for those who don't have Christian parents or whose parents prefer not to do it.

The Specially-Written Songs

The Lightbringers includes eleven brand new songs specifically written to enhance the sessions (available in the downloadable material). Written and recorded by Testricity Music Group (led by Wayne and Esther Tester, www.testricity.com) in Nashville. We think they are fantastic!

Each song comes with a lyric video to make it easy for everyone to sing along. The lyrics are also printed in this book. It's worth having a good look at them so that you can appreciate how they reflect the teaching themes on the course. They are a fantastic way of helping the key truths taught go from head to heart. Encourage dance moves as you sing and worship!

On the website you will find some ideas for making the songs even more fun: for example, teaching dance moves and submitting a video to us of your group performing them.

We've listed the songs below together with the page where you can find each one:

1.	SuperStar	page 39
2.	Gobsmacked	page 57
3.	Name Above All Names	page 75
4.	I Want You	page 95
5.	Orb Of Challenge	page 115
6.	Absolutely Fabulous	page 133
7.	Champion	page 151
8.	When I Get To Heaven	page 173
9.	I Love You Like	page 191
10.	Can't Stop	page 211
11.	God Made Me Special	page 254

People Required For A Larger Group

We have suggested below the kind of team that would be ideal for running *The Lightbringers* with a larger group in a church setting. But, of course, you can run it for much smaller groups with far less effort or for one or two children in a family home using the Family Edition (see page 8).

Registration
This is where you meet the parents. This is the initial contact point. First impressions do last so put some of your best here. This is the place to base your administrators.

Welcome Person
An adult or several adults who greet the children on arrival and give a quick-guided tour and breakdown of the format to those who are new. This is the place to base those with pastoral gifts.

Activity Supervisor
Each activity such as bouncy castle, computers, etc. needs to be supervised by an activity supervisor. This can be one of your teens as long as they are prepared to be responsible.

Technical
A person who operates sound equipment, videos etc. is invaluable. If done well, this will help you greatly; if done poorly, this can destroy your course.

Front People
A front person is needed, with the possible addition of a second for illustrations. If you work with two front people who know what they are doing and have obvious communication gifts, then introduce a third who can develop and learn. As they come to maturity in this gift, then release more to them. This is a continual process and will allow you to move or sow out into other children's works. The choice of the third person is very important. They may not be the most gifted at first, but they need to be humble, teachable, and have the heart of a servant. The front is the place for your evangelists and teachers.

Small Group Leaders
For most of the course these people float around checking that everyone is OK – talking to children, sitting with them, chilling with them, getting to know them, caring for them. The people with pastoral gifts and a heart for children thrive in this position but they come into their own during Ministry Times when they gather their small group for feedback and prayer.

Others
If you run crafts as part of your course, then you will need artistic people. A qualified first aider should not be overlooked. You may also want a person to be the team leader of each team.

During the course part of the evening, there will need to be a sprinkling of leaders in each team. Problems should not be dealt with from the front but sorted quickly from within the team. For the staff as well as for the children it will be a process of education.

Personal Prayer Of Preparation

God, You're the bedrock under my feet and I depend completely on You. You protect me and clear the ground under me so that my footing is firm. You're the one true and living God. You're a tower of salvation, a shield to all who trust in You, my refuge and my deliverer.

I humbly accept Your call to lead this *Lightbringers* Course. On my own I can do nothing whatsoever that will make a difference but I stand in the truth that all authority in heaven and earth has been given to the resurrected Christ, and because I am in Christ, I share that authority in order to make disciples and set prisoners free.

Thank You that You have cleansed me and washed away my sin. As I declare Your Word in Your strength and power, please fill me afresh with Your Holy Spirit.

Strengthen me by Your Spirit, so that I'll be able to take in to a greater degree the extravagant dimensions of Your love and grace and pass that on to others on the course.

I declare that I have a spirit of power and love and a sound mind, and that the Word of Christ dwells in me richly. I've been made holy by Your Word of Truth. The anointing I've received from You abides in me.

Your Word is an indispensable weapon to me, and in the same way, prayer is essential in ongoing warfare. So I declare that because I've made You my dwelling place, no evil shall come upon me. Your promise is that You will give Your angels charge over all that concerns me, and You will keep me in all my ways.

I welcome the kingdom of the Lord Jesus Christ afresh today into my life, my home, my family, my work, and into all I do within the ministry of making disciples in my church.

I pray all of this in the name of Jesus Christ. Amen.

Based on: 1 John 4:4; 2 Samuel 22; Psalm 51; Psalm 19:14; Ephesians 3:16; 2 Timothy 1:7; Colossians 3:16; John 17:17; 1 John 2:27; Ephesians 3:8; Psalm 91:9–11; 2 Corinthians 4:1–7.

Team Declaration

We declare that Jesus is our Lord. He's greater than the one who is in the world and He came to destroy all the devil's works, having triumphed over him by the cross.

We declare that God has given us the *Lightbringers* Course at this time to share His Word, and the gates of hell will not prevail against it. The words that come out of God's mouth will not return empty-handed. They'll do the work He sent them to do.

As those who are seated in the heavenly realms, we agree that Satan and every enemy of the Lord Jesus must not in any way interfere with the running of this course. We commit the place where the sessions will take place to Jesus. We cleanse it in Jesus' name from any impure thing.

We declare that the truth of God's mighty Word will be planted and established in [name your church or organization] and that those who come will know the truth and be set free.

We will use our powerful God-given tools for tearing down barriers erected against the truth of God, and for building lives of obedience into maturity.

We announce that what God has promised gets stamped with the "yes" of Jesus. We declare that our God can do anything – far more than we could ever imagine or guess or request. Glory to God in the Church! Glory down all the generations forever and ever!

God is striding ahead of us. He's right there with us. He won't let us down. He won't leave us. We won't be intimidated and we won't worry. The battle belongs to Him!

Based on: Colossians 2:15; John 10:10; John 8:32; Matthew 16:18; Isaiah 55:11; 2 Corinthians 10:4; 2 Corinthians 1:20; Ephesians 3; Deuteronomy 31:8, 1 Samuel 17:47.

Session 1: I Am Special, Safe, And Accepted

Session 1: I Am Special, Safe, And Accepted

Time Plan

Getting Started 30 minutes	Free Play (20 minutes)	
	Welcome (5 minutes)	
	Announcements (5 minutes)	
Worship 20 minutes	Prayer (5 minutes)	
	Game (5 minutes)	Choose one: "Pass the mint" or "Guess Who?"
	Praise (10 minutes)	SuperStar
Word 45 minutes	Bible Verse (5 minutes)	"I have come that they may have life, and have it to the full." (John 10:10)
	Interview (5 minutes)	
	Teaching Time (20 minutes) Reflective Worship (10 minutes) Explore the Bible (5 minutes) Illustration (5 minutes)	Genesis 1-3
	Story Time (15 minutes)	*The Adventures Of Lilly Pepper* – Trouble At School (video: 4.5 minutes) *The Lightbringers* – It Begins (video: 8.5 minutes)
Response 10 minutes	Prayer (5 minutes)	Remember to give out this week's activity sheet if you haven't already.
	Next Week (5 minutes)	

Overview

When Adam and Eve were created, they had life in all its fullness. God met all their needs. They were perfectly accepted, secure and significant. In the "fall" they lost their relationship with God. The result for us is that we are born with a huge need for acceptance, security and significance. Jesus came to restore the very same life, acceptance, security and significance that Adam and Eve had originally.

Getting Started

Free Play (20 minutes)

Welcome (5 minutes)

This is a chance to welcome the children but also an opportunity to have fun with them.

Announcements And Ground Rules (5 minutes)

Just as games have rules so that you can play and have fun, clear discipline guidelines are needed so the children know what is or isn't acceptable in the context of this gathering. Only two simple rules are necessary:
1. Nobody leaves their seat. If they need to go to the bathroom then they must put their hand up and ask permission from a leader.
2. When you ask for quiet, everyone sits down, focuses on the front, and makes no sound.

Worship

Prayer (5 minutes)

In two sections:
1. **Giving Thanks:** Children who have prayed for something the week before (or several weeks before) and whose prayers have been answered should be asked to come and tell the others how God answered their prayer.
2. **Bringing Needs:** Some of the children will want to pray for certain things. Allow them to come and mention what they are praying for and ask God together to answer prayer.

Session 1: I Am Special, Safe, And Accepted

Game Choose one (5 minutes)

Game 1 – Pass The Mint

PREPARATION A packet of mints with holes in them, e.g. Polo or LifeSavers, and straws.

PLAYERS Four to five per team.

SET-UP Each player has a straw. The first player has the straw through the mint.

OBJECT Each team has to pass their mint to each member of the team (via a straw) till the last team member has the mint. No hands can be used.

WINNING The first team to have the mint passed down every member.

Game 2 – Guess Who?

PREPARATION A list of questions (e.g. Do you have brown eyes? Are you wearing red? Do you have a fringe? Do you have freckles? etc.).

PLAYERS Everyone.

SET-UP Leader with a list of questions.

OBJECT All the children begin standing. After each question the children sit down if they match what is being said.

WINNING The last child standing is the winner.

Praise SuperStar (10 minutes)

The song that has been specially written for this lesson is "SuperStar", an anthem for *The Lightbringers* theme. We think your group is going to love it! See if they can come up with some actions for it. We suggest using a few praise songs for each session so you may want to introduce another song like "God Made Me Special" which will be used during the Steps to Freedom. Enjoy!

FUN FACT: Wayne Tester, who, together with his wife Esther, wrote and recorded the songs in *The Lightbringers*, won the competition to write the theme song for the Sydney Olympics where his song was performed in the opening ceremony. Ask the children to guess how many people heard that performance live…. It was an incredible 3.7 billion people in the TV audience around the world. That's half the population of the world listening to the same song at the same time!

RAP
SHOUT IT OUT LET'S MAKE SOME SOUND – GOD IS GREAT SPREAD LOVE AROUND
WE WERE LOST BUT NOW WE'RE FOUND – PARTY 'CAUSE WE'RE HEAVEN BOUND

CHORUS
YOU LIGHT UP THE NIGHT JESUS, YOU ARE THE SUPERSTAR
YOU LIGHT UP THE NIGHT JESUS, YOU ARE THE SUPERSTAR
YOU, YOU, YOU ARE THE LIGHT, LIGHT, LIGHT OF THE
WORLD, WORLD LIGHT OF MY LIFE
YOU LIGHT UP THE NIGHT JESUS, YOU ARE THE SUPERSTAR

YOU ARE GALACTICAL, SUPERNATURAL – YOU, YOU, YOU, YOU, Y'YOU, YOU
YOU ARE REMARKABLE, INCOMPARABLE – YOU, YOU, YOU, YOU, Y'YOU, YOU

PRE-CHORUS
JESUS, YOU REALLY LOVE ME – JESUS, YOU REALLY WANT ME
JESUS, I'M GONNA LET YOUR LIGHT – SHINE, SHINE, SHINE, SHINE, SH'SHINE

REPEAT CHORUS & RAP

PARTY ON LET'S COME UNWOUND – COME UNWOUND, COME UNWOUND
PARTY ON LET'S COME UNWOUND – COME UNWOUND, COME UNWOUND

FAMOUS ETERNALLY, FOR INFINITY – YOU, YOU, YOU, YOU, Y'YOU, YOU
YOU SHINE AMAZINGLY, OH SO FAITHFULLY – YOU, YOU, YOU, YOU, Y'YOU, YOU

REPEAT PRE-CHORUS & CHORUS

IN YOUR PRESENCE NIGHT IS BRIGHT AS DAY EVEN DARKNESS IS AS LIGHT

REPEAT CHORUS TWICE

PARTY ON LET'S COME UNWOUND

Words & Music by Wayne Tester, Esther Tester. © 2018 Testricity.com Music (ASCAP) / Fuzzy Socks Music (BMI) (both admin. by Testricity Music Group, www.testricity.com). ℗&© 2018 Testricity Music Group. ALL RIGHTS RESERVED.

Word

I Am Special, Safe, And Accepted – Genesis 1-3

Bible Verse To Memorize (5 minutes)

> I have come that they may have life, and have it to the full.
> John 10:10

▶ "I have come that they may have life, and have it to the full." (John 10:10)

Interview (5 minutes)

Invite one of the leaders or one of the children to come and tell the group what Jesus has done for them; how He's helped them in work/school; how He cares for them; how they first made their decision to become a Christian. If the person is very nervous, interview them. If they are more confident, allow them to speak freely – taking notice of the timing allowed for this section.

Teaching Time (20 minutes)

1. Reflective Worship (10 minutes)

2. Explore The Bible (5 minutes)

Genesis 1-3

▶ In order to find out the answer to the question, "Where did I come from?", we need to go back to the very start of the Bible, to the story of Adam and Eve in Genesis 1-3.

When Adam and Eve were created, they had everything that they needed – all their needs were met by God. Adam had a purpose (to rule over the animals), everything was provided for, and they knew they belonged to God. Verses 26 and 27 (Genesis 1) tell us that God created human beings in God's image and therefore Adam and Eve had a spiritual connection with God. But, when Adam and Eve were tricked by the devil into eating the fruit (what the Bible calls sin) they lost that connection with God. For the first time they began to have negative emotions, feeling fearful, depressed, and rejected (Genesis 3:10).

So, God sent Jesus to undo the work that the devil had done when he tricked Adam and Eve. God sent Jesus to bring us life and restore that connection with God (John 10:10).

How do you think Adam and Eve felt before they ate the fruit? What about afterwards? What had changed?

3. Illustration Choose one (5 minutes)

Illustration 1 – Who am I?

Objects Needed: Water, lemon juice, cotton bud, white card and lamp, or alternatively buy invisible ink.

Create invisible ink by mixing a few drops of water with some lemon juice. Dip the cotton bud in the lemon juice and write on the white card, "The invisible things are as real as the stuff that's visible".

Session 1: I Am Special, Safe, And Accepted

Who am I? My name is _____. I have _____ hair.
But is this who I am? What if I dyed my hair or lost my arm? Would I still be me?
What you see with your eyes are just the outer things of me.

Take this paper (*hold up blank sheet of white card*) – you can all see that this is plain white paper with no writing on it. But when I hold it to a light (*shine a desk lamp onto the paper*) you can see words (you could ask one of the children to read what it says). The invisible things are as real as the stuff that's visible.

We are made in God's image! That means that we are spiritual beings. In other words, we are made up of not just our bodies (the things you can see) but also the things that we can't see (our spirits).

Illustration 2 – God-Shaped Hole

Object Needed: Mint with hole e.g. Polo or LifeSavers.
Inside every one of us is a God-shaped hole in our hearts (hold up mint). It's a bit like this mint. This is how we were created – with a hole in the middle! Do you remember our Bible lesson about Adam and Eve? Sin separates us from God.

So how do we get our God-shaped hole filled?

A famous Mathematician (Pascal) once said, "There is a God shaped vacuum in the heart of every person, and it can never be filled by any created thing. It can only be filled by God".

Without Jesus we are empty but when we ask Jesus into our hearts He fills this hole with His Spirit, we are no longer separated from God, and we can have that connection with God. It's really easy – we just have to ask!

Illustration 3 – Safe, Special, And Accepted

Objects Needed: Cardboard Box (with no bottom) on a table with words SPECIAL, SAFE and ACCEPTED written on it. Current kids' magazines, certificate of achievement, football, pretend money.

In our life we all need to feel safe, special, and accepted (show box). We need to know that we are important. God has designed us this way. BUT, rather than looking to God, we may look to other things: good school results (*put certificate in the box*), being the best at sport (*put football in the box*); trying to be popular and following what our friends are doing (*put magazines in box*); having lots of money (*put money in box*) etc.

This might help us at first, but what happens when we are not picked for the team or we fail our test or our money runs out or our friends let us down? Kids, by filling our lives with anything other than God (*pick up box and let the contents fall*) will leave us feeling empty, just like this box. You can't feel safe, special, and accepted from this stuff. It is only God that can meet these needs. After all He created us this way and knows us better than we know ourselves!

Story Time (15 minutes)

The Story For Younger Children – *The Adventures Of Lilly Pepper*

Chapter 1 – Trouble At School

The video is 4.5 minutes. Take some time after the story to ask and listen to what the children think. Then go to the response and prayer time.

▶   Welcome to *The Adventures Of Lilly Pepper*! Are you ready? Let's go! Chapter 1, Trouble At School.

▶   Lilly Pepper was seven years old. She lived with her mum and her baby brother, Jake, and a very scruffy dog called Mop. A strange name, but that's what Lilly wanted to call him when she was just two, so mum had agreed. That was the other thing about Lilly Pepper, she was very determined. In fact, her second name wasn't really Pepper at all. She'd been called that once by mum – because she liked eating raw peppers, green, yellow, red, she liked them all – and now she refused to be called anything else.

In the first weeks of any new school year when her real name was called on the school register, she would stand up, put her hands on her hips, and proclaim:

"Mr Edwards, my name is Lilly Pepper."

And after she did that a few times, Mr Edwards – like every teacher before him – gave in. Anything for a peaceful life, but deep down Mr Edwards knew that this class was not going to give him a peaceful life. They were approaching summer break, and every morning for the whole year, with a sigh, Mr Edwards had called, "Lilly Pepper."

And Lilly would stand, smile and announce,

"Here I am, Mr Edwards, ready for action."

▶   Lilly was definitely "lively". That was the word Mr Edwards used at parents evening in describing Lilly to her mum. But, in the staff room, he simply rolled his eyes and said, "She's wild!" She wasn't wild. She simply liked to think for herself and she didn't do things just because everyone else did and she wasn't that keen on believing everything Mr Edwards showed on the whiteboard unless he could prove it, and that is why, today, Lilly found herself standing outside the Principal's office, waiting to explain what she'd done in class!

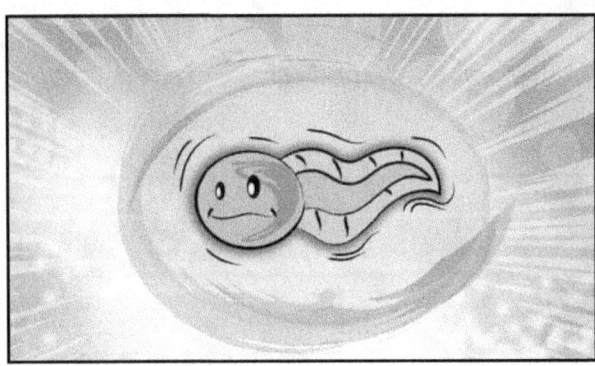

▶   It had started when Mr Edwards had shown the class a picture of a tadpole on the whiteboard. A tiny wriggly tadpole. And told the children that this is how all life once began. And then the next picture showed the tadpole with legs, and then it got bigger and bigger and by the end of the pictures it had changed into a monkey. Then more pictures of monkeys changing to eventually look like people. And Mr Edwards concluded his talk with the words,

"And that's where all people came from. Now, let's write that down in our books."

But Lilly burst out laughing. She was laughing so loud it was hard to hear anything else. And then she said it, the line that was going to get her sent straight to the Principal.

▶ "I don't think that's right, Mr Edwards. We do look a bit like monkeys, but that shouldn't make us think we came from them! God made you, Mr Edwards, just like He made everyone."

Well, Mr Edwards didn't know what to do. Lilly was still laughing because she had found the whole thing so ridiculous. The other children were now making monkey sounds. Mr Edwards was getting more and more cross, desperately trying to explain that we all came from monkeys. And with Lilly Pepper's giggles still echoing in his head he got far too angry and shouted at the top of his voice:

"You're all monkeys."

The class stopped and stared. But Lilly Pepper called out, "No we're not. We're children. God made us children, not monkeys."

And that was the last straw. Lilly was sent to see Mrs Stevens, the Principal, to explain her actions. What will Mrs Stevens do? We'll find out next time. See you soon!

Take some time to ask and listen to what the children think about the story.

Session 1: I Am Special, Safe, And Accepted

The Story For Older Children – *The Lightbringers*

Chapter 1 – It Begins

The video is 4.5 minutes. Take some time after the story to ask and listen to what the children think. Then go to the response and prayer time.

▶   The rain continued to fall. The night had come early – it always did at this time of year.

▶   Lightning flashed across the sky illuminating the solitary figure that knelt before the gravestone. Eventually she stood and walked past the overturned graves. Her feet sloshed through the mud. Thunder rumbled nearby.

She walked between the two pillars supporting the rusty gates, gates held by a loose rusty chain, but she easily squeezed through. These gates had been closed for many years. She stood on the edge of the road. The dazzling lights of a truck highlighted her bedraggled brown hair. Her clothes were wet through. Her denim jacket was completely drenched and no defence against this type of weather, but it was the only jacket she had. Her jeans clung tightly to her legs. Then the truck passed.

No one would notice the flowers on the grave. No one came to the graveyard unless it was for mischief. This graveyard had not been used for many years. Nobody remembered the people buried there now. Except one.

Lightning flashed but the girl had gone.

▶   The rain continued to fall.

Sophie woke early. Her wet clothes still hanging on the chair at the end of the bed. The Home was silent. It wouldn't be for long. But, these moments were hers and she used them to stare at the ceiling and to think.

There were some things she was sure about. She was sure there was no parallel universe where everything was different and where the accident hadn't happened. She was sure that no new parents were going to walk through the door and take her away from the Home. She used to think that when she first arrived aged five, but four years had passed since then, and nobody wanted to adopt a nine-year-old girl who was considered "unusual". And finally she was sure that Thomas, who lived across in the boys' house, was always going to be crazy – in a good way, but definitely crazy. She was just sure.

▶   But there were some things about which she was less sure. God. God was one of those areas in which she was less sure. She used to be absolutely sure. If God existed then He wouldn't have let the accident happen, and since the accident did happen, there couldn't possibly be a God. But now she was less sure. Particularly now that the new care-worker had arrived in the Home. She was used to new care-workers. They didn't stay for long, a few buckets of wallpaper paste above the door that would fall onto an unsuspecting man or woman as they came into the kitchen, itching powder gently poured down their back and a worm or two dropped into their cup of tea was usually enough to see them off. But, Mr Dundenter was different. They had placed the bucket of paste above the door, but no matter how many times he went in and out the bucket didn't move. But one walk through by Thomas and squelch/splat! He was covered. And Mr Dundenter didn't seem to notice the itching powder at all, even though Sophie had put a whole handful down his neck when she had pretended to bump into him. And when he had got to the end of his cup

Session 1: I Am Special, Safe, And Accepted

of tea to see the worms wiggling at the bottom, he simply smiled, said, "Oh worms. My favourite," and lifted his cup one more time and swallowed the worms... Leaving Sophie and Thomas feeling slightly sick.

▶ But that wasn't what made her unsure. It was what happened the day before. She had come home from school, sat in her room reading her library book and completely lost track of time. When she did look at the clock it was past dinner time and Cook was strict on meal times. She jumped up, ran to the stairs and realizing too late that her laces were untied, she tripped and tumbled down 20 stairs before landing in a crumpled heap at the bottom.

The Home had been built specially to look after orphan children. Children who had no other family. It had a boys' house and a girls' house. Well that's what they were called – they were not separate houses. There was a central area where they ate their food and played their games, and in two different directions from that area there were stairs, one set to the left that led to the boys' rooms and one to the right that led to the girls'.

And now everyone was looking up from their food to see poor Sophie in a heap on the floor, at the bottom of the girls' stairs, moaning pitifully.

"She's dead," announced Stacey, who always thought the worst.

"She can't be dead," proclaimed Thomas, "I can hear her moaning. And you don't moan when you're dead...."

"She's not dead." It was Cook's voice, "But she has hurt herself badly." Everyone ran towards Sophie. But they hadn't got particularly far before Mr Dundenter sent them back to their seats. It was Mr Dundenter who walked over to Sophie and he knelt beside her. Sophie was crying. It hurt. It hurt a lot.

"It's my leg," Sophie sobbed.

Mr Dundenter took hold of her hand, closed his eyes and said,

"Jesus, you healed so many people in the Bible. Please make Sophie's leg better."

Immediately, she felt calm and peaceful. When she looked down, her leg looked completely normal. No pain at all. She stared at Mr Dundenter. He winked. Winked! Nothing else was said. She stood up walked to the table, ate her dinner, and everything carried on as normal.

48 THE LIGHTBRINGERS

So, she wasn't sure anymore. Actually, she was really, really confused. If there wasn't a God, what had happened yesterday? Who fixed her leg?

She turned over and looked at the clock. 5:30 am. She had crept back through her window just after midnight. But there was no getting around it. She was wide awake. Enough thinking. Time to get up. This was a Saturday. It was curious how she always found it easier to get up when there was no school. But this was a girl with a mission. Today she was going to find Mr Dundenter and ask him how he did it…

Find out what happens next in next week's instalment of *The Lightbringers*.

Take some time to ask and listen to what the children think about the story.

Response

Prayer (5 minutes)

Invite the children to stand and ask if anyone wants to ask Jesus to be their forever friend using the ABC prayer (this can be done in small groups or as one large group):
A – Admit your sins and ask for forgiveness;
B – Believe in Jesus;
C – Choose to follow Jesus for the rest of your life.

Dear God, I admit I have done wrong things and I need You. Please forgive me for my sins. I believe Jesus died and rose again for the things I've done wrong. I declare that Jesus Christ is now my Lord and Saviour. Thank You for saving me. I choose to follow You for the rest of my life. In Jesus' name, Amen.

Ask the children to speak to a leader if they prayed that prayer and have booklets to give out. There is also an example parent letter available in the downloads.

Session 1: I Am Special, Safe, And Accepted

Pray that everyone will hear the truth God wants to show them today. Then encourage all the children to say the following prayer:

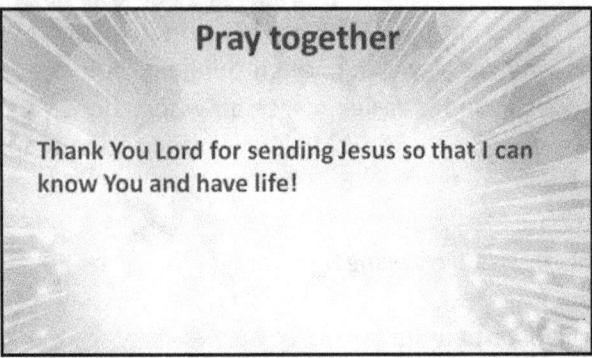

Pray together

Thank You Lord for sending Jesus so that I can know You and have life!

▶ Thank You Lord for sending Jesus so that I can know You and have life!

Special, Safe, And Accepted

What does God say is true? Read together the list of "Special, Safe, And Accepted" truths from their activity sheets or from the PowerPoint. Pause after each section for a quiet moment of reflection. At the end you could ask if any child is willing to share which truth was particularly special for them.

Special, Safe, And Accepted

I am SPECIAL because God says...
His Holy Spirit lives inside me (1 Corinthians 3:16)
He has made me to do good things (Ephesians 2:10)
I can always come to God and talk with Him (Ephesians 3:12)
I can do things I find hard because God gives me strength and helps me (Philippians 4:13)

▶ I am **SPECIAL** because God says:
His Holy Spirit lives inside me (1 Corinthians 3:16)
He has made me to do good things (Ephesians 2:10)
I can always come to God and talk with Him (Ephesians 3:12)
I can do things I find hard because God gives me strength and helps me (Philippians 4:13)

Special, Safe, And Accepted

I am SAFE because God says...
I am not guilty or bad because God has forgiven me (Romans 3:31-34)
Nothing can come between God and me (Romans 8:35-39)
He will finish the good work He started in me (Philippians 1:6)
I am safe with Jesus and in God (Colossians 3:3)
I am a child of God and I am safe from evil (1 John 5:18)

THE LIGHTBRINGERS

▶   I am **SAFE** because God says:
I am not guilty or bad because God has forgiven me (Romans 3:31-34)
Nothing can come between God and me (Romans 8:35-39)
He will finish the good work He started in me (Philippians 1:6)
I am safe with Jesus and in God (Colossians 3:3)
I am a child of God and I am safe from evil (1 John 5:18)

> **Special, Safe, And Accepted**
>
> **I am ACCEPTED because God says...**
>
> I am His child (John 1:12)
>
> Jesus chose me to be His friend (John 15:15)
>
> I am a saint – a special person set aside by God (Ephesians 1:1)
>
> I have been forgiven for all the things I've done wrong (Colossians 1:14)

▶   I am **ACCEPTED** because God says:
I am His child (John 1:12)
Jesus chose me to be His friend (John 15:15)
I am a saint – a special person set aside by God (Ephesians 1:1)
I have been forgiven for all the things I've done wrong (Colossians 1:14)

Make sure you hand out the activity sheet. As time allows spend some time together completing the activity sheet. The children can also take it home to complete.

Next Week (5 minutes)

Highlight next week's course. Keep it exciting:
"Next week everyone who comes will get a _____", "Next week we'll hear the next part of this exciting story", etc.

Session 2: I Am A New Creation

Session 2: I Am A New Creation

Time Plan

Getting Started 30 minutes	Free Play (20 minutes)	
	Welcome (5 minutes)	
	Announcements (5 minutes)	
Worship 20 minutes	Prayer (5 minutes)	
	Game (5 minutes)	Choose one: "Can you build it?" or "Happy families"
	Praise (10 minutes)	Gobsmacked
Word 45 minutes	Bible Verse (5 minutes)	I praise you because you made me in an amazing and wonderful way. (Psalm 139:14 NCV)
	Interview (5 minutes)	
	Teaching Time (20 minutes) Reflective Worship (10 minutes) Explore the Bible (5 minutes) Illustration (5 minutes)	I am a new creation – Acts 9:1-22
	Story Time (15 minutes)	*The Adventures Of Lilly Pepper* – Mrs Stevens' Decision (video: 5.5 minutes) *The Lightbringers* – Wonderfully Designed (video: 13.5 minutes)
Response 10 minutes	Prayer (5 minutes)	Remember to give out this week's activity sheet if you haven't already.
	Next Week (5 minutes)	

Overview

The Bible makes it clear that, because of what Jesus has done for us, we are new creations in Christ. Knowing that we are children of God who can come boldly into God's presence changes everything.

Getting Started

Free Play (20 minutes)

Welcome (5 minutes)

This is a chance to welcome the children but also an opportunity to have fun with them.

Announcements And Ground Rules (5 minutes)

Remind them of the two simple rules:
1. Nobody leaves their seat. If they need to go to the bathroom then they must put their hand up and ask permission from a leader.
2. When you ask for quiet, everyone sits down, focuses on the front, and makes no sound.

Worship

Prayer (5 minutes)

In two sections:
1. **Giving Thanks:** Children who have prayed for something the week before (or several weeks before) and whose prayers have been answered should be asked to come and tell the others how God answered their prayer.
2. **Bringing Needs:** Some of the children will want to pray for certain things. Allow them to come and mention what they are praying for and ask God together to answer prayer.

Session 2: I Am A New Creation

Game Choose one (5 minutes)

Game 1 – Can You Build It?

PREPARATION Lego.

PLAYERS Four to five per team.

SET-UP Using the Lego, build two simple Lego structures.

OBJECT Put out a big bowl of Lego, set a timer, and see how fast the kids can recreate each example.

WINNING The first team to build a duplicate structure.

Game 2 – Happy Families

PREPARATION Make happy families cards e.g. Mrs Elephant, Mr Elephant, Baby Elephant, Granny Elephant, Mr Monkey, Mrs Monkey, Baby Monkey etc.

PLAYERS The number of players needs to be divisible by four.

SET-UP Leader hands out a card to each player.

OBJECT Children have to pair up with their family.

WINNING The first team to do this is the winner.

Praise Gobsmacked (10 minutes)

The song that has been specially written for this lesson is "Gobsmacked" (a slang British-English expression equivalent to "overwhelmed with wonder"), which is what Saul was when he met Jesus on the road to Damascus.

YOU SPEAK WITH BLAZING WORDS
AND MAKE THE LIGHT APPEAR
CREATOR OF THE EARTH
I STAND IN AWE AND FEAR
YOU ARE ALL-POWERFUL
AND I AM SO AMAZED
YOUR TRUTH IS WONDERFUL
I CAN'T CONTAIN MY PRAISE

CHORUS
OH, I'M GOBSMACKED!
I'LL NEVER GO BACK
TO PLAIN BLACK
I'M SEEING IN COLOR
LIKE KODAK
YOU MAKE MY FEET DANCE
I'M GOBSMACKED!

REPEAT CHORUS

YOU MADE THIS ALL FOR ME
YOU MADE ME ALL FOR YOU
YOU GAVE ME ALL I NEED
NOW ALL I NEED IS YOU
YOUR LIFE IS BEAUTIFUL
MY HEART IS FILLED WITH THANKS
YOUR LOVE HAS MADE ME WHOLE
I CAN'T CONTAIN MY RAVE

REPEAT CHORUS 2 TIMES

I'LL NEVER GO BACK
I'M SEEING IN COLOR
YOU MAKE MY FEET DANCE

REPEAT CHORUS 3 TIMES

Words & Music by Wayne Tester, Esther Tester. © 2018 Testricity.com Music (ASCAP) / Fuzzy Socks Music (BMI) (both admin. by Testricity Music Group, www.testricity.com). ℗&© 2018 Testricity Music Group. ALL RIGHTS RESERVED.

Remember, we suggest using a few praise songs for each session. As well as the specific song here, you may want to reintroduce one or both of the songs from last week. Enjoy!

Session 2: I Am A New Creation

Word

I Am A New Creation

Bible Verse To Memorize (5 minutes)

▶ I praise You because You made me in an amazing and wonderful way. (Psalm 139:14 NCV)

Interview (5 minutes)

Invite one of the leaders or one of the children to come and tell the group what Jesus has done for them; how He's helped them in work/school; how He cares for them; how they first made their decision to become a Christian. If the person is very nervous, interview them. If they are more confident, allow them to speak freely – taking notice of the timing allowed for this section.

Teaching Time (20 minutes)

1. Reflective Worship (10 minutes)

2. Explore The Bible (5 minutes)

Acts 9:1-22

▶ When we decide to follow Jesus we are not only forgiven but we become totally new creations (2 Corinthians 5:17). Our old self has gone and we are made new – our lives are transformed. We became a completely new person deep down inside.

In Acts 9:1-22 we see how Jesus transforms Saul's life. Saul was an angry man who hated Christians, so much so that he beat them and killed them. Saul was travelling to the city of Damascus to arrest and imprison believers when suddenly, from heaven, came the brightest light he had ever seen. Trying to cover his eyes he then heard a voice saying, "SAUL! SAUL! Why do you persecute me?" Saul, not recognizing the voice, said, "Who are you, Lord?" The answer came back, "I am Jesus."

Saul had a dramatic encounter and met Jesus. God transformed his life! It wasn't long before Saul became a preacher teaching people about Jesus. Everyone was amazed. They couldn't believe that this was the same person that had hated them so much and wanted to kill them.

And so, like Saul, God completely transforms our life when we ask Him into our hearts.

3. Illustration Choose one (5 minutes)

Illustration 1– Changed For Good

Object Needed: Picture of caterpillar changing into a butterfly or, even better, a video clip.

Do you know what this is? *(Hold up a caterpillar or a picture of one)*. Right, a caterpillar. What do caterpillars become? Butterflies. They become transformed from a fuzzy, slow, hairy caterpillar into a beautiful, colourful butterfly. What an amazing transformation! Can a butterfly change back into a caterpillar? No, it can't. Once it's a butterfly it will always be a butterfly.

We can be changed too. God wants to work in our lives so that we are changed. The Bible says that, if we are in Christ, we are new creations – just like the butterfly "the old things are gone," it says, "and the new has come."

Illustration 2 – Adopted By Father God

Object Needed: A football or some other sport object.

Do you like sports? Which one do you like best? Are you a good player? Not everyone is, you know. When I was at school I wasn't good at sports. What I hated the most about sports was not the playing of the games but being picked for the team. I don't know how you get picked for teams but when I was at school the team captains would pick. They would always start by picking the best players and I was always one of the last to be chosen. As I would stand with my friends I always pretended that it didn't bother me but, one-by-one my friends were chosen, and I was always the one left at the end. If the truth be known, it really hurt. Has that happened to you? How did you feel?

The Bible tells us that when we ask Jesus into our lives we become adopted by God, therefore, we are now children of God! How would you like to be in God's family? Well, you can all be in God's family and you don't have to worry that you might be the last one chosen either. The Bible tells us that before He even made the world, God loved us and chose us. Before we were even born, God decided to adopt us into His own family (Ephesians 1:4-5).

God has chosen us – now it is up to each one of us to say, 'Yes, I believe that I am a Child of God with direct access to my Father God.'

Illustration 3 – Believing Who I Am

Objects Needed: Two identical balloons – one filled with air and the other filled with helium.

Who are we now? When we ask Jesus into our hearts, God's Spirit lives inside us. BUT, our outside being is still the same. We have the same old ways of thinking which the Bible calls our "flesh". Our spirits now want to do the good things that God wants us to do but our flesh still wants to do some of its old habits. We start to think maybe we aren't new after all! It makes it hard for us to believe the truth that we really are new creations.

It is kind of like this balloon *(hold up the helium balloon)*. When we are living for God we're like this balloon filled with helium. We rise, soar and live as God intended us to live. However, when we don't believe the truth and start living like our old selves, look what happens *(hold up the balloon filled with air)*. We might look the same on the outside but we just end up being tied down and not able to live the life God intends for us.

Story Time (15 minutes)

The Story For Younger Children – *The Adventures Of Lilly Pepper*

Chapter 2 – Mrs Stevens' Decision

The video is 5.5 minutes. Take some time after the story to ask and listen to what the children think. Then go to the response and prayer time.

▶ Hello again! When we last saw Lilly she had just been sent to see Mrs Stevens, the Principal. How much trouble is she in? We'll find out in Chapter 2, Mrs Stevens' Decision.

Lilly wasn't sure what was going to happen next. She sat outside Mrs Stevens' office and waited. She had only been there a few minutes but it seemed like forever.

▶ Eventually, the door opened and Mrs Stevens invited Lilly to come into her office and sit down. The school was very old. Lilly knew that her grandmother had come to this school and so had her mum. The walls in Mrs Stevens' office were lined with shelves made out of very old and very dark wood. The books that sat on them looked even older. There was an old fireplace and curled in the corner next to it was Mrs Stevens' cat. Lilly wasn't sure you were supposed to have cats in school, but Mrs Stevens didn't seem to worry about that at all.

Mrs Stevens sat behind an old wooden desk and leaned across the table towards Lilly. Beside her was a chair. She wondered if her mother was going to be called soon to sit next to her and hear her punishment from Mrs Stevens.

▶ "So Miss …umm Pepper," Mrs Stevens began, "Mr Edwards said that you were very disruptive in his class earlier. And you were very rude."

Lilly looked at her feet and mumbled, "Yes, Mrs Stevens."

That was the part that was troubling Mrs Stevens. Lilly was loud, excitable, sometimes a little overwhelming but very smart, very helpful and never rude."

"So Lilly, What exactly did you say to Mr Edwards?"
Still looking at her feet Lilly mumbled, "That we're not monkeys."

Lilly was pretty sure this wasn't all her fault and she could tell this wasn't going well, so she lifted up her head, and with that fiery determination in her eyes, she looked at Mrs Stevens and it all poured out:

"Mr Edwards called me a monkey and he called the whole class monkeys. So, I told him that he was the monkey, not us, and that God made us. We didn't come from a tadpole that walked, we came from God who made us and made us in a very special way. And it wasn't my fault that everyone started making monkey sounds. And then he sent me out and I really hadn't done anything wrong except say he was wrong, and that was because he was wrong."

She'd delivered that all a little louder than she wanted to and she wasn't sure if Mrs Stevens was going to be even more cross. She wished she knew how to keep quiet sometimes, but she knew that God had made her, and loved her, and accepted her. She'd known it all along really. When she was four she had stood up in the Bible Club to say that she wanted to be Jesus' friend and she knew Jesus died for her to take away all the bad stuff she had done and was with her and looked after her. And she knew for sure that she was a girl who God had made.

▶ Lilly wondered what the punishment would be. Would her mum be called in to tell her off? Would she have to sit outside Mrs Stevens office every lunchtime like David and Gary had to when Mr Edwards caught them fighting. She had no idea.

But what Mrs Stevens decided was scarier than anything Lilly could ever thought of. It had taken Mrs Stevens a little while to understand, but now she'd got it. Lilly was sure that God had made her and everything else but Mr Edwards thought something different. Mrs Stevens face was still serious but her eyes looked sparkly. Eventually she smiled at Lilly, she couldn't help it:

"Ok Lilly. This is what we are going to do. Tomorrow I will ask Mr Edwards to again explain his idea to the class. Tadpoles and monkeys and the rest of it. And then I would like you to explain your idea to the class, what you think about God making you. And then we'll let the class decide what they think."

▶ Lilly was on the edge of objecting because she wasn't a teacher and although she was good at "show and tell" especially when she'd brought in a wiggly worm, she wasn't sure she could do this. But it really didn't seem to be a choice. She was ushered out of Mrs Stevens' office and ran outside to see her slightly anxious mother with Jake, wondering why the rest of Lilly's class had come out and Lilly hadn't.

Eventually they were on their way home, Lilly beginning to feel very nervous indeed.

How do you think she'll get on? I'll tell you what happens next time. Bye!

Take some time to ask and listen to what the children think about the story.

Session 2: I Am A New Creation

The Story For Older Children – *The Lightbringers*
Chapter 2 – Wonderfully Designed

The video is 13.5 minutes. Take some time after the story to ask and listen to what the children think. Then go to the response and prayer time.

▶ It was only 5:30am when she got out of bed. She really didn't expect to find anyone else up. The rain hadn't slowed down all night, and now relentlessly hammered on her bedroom window. Dawn had arrived, albeit reluctantly. The sun was making an effort, but darkness still seemed to be winning the fight outside. Her denim jacket was still damp and sat on top of the box.

▶ That box. A heavy metal box with a big key hole and no key. It wasn't all she owned. But, it was all she arrived with. She'd been given lots since and now had books and games and new toys every Christmas. The Home did look after her well. But the box was the only thing she brought with her from before. That stupid box. That stupid metal box that nobody could open! She'd kicked it. Banged it. Hammered it. She even tried using the caretaker's drill but the box just glared at her. If a box could glare? The metal box that remained completely unmarked by everything she tried to do to it.

She left her room. But as she reached the top of the stairs, still wearing her fluffy PJs and robe, she could clearly see Mr Dundenter at the bottom of the stairs.

▶   He was sitting at the kitchen table looking ridiculously wide awake. She wiped the sleep from her eyes and being very careful this time she began to descend the stairs.

The central area was all open. In the centre were two very large tables surrounded by chairs. The counter from where they served the food was nearby and the large stove, sink and work surfaces were all visible against the far wall. The stove was on and in front of it Cook was making her legendary oatmeal porridge. At least she called it oatmeal porridge. It certainly didn't look or taste like any oatmeal porridge Sophie had eaten at any of her friends' homes and rumour had it that if you wanted you could use it instead of cement – but Sophie was fairly sure that was made up, probably by Stacey who was good at making things up. Cook stood there with the enormous saucepan, stirring it with a wooden spoon and singing to herself.

As Sophie entered the room Mr Dundenter whispered without looking up, "Good morning Sophie. I hope you slept well. I have been expecting you. Come and sit down."

His eyes didn't leave the book that he was reading. An old book, it looked like it was held together with various bits of sticky tape. But, as she sat she could see the book more clearly. Not just a book, but a great big Bible. And then he looked up. That enormous smile made her feel relaxed almost at once. But she wouldn't be put off. She had a question to ask and she was going to ask it.

"Mr Dundenter. What did you do to my leg? It was really painful. You and I know it was. And you fixed it! How?"

He shrugged his shoulders, "I didn't do it."

But she was insistent, "You know you did. You got it back to normal."

"Nope." He shook his head. "Not me."

She was about to protest when he moved his head back down to look at his Bible and he began to read:

> God You know me, You see my heart
>
> You know when I stand up and sit down.
>
> You are all around me.
>
> If I went into space, You would be there.

> If I hid in the depths of the earth
>
> You would find me
>
> And You would protect me.
>
> Not even the darkness can hide me.
>
> You made every part of me
>
> You put me together inside my mother's tummy
>
> And I praise You because I am made in an
>
> amazing and wonderful way.[1]

"Cool hey? It's in one of the older parts of the Bible; a book of songs and poems. It's called Psalms."

"But," Sophie protested, "What's that got to do with anything Mr Dundenter? What's that got to do with my leg?"

But Mr Dundenter smiled again. He really did have the sort of smile that could light up a room. And in response to his smile Sophie was sure that Cook was singing louder and even if she wasn't, she was definitely grinning, grinning like a Cheshire cat. What was going on here?

"Sophie. Weren't you listening? This is about God creating you. It says, 'He put you together inside your mum's tummy.' Of course He can fix twisted legs. He made you in the first place."

And before she could stop it, the thought jumped into her head, "He didn't fix my parents, did He?" But she pushed the thought to one side and fixed her mind on a different thought. "You mean Jesus fixed me?"

He nodded, "You know He did. You heard my prayer. He made you. He loves you. He even died for you to get rid of all the bad stuff. He looks after you, and He wants to be close to you."

"Stop!" shouted Sophie. "Too much. I'm still not sure God even exists!"

"Oh He exists Sophie. And if you're willing He wants you to get to know Him. Shall we have a chat with Him?"

Now Sophie was even more confused, Mr Dundenter was unfazed, however. He closed his eyes and prayed. Sophie stared at him speechless. What was she supposed to do now? She didn't think she had any choice.

---

[1] Inspired by and adapted from 'Always Near Me' by Susie Poole. Used with permission.

▶   So she closed her eyes and listened to Mr Dundenter's prayer: "God, Sophie isn't sure about all this. But can You come now and fill her with more of You so she feels peaceful and safe and so that she knows she belongs to You and how much You love her? And help her to know that she is Your special child. Amen."

And it happened. It really happened. She felt calm and peaceful and knew that God loved her and she felt that same feeling she had felt when her leg stopped hurting, like she was wrapped in love. And she was crying and didn't know why. And she felt happy and strange and accepted and important all at the same time.

When she looked up Mr Dundenter was looking at her and Cook was smiling at her. She was definitely having a strange few days. But she absolutely believed it. God loved her and created her and was with her….

She felt as if she was in a dream when she mumbled, "I need to get changed," and she walked towards the stairs.

But Mr Dundenter called behind her, "Sophie, that bit in the Bible that said, 'Not even the darkness can hide me,' well that goes for graveyards too."

Her mouth dropped open. How did he know? She just kept walking. And then he said mysteriously:

"Uh, I think you'll find the Captain has the key to the box."

What? She definitely didn't understand that. When she got back to her room she threw herself on her bed and looked around. And then her eyes landed on the box. "The Captain has the key to the box." What does that mean?

It was a strange day. She'd got dressed, gone back downstairs, and eaten breakfast without saying a word. She wondered what went on in Stacey's head when she heard her proclaim that Cook's oatmeal porridge could turn you into a monster, but she didn't respond. The sun eventually broke through the clouds just after lunch, but only for a few hours before the rain came back even heavier than before. In those few hours Sophie managed to go out into the garden for some fresh air. She hadn't been there long when, to her absolute disbelief, she witnessed Thomas halfway up his favourite climbing tree… again! Her disbelief was because she knew he couldn't get back down and, worse than that, Thomas knew that he couldn't get back down. But he had still climbed the tree.

Sophie sighed, "At least some things haven't changed. Thomas is still nuts."

But she was more than intrigued as she sat on the swing to see that, unlike the other helpers who would call the fire department at this moment, Mr Dundenter did the most ridiculous thing.

▶ He actually climbed up after Thomas and, instead of trying to bring him down, he sat with him on the branch for a full 30 minutes just chatting. She didn't know what to make of all this. She still couldn't quite work out if Mr Dundenter was some sort of superman, or whether he was plain nuts just like Thomas. But she couldn't deny that she felt different, and she couldn't deny that she was now absolutely convinced that God existed and was looking after her. And she had to admit that she was really impressed when, 30 minutes later, both Mr Dundenter and Thomas successfully climbed back down the tree.

It had indeed been an unusual day, but it wasn't until dinner that the thought eventually lodged itself in her head. She was half way through her dinner when she announced, "Of course!" She said it so loud that everyone stared. She ignored them and carried on eating. But she'd got it. She knew where the Captain was. The one with the key. She knew….

She went to her bedroom. But she didn't intend to sleep. And then at midnight when the house was quiet and the only sounds that could be heard was the rain battering her window and the wind threatening to drag the trees out of the ground, she put on her jeans and her still damp jacket, crept down the stairs, opened the front door and stepped once more into the night. She was going to see the Captain…

Find out what happens next in next week's instalment of *The Lightbringers*.

Take some time to ask and listen to what the children think about the story.

Response

Prayer (5 minutes)

Now that we're friends of Jesus, we are completely new, just like the butterfly. We have a heavenly Father who is always there for us and wants the best for us.

> **Pray together**
>
> Dear God,
> Show me and each one of us the truth of who You are as our Heavenly Father.

▶ Dear God, show me and each one of us the truth of who You are as our Heavenly Father.

Encourage all the children to stand and read out together "The Truth About My Father God" list from their activity sheet or the PowerPoint slides (also on the following page). Read across each line together. Afterwards, ask them if any truth from the list particularly struck them. Encourage them to read their favourite one every day this week and to try to look up the Bible verse(s) associated with it.

▶ **The Truth About My Father God**

The Truth About My Father God

I say NO to the lie that Father God:	*I say YES to the truth that Father God:*
is distant and not interested in me	is close to me and cares for me (Psalm 139:1-18)
is grumpy and strict	loves me and is kind all the time (Psalm 103:8-14)
is too busy for me or not there for me	is always there for me and is full of joy and love (Hebrews 13:5; Zephaniah 3:17)
is angry or never happy with what I do	is patient and slow to get cross (Exodus 34:6; 2 Peter 3:9; Psalm 147:11)

The Truth About My Father God

I say NO to the lie that Father God:	*I say YES to the truth that Father God:*
is mean and cruel	is loving and protects me (Isaiah 42:3; Psalm 18:2)
doesn't want me to have fun	wants me to have the best life (John 10:10; Romans 12:1-2)
won't forgive me	is always kind and forgives me (Psalm 130:1-4; Luke 15:17-24)
is looking for when I get things wrong	is proud of me (Romans 8:28; Hebrews 12:5-11)

Session 2: I Am A New Creation

I say NO to the lie that Father God:	I say YES to the truth that Father God:
is distant and not interested in me	is close to me and cares for me (Psalm 139:1-18)
is grumpy and strict	loves me and is kind all the time (Psalm 103:8-14)
is too busy for me or not there for me	is always there for me and is full of joy and love (Hebrews 13:5; Zephaniah 3:17)
is angry or never happy with what I do	is patient and slow to get cross (Exodus 34:6; 2 Peter 3:9; Psalm 147:11)
is mean and cruel	is loving and protects me (Isaiah 42:3; Psalm 18:2)
doesn't want me to have fun	wants me to have the best life (John 10:10; Romans 12:1-2)
won't forgive me	is always kind and forgives me (Psalm 130:1-4; Luke 15:17-24)
is looking for when I get things wrong	is proud of me (Romans 8:28; Hebrews 12:5-11)

Make sure you hand out the activity sheet. As time allows spend some time together completing the activity sheet. The children can also take it home to complete.

Next Week (5 minutes)

Highlight next week's course. Keep it exciting:
"Next week everyone who comes will get a _____", "Next week we'll hear the next part of this exciting story", etc.

Session 3: I Can Trust Father God

Session 3: I Can Trust Father God

Time Plan

Getting Started 30 minutes	Free Play (20 minutes)	
	Welcome (5 minutes)	
	Announcements (5 minutes)	
Worship 20 minutes	Prayer (5 minutes)	
	Game (5 minutes)	Choose one: "Minefield" or "Blind ball retrieval"
	Praise (10 minutes)	Name Above All Names
Word 45 minutes	Bible Verse (5 minutes)	Without faith it is impossible to please God, because anyone who comes to Him must believe that He exists and that He rewards those who earnestly seek Him. (Hebrews 11:6)
	Interview (5 minutes)	
	Teaching Time (20 minutes) Reflective Worship (10 minutes) Explore the Bible (5 minutes) Illustration (5 minutes)	1 Kings 18
	Story Time (15 minutes)	*The Adventures Of Lilly Pepper* – At Home (video: 5 minutes) *The Lightbringers* – Return To The Graveyard (video: 13 minutes)
Response 10 minutes	Prayer (5 minutes)	Remember to give out this week's activity sheet if you haven't already.
	Next Week (5 minutes)	

Overview

Everyone lives by faith, even those who are not Christians. It's who or what we put our faith in that determines whether or not it will be effective. As Christians, it's essential that what we believe is in agreement with what God has revealed in His Word.

Getting Started

Free Play (20 minutes)

Welcome (5 minutes)

This is a chance to welcome the children but also an opportunity to have fun with them.

Announcements And Ground Rules (5 minutes)

Remind them of the two simple rules:
1. Nobody leaves their seat. If they need to go to the bathroom then they must put their hand up and ask permission from a leader.
2. When you ask for quiet, everyone sits down, focuses on the front, and makes no sound.

Worship

Prayer (5 minutes)

In two sections:
1. **Giving Thanks:** Children who have prayed for something the week before (or several weeks before) and whose prayers have been answered should be asked to come and tell the others how God answered their prayer.
2. **Bringing Needs:** Some of the children will want to pray for certain things. Allow them to come and mention what they are praying for and ask God together to answer prayer.

Game Choose one (5 minutes)

Game 1 – Minefield

PREPARATION Items which can be used as obstacles, e.g. cones, tables, toys; two blindfolds.

PLAYERS Two players per team.

SET-UP Set up a "minefield" using the obstacles. One player will be the walker (and wears the blindfold) the other player will be the instructor.

OBJECT The walker must walk backwards through the minefield without stepping on or bumping into anything. They must also avoid bumping into other children walking through the minefield. They must trust the player telling them how many steps and in which direction.

WINNING The first team to be guided safely through the minefield.

Game 2 – Blind Ball Retrieval

PREPARATION Two containers of balls and two blindfolds.

PLAYERS Two teams of 4-8 players.

SET-UP Place the container of balls about six feet in front of the team.

OBJECT The first player will put on the blindfold and then the balls will be dumped out. Each player will try to retrieve three balls and place them back into their own container by following instructions given by the rest of the team. Once they have done this they can remove their blindfold and give it to the next person in line. That person will put on the blindfold and the balls will be dumped again. They too must retrieve three balls and put them in their container. The balls can be any balls that they find but they have to go into their own container. If they put a ball into the wrong container it will count for the other team.

WINNING The first team where everyone has retrieved their balls is the winner.

Praise Name Above All Names (10 minutes)

The song that has been specially written for this lesson is "Name Above All Names" which emphasizes that God is above all other gods (e.g. Baal) and that only God is real which is why we can trust Him. It uses some of the Hebrew names for God from the Old Testament (translations below).

EL HANNE'EMAN – FAITHFUL GOD, YOU HAVE AN EVERLASTING NAME
EL SALI – YOU ARE MY FORCE FIELD AND MY STRENGTH
EL ROI – YOU KNOW ME, YOU SEE ME, MY NAME IS CHILD
EL ELYON – YOU ARE ALWAYS STRONG AND NEVER WRONG

CHORUS
JESUS
THE NAME ABOVE ALL NAMES
YOU ARE HOLY
WORTHY OF ALL OUR Praise, WHOA-O-O-O
JESUS
THE NAME ABOVE ALL NAMES
YOU ARE HOLY
I'LL BE YOURS ALL MY DAYS, WHOA-O-O-O

EL YISRAEL – I AM YOUR SANCTUARY
EL HAKKAVOD – YOU ARE THE GOD OF GLORY
EL ECHAD – THERE IS NO ONE LIKE YOU, NO ONE CAN REPLACE YOU
IMMANUEL – FATHER, YOU ARE ALWAYS WITH US

REPEAT CHORUS

YOU HAVE SAVED ME, YOU GIVE ME LIFE
YOU RAISED ME FROM GROUND, YOU PULL ME TO SKY

REPEAT CHORUS

Words & Music by Wayne Tester, Esther Tester. © 2018 Testricity.com Music (ASCAP) / Fuzzy Socks Music (BMI) (both admin. by Testricity Music Group, www.testricity.com). ℗&© 2018 Testricity Music Group. ALL RIGHTS RESERVED..

EL HANNE'EMAN – The Faithful God
EL SALI – God My Rock
EL ROI – The God Who Sees Me
EL ELYON – God Most High
EL YISRAEL – The God Of Israel
EL HAKKAVOD – The God Of Glory
EL ECHAD – The One God
IMMANUEL – God Is With Us

Remember, we suggest using a few praise songs for each session. As well as the specific song here, you may want to reintroduce some of the songs that have already been used. Enjoy!

Session 3: I Can Trust Father God

Word

I can trust Father God

Bible Verse To Memorize (5 minutes)

> Without faith it is impossible to please God, because anyone who comes to Him must believe that He exists and that He rewards those who earnestly seek Him.
> Hebrews 11:6

▶ Without faith it is impossible to please God, because anyone who comes to Him must believe that He exists and that He rewards those who earnestly seek Him. (Hebrews 11:6)

Interview (5 minutes)

Invite one of the leaders or one of the children to come and tell the group what Jesus has done for them; how He's helped them in work/school; how He cares for them; how they first made their decision to become a Christian. If the person is very nervous, interview them. If they are more confident, allow them to speak freely – taking notice of the timing allowed for this section.

Teaching Time (20 minutes)

1. Reflective Worship (10 minutes)

2. Explore The Bible (5 minutes)

1 Kings 18

▶ There is nothing you can do that will make God love you any more or any less. That's a fact! But, how much you grow as a Christian will depend on how much you believe God's Word and act on it. This is called faith – believing the truth and choosing to follow Him.

There's a story about Elijah in the Bible (1 Kings 18), where he had a big faith showdown with the prophets of a false god called Baal. As the people were watching, he encouraged them to ask their god to throw down fire on their pile of sacrificed bull. The prophets shouted, danced and did everything they could to make Baal hear them. Nothing happened. After a few hours of this Elijah teased them saying, "Maybe Baal's gone on vacation? Or maybe he's asleep!"

When the evening came, Elijah took to the stage. He built an altar for his sacrifice, and then soaked the whole thing in water – three times over. There was no way this could be set alight without God doing a miracle. Then he prayed a simple prayer, and God threw down fire that consumed the entire altar!

It wasn't that Elijah had a stronger faith than the prophets of Baal – the difference was whom he had put his faith in. Baal couldn't answer because he is not real, but our God proved how real and powerful He really is. We need to believe this and know that God can do miracles in our lives.

3. Illustration Choose one (5 minutes)

Illustration 1 – The importance of faith

Objects Needed: Chair, glass, piece of card.

How many of you sat down on a chair today? How many of you thought, "I hope this chair is made well so that I won't fall on the floor"? Most of us have faith that our chair is going to hold us as we sit down *(sit on chair)*. We don't think about it, it's just there.

But it's harder to have faith in something that we can't see – like God. You cannot see God because He is Spirit, but you can still know that He is real. Something else that you cannot see, but is real is air and I'll prove to you that the air in this room is real!

Pour water into a glass until it is almost full. Place a piece of cardboard, cut too slightly larger than the top of the glass, over the top. Hold cardboard in place, and invert the glass. Take away your hand from the cardboard.

The gravity is still at work trying to make the water fall on the floor, but that the air – which we cannot see – is stronger than gravity and is keeping the cardboard in place. You see kids, faith is simple – it's believing in something that you can't see but nevertheless is real.

Illustration 2 – Effective Faith

Objects Needed: Mustard seeds.

How much do you think a mountain weighs? Do you think it weighs more than you? Do you think it weighs more than your car? How about more than your house? How hard do you think it would be to move a mountain? If you did you would probably need dynamite, heavy machinery, hundreds of workers and it would still take years and years to move!

Did you know that Jesus tells us how to move mountains? *(Pour some mustard seeds into your hand and show how small they are).* Jesus told His disciples (Matthew 17:20-21) that if they had faith the size of a mustard seed they could tell a mountain to jump into the ocean and it would! Imagine that! You wouldn't need dynamite or heavy machinery – it would just jump into the ocean.

Why do you think that Jesus used a mustard seed? Because it is really small, but it has big potential. It may not look like much, but there is a big tree in this little seed. Kids, the size of our faith doesn't matter so much as who we put our faith in. It's not our power that moves the mountain – it's God's.

Now, Jesus wasn't talking about a real mountain. He was talking about the obstacles and difficulties that we will face in our life. It doesn't take a huge amount of faith to move the mountains in our life. All we really need is a little bit of faith in God and He will move the mountains we face.

Illustration 3 – Growing In Faith

Objects Needed: volunteer (*choose a child who trusts you and give him/her instructions ahead of time*), blindfold and chair/step ladder, Bible.

Our faith can only grow when we put it into action. If we take small steps of faith and see that God is trustworthy, our faith will grow. *Ask for your volunteer. Begin by asking if he/she trusts you. Then blindfold them and challenge them to fall straight backwards telling them you will catch them.* You see, ____'s faith in me grew when he/she came up and dared to trust me. We need to trust God in the little things and when we do, only then will our faith grow. Now, we want to take our little faith and grow it more.

Take the chair or ladder and ask the volunteer (blindfolded) to stand on the chair or a few steps on a ladder so they are off the ground. Then ask them to fall straight backwards again, telling them you will catch them again. Just like _____ trusted me and took a huge risk that I was going to catch him/her, we need to dare to take a risk for God – take little steps which will turn into big leaps! Our actions, what we do, will show what we really believe, what we have put our faith in. Everyone here can grow in their faith. All we need to do is to know what's already true *(hold up the Bible)*, choose to believe it, and then act on it!

Story Time (15 minutes)

The Story For Younger Children – *The Adventures Of Lilly Pepper*

Chapter 3 – At Home

The video is 5 minutes. Take some time after the story to ask and listen to what the children think. Then go to the response and prayer time.

▶   Hi! Welcome back to *The Adventures Of Lilly Pepper*. Chapter 3, At Home. Last time we left Lilly feeling very nervous because she's got to teach a lesson to her class.

▶   Lilly had been quiet all the way home. She'd sat watching television for a little while, read her book, played with Jake on his activity mat and now sat down with mum to eat. They were half way through dinner – and Jake was completely finished with the mushy mix that mum had made him – before mum said, "Lilly, what's wrong? And don't say 'nothing' because you've never ever been this quiet unless something is wrong. You haven't been this quiet since Mop ate the goldfish."

Lilly knew that her mum would get it out of her eventually, so she might as well own up. So out came the whole story. Mum frowned and then smiled and then frowned again as Lilly went through the whole account and then at the end mum simply said, "Oh!"

Session 3: I Can Trust Father God

▶ What am I supposed to do? Mr Edwards is going to make me look silly. Can't you help me just a little bit?"

"Ok" replied mum, "I'll tell you what you have to do."

Lilly wasn't sure if she should write it down, but was a little surprised by her mum's advice.

"Pray. You will have to pray and ask Jesus what to do because I don't know, and I don't think Jake and Mop are going to help much either."

Lilly became even quieter. She was now more nervous than ever. But after dinner, after she had helped load the dishwasher, up to her room she went, to pray. She wasn't really sure what that looked like. She knelt on the floor, put her hands together:

"Dear God. It's me, Lilly Pepper. I'm in trouble again. But this time it's not really my fault. In fact, it's more Your fault. Mr Edwards told everyone that we came from monkeys. And I told them that You made us. And now I have to tell the class that. So could You help me please? Amen!"

She sat and waited and waited. But nothing. No angels came, which was very disappointing, no voice from heaven, just silence. No answer.

▶ She picked up her Bible. But there are so many pages. She had read lots of other books, but where should she start with this? She put it down on the desk so hard it opened. It opened at a book called 'Psalms'. To be precise, it opened at Psalm 139 . So Lilly read it and she couldn't believe what she was reading:

> God You know me, You see my heart
>
> You know when I stand up and sit down.
>
> You are all around me.
>
> If I went into space, You would be there.
>
> If I hid in the depths of the earth
>
> You would find me
>
> And You would protect me.
>
> Not even the darkness can hide me.
>
> You made every part of me
>
> You put me together inside my Mum
>
> And I praise You because I am made in an
>
> amazing and wonderful way. [2]

Wow. There it was. Right in front of her. "You made every part of me."

Lilly was delighted. She knew it. And now she had it in writing. She put her hands together again, closed her eyes and prayed, "Thank you God. I knew I could trust You." And went to sleep!

How will she get on teaching a lesson at school? I'll tell you next time.

Take some time to ask and listen to what the children think about the story.

---

[2]   Inspired by and adapted from 'Always Near Me' by Susie Poole. Used with permission.

Session 3: I Can Trust Father God

The Story For Older Children – *The Lightbringers*
Chapter 3 – Return To The Graveyard

The video is 13 minutes. Take some time after the story to ask and listen to what the children think. Then go to the response and prayer time.

▶   Sophie had slipped quietly out of the front door and onto the street. The sound of the rain dancing on the road was punctuated by the bark of a dog and then silence again. The splash and trickle of water. And then:

"Boo!"

Sophie almost jumped out of her skin. Someone had crept up beside her. He must have been sheltering under part of the house. He was wearing a red hoodie. Her heart was beating faster than a very fast train and she was shaking and then she saw those words written across the hoodie:

KEEP CALM AND WEAR A HOODIE!

▶   She couldn't believe it. "Thomas. What are you doing?"

The bedraggled figure pulled down the hood to reveal the smiling face of Thomas.

"Hey Sophie, how are you? I've been waiting ages for you." All delivered calmly and with a smile.

"But why, Thomas? Why? Don't you know it's midnight and it's raining and sensible people should be in bed."

"Well", he responded. "You're sensible and you're not in bed. And anyway, I saw you at dinner and I knew you were up to something. I could see you thinking, you were doing your funny thinking face. And I saw you creep in the other night when I was coming from the bathroom."

"Whoa… too much information, Thomas," Sophie interjected, "Way too much. But this is nothing to do with you. Go back to bed."

Thomas was in the same school class as Sophie. He had been ever since she could remember and he was a boy, so, as far as Sophie was concerned, that meant he was automatically annoying. But despite the fact that he climbed trees he couldn't get down from and the fact that he was definitely a little bit nuts, he was also quite likeable. And she had to admit, he was very clever. He did seem to know the answers to most questions asked in the classroom. He had dark hair with a fringe that desperately needed cutting, brown eyes, freckles and right now, increasingly wet clothes. He looked at her through his fringe.

"I'm definitely coming. It's dark and wet and I can protect you."

Sophie laughed. She didn't need protecting and certainly not by Thomas.

But what could she do? She was worried that, if he went back in, then he would wake people up. He wasn't known for being the most graceful of boys – although she wasn't sure there was such a thing as a graceful boy.

She sighed, "Come on then. Let's go."

▶   "Great! This is fun", said Thomas as he splashed along beside her. Although, splashing in canvas shoes was not a great idea. "So where are we going?"

She quickened her pace, "The Old Graveyard."

"Well, see you in the morning!" And with that, Thomas turned and pretended to walk off in the other direction, but he was soon back, "Why? Why?"

She wasn't giving too much away. But even as she said the words she knew how ridiculous it all sounded: "We're going to see the Captain because Mr Dundenter says he has the key to the metal box in my bedroom." She waited for the laughter or at least the comments of disbelief. But none came. She stopped and looked at him. He shrugged his shoulders and eventually said, "If Mr Dundenter said it, then I believe it. I guess it's a faith thing really. Believing in what someone says even without proof."

Well, this set of words certainly caught Sophie by surprise and she must have looked particularly puzzled. She suspected that she definitely had the funny thinking face on so Thomas carried on talking,

"I had a long chat with Mr Dundenter up the tree. He told me to climb down, and he said it was a faith thing. He said that he would catch me if I fell and if I had faith in him I would climb down. So I did. The first time ever that I did it without the firemen." He looked a little embarrassed at that point. "Faith. I trusted what he said was true. So, if he said we should go to the graveyard, then we should go to the graveyard."

It was Sophie's turn to shrug her shoulders. "Mr Dundenter didn't exactly say 'we' and he didn't exactly suggest we do it at midnight," but on a night like this she was glad of the company. She turned to Thomas, "I do have faith in Mr Dundenter, but I think I may also have faith in God, who apparently put me together in my mother's tummy and told Mr Dundenter to tell me about the graveyard. Do you really think God made us Thomas?"

At this point Thomas laughed out loud. "Of course He did, you banana. What else could have happened? Of course God made us and loves us and protects us... otherwise I would have fallen out of the tree and died lots of times. Stacey is of course pretty convinced I'm going to fall out of the tree and die anyway, but she doesn't have a clue."

With that, Sophie and Thomas walked on in silence. It was 20 minutes later when they arrived at the metal gates. The chain still connected the two gates together and the padlock held the chain shut, but Sophie had long ago worked out that the gates could still be opened far enough to allow her through. There was nothing else for it, into the graveyard they went.

▶   It continued to rain. Of course it did. It hadn't stopped for days. But now the storm had returned and was determined to make its presence felt. Lightning illuminated everything and then loud rumbling thunder followed almost instantly. Rain poured off Sophie and Thomas as they walked. "Why does it never stop raining?" Sophie thought as another streak of lightning flashed across the sky.

The graveyard was never a pleasant place to visit in the dark, but Sophie had got used to it. She had been here many times before. However, tonight was particularly eerie. It felt as if darkness had somehow become thicker and the statues seemed to be alive. Yes, the statues...

Another flash of lightning silhouetting further statues. She had always found the statues strange. She understood the angel statues. There were lots of them at the end of the graves. She understood why people would want to make angel statues. She thought they might be guardian angels. And she particularly liked the angel at the end of the grave she visited. It was big. Well, twice her size and it had a sword by its side. It looked very, very tough, but somehow nice anyway.

Sophie had been wondering if Mr Dundenter might be an angel. But, she definitely didn't see any bumps on his back where his wings could be. However, maybe angels could do disguises. She would ask him. Next time she saw him she would ask him.

The angel statues made sense. But who would put those other statues next to their graves. There were statues that looked like, well they looked like they had the body of a person and the head of a wolf.

She'd hoped to go straight to the Captain. But Thomas had found it. He shouted,

"Hey Soph, these people have the same name as you, 'Harold Stanmore and Bethany Stanmore'. Who are they? Are they the reason you've come?"

Well, they were. They were her grandparents. She didn't know where her mum and dad were put after the accident, so this was the only family she knew of. And so she visited. But to Thomas she replied, "Come on, we're looking for the Captain."

▶   Slowly, he made his way over to her. His shoes were now squelching. Mud splattered both of them. Sophie was standing in front of it, 'Captain Valiant'. This was his grave and sure enough they're above his coat of arms, the symbol of House Valiant, a large circle, with a small circle inside and a key above it. But, all made of stone. What was she supposed to do with this? And then she saw it. Or thought she saw it. In the corner of her eye, something moved. And then the lightning flashed again and her heart jumped. The wolf statue. It had moved. And it continued to move.

They had trusted Mr Dundenter, they had faith in him and they had faith in God. Sophie knew that they were here on a mission that God had sent them on. But now they were about to get eaten by a wolf creature. Maybe it wasn't such a good thing to have faith in God after all?

It was clearly moving now. Before it had made stumbling movements. Now it moved towards Sophie, making huge strides. Mouth open. She wondered how a statue could have so many real teeth. It dived towards her. But Thomas dived too. He grabbed Sophie and the two of them stumbled away from the glistening teeth. But, they landed on the ground hard, Thomas banging into the grave of Captain Valiant. There was a strange grinding noise and the stone key fell off and landed beside Sophie. Her eyes were wide. But, what use was a key when a wolf thing was about to have

Session 3: I Can Trust Father God

you for early breakfast?

For his part, the wolf thing knew that he had cornered his prey. He was expecting one, he'd got two. Still, he could eat two; he was hungry. He moved closer. More lightning, this time glinting off those huge teeth. He sprang at them, mouth wide, getting closer and closer to the trapped Thomas and Sophie…

I'll tell you what happens next in next week's instalment of *The Lightbringers*.

Take some time to ask and listen to what the children think about the story.

Response

Prayer (5 minutes)

Ask the children to stand and hold out their hands. Place a mustard seed in each child's hands. Remember the story of the mustard seed. Let's ask God to help us increase our faith in Him so that our faith would increase, just like this mustard seed will grow.

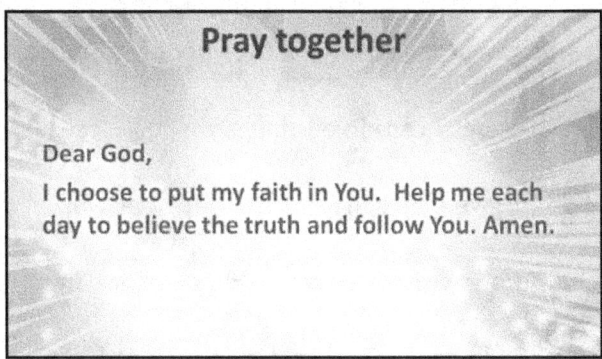

▶ Dear God, I choose to put my faith in You. Help me each day to believe the truth and follow You. Amen.

Encourage all the children to stand and read out together the "What I Can Do" list from their activity sheet or the PowerPoint (also on the following page). Afterwards, ask them if any truth from the list particularly struck them. Encourage them to read their favourite one every day this week and to try to look up the Bible verse associated with it.

Session 3: I Can Trust Father God

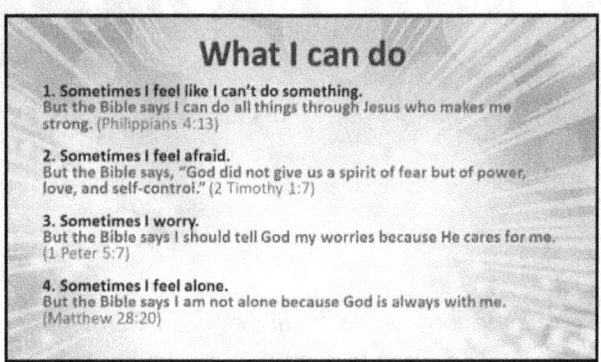

▶ **What I Can Do (5-to-8-Year-Olds)**

We have a choice to make. We can believe what God says about us, or what other people and the world say.

1. Sometimes I feel like I can't do something. But the Bible says I can do all things through Jesus who makes me strong. (Philippians 4:13)
2. Sometimes I feel afraid. But the Bible says, "God did not give us a spirit of fear but of power, love, and self-control." (2 Timothy 1:7)
3. Sometimes I worry. But the Bible says I should tell God my worries because He cares for me. (1 Peter 5:7)
4. Sometimes I feel alone. But the Bible says I am not alone because God is always with me. (Matthew 28:20)

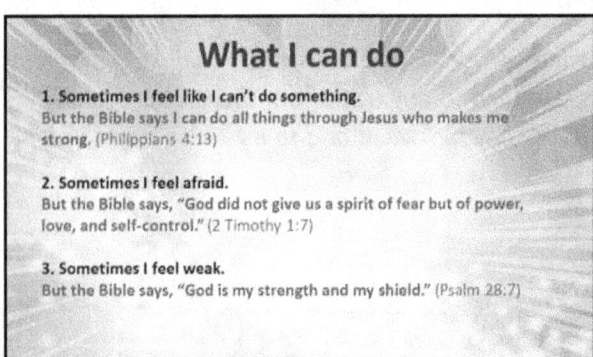

▶ **What I Can Do (9-to-11-Year-Olds)**

We have a choice to make. We can believe what God says about us, or what other people and the world say.

1. Sometimes I feel like I can't do something. But the Bible says I can do all things through Jesus who makes me strong. (Philippians 4:13)
2. Sometimes I feel afraid. But the Bible says, "God did not give us a spirit of fear but of power, love, and self-control." (2 Timothy 1:7)
3. Sometimes I feel weak. But the Bible says, "God is my strength and my shield." (Psalm 28:7)

88 THE LIGHTBRINGERS

> **What I can do**
>
> **4. Sometimes I worry.**
> But the Bible says I should tell God my worries because He cares for me.
> (1 Peter 5:7)
>
> **5. Sometimes I feel guilty.**
> But the Bible says I am not guilty because I am free in Jesus. (Romans 8:1)
>
> **6. Sometimes I feel alone.**
> But the Bible says I am not alone because God is always with me.
> (Matthew 28:20)

4. Sometimes I worry. But the Bible says I should tell God my worries because He cares for me. (1 Peter 5:7)
5. Sometimes I feel guilty. But the Bible says I am not guilty because I am free in Jesus. (Romans 8:1)
6. Sometimes I feel alone. But the Bible says I am not alone because God is always with me. (Matthew 28:20)

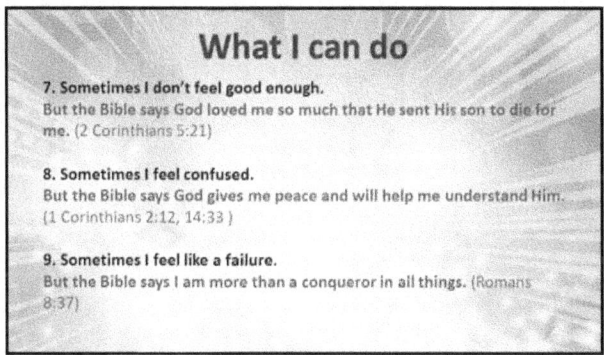

> **What I can do**
>
> **7. Sometimes I don't feel good enough.**
> But the Bible says God loved me so much that He sent His son to die for me. (2 Corinthians 5:21)
>
> **8. Sometimes I feel confused.**
> But the Bible says God gives me peace and will help me understand Him.
> (1 Corinthians 2:12, 14:33)
>
> **9. Sometimes I feel like a failure.**
> But the Bible says I am more than a conqueror in all things. (Romans 8:37)

7. Sometimes I don't feel good enough. But the Bible says God loved me so much that He sent His son to die for me. (2 Corinthians 5:21)
8. Sometimes I feel confused. But the Bible says God gives me peace and will help me understand Him. (1 Corinthians 2:12, 14:33)
9. Sometimes I feel like a failure. But the Bible says I am more than a conqueror in all things. (Romans 8:37)

Hand out the activity sheet and as time allows spend some time together completing the activity sheet. The children can also take it home to complete.

Next Week (5 minutes)

Highlight next week's course. Keep it exciting:
"Next week everyone who comes will get a _____", "Next week we'll hear the next part of this exciting story", etc.

Session 3: I Can Trust Father God

Session 4: I Can Choose To See Things As God Says They Really Are

Session 4: I Can Choose To See Things As God Says They Really Are

Time Plan

Getting Started 30 minutes	Free Play (20 minutes)	
	Welcome (5 minutes)	
	Announcements (5 minutes)	
Worship 20 minutes	Prayer (5 minutes)	
	Game (5 minutes)	Choose one: "Human maggot" or "Shoe scramble"
	Praise (10 minutes)	I Want You
Word 45 minutes	Bible Verse (5 minutes)	Do not conform to the pattern of this world, but be transformed by the renewing of your mind. (Romans 12:2)
	Interview (5 minutes)	
	Teaching Time (20 minutes) Reflective Worship (10 minutes) Explore the Bible (5 minutes) Illustration (5 minutes)	Genesis 6
	Story Time (15 minutes)	*The Adventures Of Lilly Pepper* – The Lesson (video: 8 minutes) *The Lightbringers* – Wolf Food! (video: 10.5 minutes)
Response 10 minutes	Prayer (5 minutes)	Remember to give out this week's activity sheet if you haven't already.
	Next Week (5 minutes)	

Overview

Depending on where they were brought up, children will have learned to look at the world in a way that seems right to them. But is it? We need to teach children to start seeing the world from God's perspective.

Getting Started

Free Play (20 minutes)

Welcome (5 minutes)

This is a chance to welcome the children but also an opportunity to have fun with them.

Announcements And Ground Rules (5 minutes)

Remind them of the two simple rules:
1. Nobody leaves their seat. If they need to go to the bathroom then they must put their hand up and ask permission from a leader.
2. When you ask for quiet, everyone sits down, focuses on the front, and makes no sound.

Worship

Prayer (5 minutes)

In two sections:
1. **Giving Thanks:** Children who have prayed for something the week before (or several weeks before) and whose prayers have been answered should be asked to come and tell the others how God answered their prayer.
2. **Bringing Needs:** Some of the children will want to pray for certain things. Allow them to come and mention what they are praying for and ask God together to answer prayer.

Game Choose one (5 minutes)

Game 1 – Human Maggot

PREPARATION Some sleeping bags.

PLAYERS Four to five per team.

SET-UP Each team has a sleeping bag. The first player of each team climbs into their sleeping bag and lies down on the ground with feet touching the starting point.

OBJECT The players must worm their way to the finishing line which will be at the opposite end of the room. Hands must be kept in the sleeping bag at all times.

WINNING The first team to have all their team across the line.

Game 2 – Shoe Scramble

PREPARATION None.

PLAYERS Four to five per team.

SET-UP Everyone takes off their shoes and tosses them into a pile at the opposite end of the room. The teams form a line.

OBJECT The players, in turn, must run to the pile and put on their shoes.

WINNING The first team to have all their team across the line with their shoes on.

Praise I Want You (10 minutes)

The song that has been specially written for this lesson is "I Want You" which is about CHOOSING God even when no one else does.

There is space to insert spoken Bible verses. You don't have to use the same verses as in the recording. Ask God which verses He would have you use for your group.

CHORUS
I WANT YOU – YOU ARE THE WAY
I WANT YOU – DAY AFTER DAY

VERSE
MONDAY, TUESDAY, WEDNESDAY, THURSDAY
FRIDAY, SATURDAY, SUNDAY
MONDAY, TUESDAY, WEDNESDAY, THURSDAY
FRIDAY, SATURDAY, SUNDAY
MONDAY, TUESDAY, WEDNESDAY, THURSDAY
FRIDAY, SATURDAY, SUNDAY
MONDAY, TUESDAY, WEDNESDAY, THURSDAY
FRIDAY, SATURDAY, SUNDAY

I Praise YOU BECAUSE I AM FEARFULLY AND WONDERFULLY MADE
YOUR WORKS ARE WONDERFUL, I KNOW THAT FULL WELL.
PSALM 139:14

REPEAT CHORUS

REPEAT VERSE

DO NOT CONFORM TO THE PATTERN OF THIS WORLD
BUT BE TRANSFORMED BY THE RENEWING OF YOUR MIND
ROMANS 12:2

REPEAT CHORUS

REPEAT VERSE

REPEAT VERSE & CHORUS

I WANT YOU

Words & Music by Wayne Tester, Esther Tester. © 2018 Testricity.com Music (ASCAP) / Fuzzy Socks Music (BMI) (both admin. by Testricity Music Group, www.testricity.com). ℗&© 2018 Testricity Music Group. ALL RIGHTS RESERVED.

Remember, we suggest using a few praise songs for each session. As well as the specific song here, you may want to reintroduce some of the songs that have already been used. Enjoy!

Session 4: I Can Choose To See Things As God Says They Really Are

Word

I Can Choose To See Things As God Says They Really Are

Bible Verse To Memorize (5 minutes)

> Do not conform
> to the pattern of this world,
> but be transformed by the
> renewing of your mind.
> Romans 12:2

▶ Do not conform to the pattern of this world, but be transformed by the renewing of your mind. (Romans 12:2)

Interview (5 minutes)

Invite one of the leaders or one of the children to come and tell the group what Jesus has done for them how He's helped them in work/school; how He cares for them; how they first made their decision to become a Christian. If the person is very nervous, interview them. If they are more confident, allow them to speak freely – taking notice of the timing allowed for this section.

Teaching Time (20 minutes)

1. Reflective Worship (10 minutes)

2. Explore The Bible (5 minutes)

Genesis 6

▶ There was a man in the Bible named Noah. Noah lived in a time when people didn't care about God and did not obey God's Word. But Noah was different. He loved God and God was pleased with him. One day God told Noah His plan to destroy the whole earth. He was going to put an end to all people and everything on earth because of all the evil. BUT, Noah and his family were going to be saved. God was going to give Noah instructions on how to build an ark and they had to put two animals of each kind in it.

Now, kids, an ark is a huge boat. No boat of this size had ever been built! It had never rained on the earth while Noah lived. Now, imagine what people were thinking about Noah. He was building a boat that would never fit on any river and they were some distance from the sea. What do you think people said to Noah? They probably laughed at him. They probably told him how stupid he was. They probably told Noah to stop building the ark. So, kids, was Noah going to believe the people or listen to God?

"Noah did everything just as God commanded him." Noah listened to God's Word rather than the world and he built the ark. After it was complete, he let in all of the animals. The rain came and the entire world was flooded. The only survivors were Noah, his family, and the animals. If Noah had disobeyed God's Word, the whole world would have died. We need to be like Noah and listen and obey His Word today.

3. Illustration Choose one (5 minutes)

Illustration 1 – Tinted glasses?

Objects Needed: Sunglasses with yellow (or another strange colour) lenses *(wear the glasses when delivering the illustration)*.

I am wearing these glasses today. When I am wearing these glasses what colour does everything look? Yellow! The room looks yellow, the chairs look yellow, even YOU look yellow! If I never took these glasses off everything would always be yellow. But, is this the truth....is everything yellow?

NO, *(take off the glasses)* the truth is that everything isn't yellow, we just get used to seeing things depending on the "filters" we are wearing. So, how we look at the world can depend on where and how we were raised. BUT, when we become Christians, God wants us to stop looking at the world through our filters and look at the world as it really is – how God says it is.

Illustration 2 – Focus On Jesus

Object Needed: Optical Illusion (find a suitable one you can project)

I want to show you an optical illusion (you could use the popular one which uses the name of JESUS in two colours). An optical illusion is a picture which kind of tricks your brain into seeing something which isn't there. Ask them to say what they see.

Kids, in our lives we need to keep our focus on Jesus and not focus on what the world thinks. We all have distractions in our lives which try to pull us away from the truth – maybe our friends, TV, Xbox etc. It can be easy to lose our focus. BUT, if we keep our eyes on Jesus, our lives will be transformed and we will know the truth.

Illustration 3 – Know The Truth

Objects Needed: Flashlight, Bible.

Imagine you were walking through a dark forest (you could turn all the lights out so it is dark) and you didn't know where you were or where you were going. You cannot see ahead, because it is so dark, but you keep walking. Then, you realize that you have had a flashlight in your pocket the whole time! You forgot! Whenever you turn the light on, you can see the path that was always close to you. As you follow the path with the light you wonder how you ever lost it, but, because it is so dark you could never find it!

Psalm 119:105 says that the Bible is like a light to us, it guides us and shows us the truth. The Bible *[hold the Bible up]* is our light in darkness. The Bible is God's Word to us. By reading and memorizing the Bible we are able to carry our flashlight with us at all times and will always know the truth!

Story Time (15 minutes)

The Story For Younger Children – *The Adventures Of Lilly Pepper*

Chapter 4 – The Lesson

The video is 8 minutes. Take some time after the story to ask and listen to what the children think. Then go to the response and prayer time.

▶   Welcome back! So, Lilly has to teach her class. Let's find out what happens in Chapter 4, The Lesson.

▶   Lilly woke early. She reached up to her top shelf and pulled down her toy monkey which a neighbour had given her when she was little. She liked the way he always smiled. She dressed, went downstairs, and got her cereal, got herself a yoghurt from the fridge and then she was ready. Mum walked Lilly to school with Jake.

Session 4: I Can Choose To See Things As God Says They Really Are

▶ Mum wouldn't let her go straight in. She hugged Lilly and then she prayed for her, a very simple prayer, "God, please will You help Lilly." And that was that. Into the classroom Lilly marched. The other children were very excited. They all wanted to know what punishment Mrs Stevens had given her. Lilly shrugged and said, "She didn't give me a punishment, instead she decided to make me a temporary teacher." They were a little confused, but Lilly would say no more because Mr Edwards had arrived and he did not look pleased. He stood in front of the class and announced,

"Well class, an unusual thing has been suggested. Miss Lilly Pepper is going to be a teacher just for this morning."

And Lilly looked around the class with a very clear look of, "I told you so".

Mr Edwards went on, "Mrs Stevens has decided that I should do yesterday's lesson again and you can listen, and then Lilly will tell you her idea and then you get to decide which one you believe. It's an unusual idea, but that's what Mrs Stevens wants, so that's what we'll do." And as if rehearsed, Mrs Stevens walked into the class at exactly that moment, and the children immediately went quiet as she walked to the back of the class and sat down. She said nothing, she simply sat down and nodded at Mr Edwards.

And with that Mr Edwards explained his lesson again. And concluded with the words, "And that's the truth." He sat down and nodded at Lilly.

▶ She walked to the front with her carrier bag and her lunch. She cleared her throat and looked at everyone and began.

"Mr Edwards says that you and I came from one of these." And out of the carrier bag Lilly pulled her very cuddly, very smiley, toy monkey. She continued, "His name is Monty." And then she opened her lunch box and took out her strawberry yoghurt, "And he says that before that we were all gooey like this yoghurt, and then we were like fish – and Mop who's my dog ate my fish, but that's not important. That is what Mr Edwards says, and he knows lots of things. He is very much older and wiser." Some of the class giggled. Mr Edwards looked a little annoyed but Mrs Stevens just smiled.

"So you can believe that if you want. Or you can believe what someone else said, someone who is much older than Mr Edwards. And even older than Mrs Stevens." The class didn't laugh at that at all, they were all slightly frightened of Mrs Stevens. But to their surprise, Mrs Stevens did laugh.

"I am talking about God. He is very, very old. And very, very smart. And this is what it says in the Bible about how He made us…"

▶ And with that she read Psalm 139:

God You know me, You see my heart
You know when I stand up and sit down.
You are all around me.
And if I went into space, You would be there.

If I hid in the depths of the earth
You would find me
And You would protect me.
Not even the darkness can hide me.

You made every part of me
You put me together inside my Mum
And I praise You because I am made in an
amazing and wonderful way.

And then:

"So, you get to choose. You can either believe that you came from goo, or a fish, or a monkey, or you can believe that God made you. And you were put together by Him. And He put you together in your mum and He made you very special. But you have to decide."

And with that Lilly Pepper took a bow and went back to her seat. The rest of the class looked at each other, shrugged and then started clapping but quickly coming to an abrupt stop as Mrs Stevens reached the front of the class.

Session 4: I Can Choose To See Things As God Says They Really Are

"Well class, that was very interesting. But you have to decide who you believe is right."

"Firstly, hands up if you believe what Mr Edwards said." There was gentle shuffling and lots of exchanged glances. But, nobody raised a hand.

"And who believes what Lilly said?"

Every hand went up. Lilly expected that. She knew God was with her. Mum had prayed after all. But the thing that happened next was surprising. As the whole class watched, Mrs Stevens lifted up her hand.

"Yes," Mrs Stevens began. "I quite agree with Lilly too. By far the most sensible answer."

And with that she thanked the class for listening so well, thanked Mr Edwards for allowing it and then left the classroom. Lilly's hand went straight up. There was something that was worrying her. When Mr Edwards eventually pointed to his now least favourite member of his class she quickly asked for permission to go speak to Mrs Stevens.

▶   She ran up the corridor, nearly knocking into a teacher and eventually caught up with her.

Mrs Stevens could see something was wrong. The usually very confident Lilly was almost shaking and looked very worried indeed.

"What is it?", Mrs Stevens asked, "Why are you so worried?"

It took Lilly a little while to respond and then eventually she managed to ask, "Mrs Stevens, I know I was a very good teacher today. But, that was with God helping me. But, you don't need me to teach arithmetic as well, do you, because numbers are a bit scary and Mr Edwards is very good at numbers and I'm not?"

And with that she stood looking up at Mrs Stevens, who burst out laughing. "Lilly Pepper you are priceless. No, we'll leave numbers to Mr Edwards. And with that she continued walking up the corridor but still laughing out loud."

"Phew!" thought Lilly. "That is such a relief" and she returned to class.

A week later, without any further incidents school was finished for summer. With a sigh of relief and a gentle prayer that God might give her a different teacher when she returned after the summer break, Lilly picked up her lunch box and left her classroom ready to enjoy some summer fun.

Little did she know that this was going to be a very interesting summer indeed. And I'll tell you about it when I see you next time. Bye for now!

Take some time to ask and listen to what the children think about the story.

Session 4: I Can Choose To See Things As God Says They Really Are

The Story For Older Children – *The Lightbringers*

Chapter 4 – Wolf Food

The video is 10.5 minutes. Take some time after the story to ask and listen to what the children think. Then go to the response and prayer time.

▶   Thomas was very afraid, Sophie more so. It was well past midnight, the storm was relentless, the rain hammered down,. They were cold, soaked through to the skin, huddled together, their backs pressed hard against a cold gravestone, and if all that wasn't enough, they were about to be eaten by a wolf thing.

Then it occurred to Sophie. The strangest thought. She had no idea why it landed in her mind, but it was there and she had nothing to lose and He'd fixed her leg, so why not. So with a quivering voice she spoke:

"I belong to Jesus. Go away!"

The wolf creature looked as if he had been punched. It took a step back and then stared. It looked from side to side, trying to work out what had happened. Sophie was beginning to understand who she was. Who God had created her to be. A child of God. And this was no time for doubt. Jesus was real, and He loved her and he loved Thomas – that's what Mr Dundenter had said – so He might just be interested in keeping them safe. And what did she have to lose? So again, with a new boldness, "I belong to Jesus. Go away!"

This time the wolf creature almost toppled. And now she stood up.

"I belong to Jesus. Go away!"

▶ There was a huge flash. And then the Wolf thing crumbled and was gone.

Thomas stood in silence and walked to the mess on the ground that used to be the wolf creature. Then he looked at Sophie, and then back at the mess and then back at Sophie and then he said, "Wow, Soph. That was very, very cool."

Sophie stood there trembling. "It worked Thomas. I can't believe it worked. I remembered what Mr Dundenter said. I remembered I was created by God and spoke out the truth that I belong to Him and it worked. The bad thing went away. Did you see that Thomas? Did you?"

Well he had and he nodded, but his eyes were wide. And then he asked the question that Sophie did not want to hear: "Um, Soph, do you think you can do that again?"

She shrugged. "I guess. Why?"

Thomas simply pointed. The whole graveyard was moving. There were wolf things coming to life and walking towards them from every corner.

"Oh!" was all Sophie could manage.

And then she stammered, "I can't do it. Not by myself, I'm afraid. I think we're in big trouble Thomas."

And more and more wolf things advanced towards them. Now they were surrounded. There must have been at least twenty of them.

And the rain kept falling. All Sophie wanted was to go home, get warm and not get eaten by wolf things. Surely, this wasn't too much to ask. Thomas was holding her hand. Normally that would be the worst thing she could possibly imagine, but facing a pack of wolf things did make worrying about holding hands seem slightly silly.

What was she to do? She searched her mind for ideas. Thomas was also thinking. Maybe the key, maybe the key was a magic key. He lifted it up above his head and waved it at the wolf things. He wasn't sure it was possible but it certainly seemed that they were laughing at him.

"Great," Thomas thought, "Laugh at us and then eat us. Not my best day ever."

"It needs to be you as well, Thomas," said a whisper from behind. "It needs to be you as well. Speak out the truth of who you are. You can do it, Thomas."

Session 4: I Can Choose To See Things As God Says They Really Are

Thomas looked for the whisper. He looked behind the gravestone... no, it couldn't be. She wore a hooded top, the string was pulled tight, she too was very wet, but it was her face. She whispered again, "You can do it."

His mind was racing. He was much happier when Sophie was doing amazing things. What was he supposed to do? He looked at her and shrugged. He figured that there was no point in all this talk of God if God didn't do stuff.

"Thomas, what are you doing?" whispered Sophie, nothing but alarm in her voice.

"We can do this together," Thomas replied, "These are enemies of God, so we need to speak out truth."

And Sophie agreed and did as Thomas asked and together with slightly quivering voices they said as confidently as they could. "We belong to Jesus, go away!" The wolf things just stood there and laughed.

"Again, Soph, but this time let's remember God is with us, and that's true even if it doesn't feel true."

So they declared again. But this time believing the truth that they belonged to God and He was really with them. "We are children of God so go away and leave us alone!"

The wolf creatures didn't laugh this time. Instead, they took a step backwards and exploded, leaving nothing to show that they were ever there.

Sophie sat and shook her head. "What is going on here? I've been to the graveyard again and again and never seen anything like this."

"But you weren't taking the key then, were you?" replied Thomas.

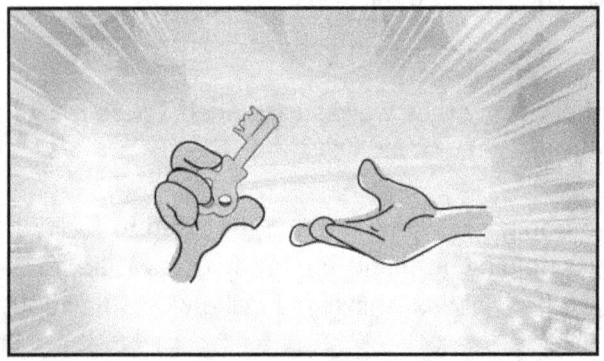

▶ And of course he was right. That was the only difference. Thomas held out his hand, helped Sophie up. With shoes squelching/sloshing, clothes dripping, they stumbled towards the gate and then they were out. A late night truck drove past. Everything looked so normal. But, Sophie and Thomas now knew better. The world wasn't how they had thought it was. There was God and there were angels but also some bad things too. They walked in silence for a few minutes. The sun was trying to rise but it wasn't going to make a dent in a night this wet and cold. Eventually, Sophie broke the silence. "Thomas, how did you do that? How did you know what to do?"

Thomas looked at the floor as he walked. He wasn't at all sure how to explain what had happened. But he did his best, "Someone told me Sophie. Someone appeared behind the grave and told me that we needed to remember the truth that we belong to Jesus."

But, Sophie knew that Thomas was leaving something out. She had known him long enough to know when he was hiding something. "Thomas what aren't you telling me?"

Thomas continued to look at his shoes as they squelched/sloshed along. Just then, he became aware of something heavy in his pocket. He reached in and pulled out the key. He handed it to Sophie. She took it with a nod. But, he needed to tell her: "Soph, the person who spoke to me from behind the grave. It was you!"

▶ "What?" Sophie responded, puzzlement in her voice. "What? But, I was next to you Thomas."

The famous Thomas shrug, but he saw what he saw. "She looked exactly like you Soph. Exactly like you. Same nose. Same eyes. Same lips."

Sophie was a little worried that Thomas seemed to remember her in such detail but she put that aside as she tried to get her head around what he'd actually said.

"Well, she couldn't have been me, could she? Unless I time travelled, and there's no such thing as time travel. So how?"

They were nearly home. Hopefully nobody was up yet. They still had time to sneak in, dump their wet clothes, and sleep. At least, Sophie would try to sleep. She needed to sleep. The key would have to wait. As would solving the mystery of the second Sophie in the graveyard.

What a night!

What's in the box? And who is the second Sophie? And why does Thomas remember Sophie's face so well? All will be revealed soon…

Take some time to ask and listen to what the children think about the story.

Session 4: I Can Choose To See Things As God Says They Really Are

Response

Prayer (5 minutes)

Ask the children to stand and read out together Psalm 119:105: "Your word is a lamp for my feet, a light on my path."

Before you pray this prayer explain that you will give them a moment to listen and then respond to God. Give them examples of what they might say "I choose not to feel lonely… afraid… stupid…."

> **Pray together**
>
> Dear God,
> Help me to start seeing the world as You do. Show me any ways I've let the world around me change how I see myself and You.
>
> Take a quiet moment to reflect.

▶ Dear God, help me to start seeing the world as You do. Show me any ways I've let the world around me change how I see myself and You.

Allow a quiet moment to reflect and then ask them to say the following prayer silently, filling in anything that has come to mind.

> **Pray together**
>
> I choose not to feel _____ anymore. Thank You that I can now walk in the truth of who I am in You. Amen.

▶ I choose not to feel …… anymore. Thank You that I can now walk in the truth of who I am in You. Amen.

Use the "Special, Safe, And Accepted", "The Truth About My Father God", or "What I Can Do" lists in smaller groups or encourage them to look at them at home this week.

Hand out the activity sheet and as time allows spend some time together completing the activity sheet. The children can also take it home to complete.

Next Week (5 minutes)

Highlight next week's course. Keep it exciting:
"Next week everyone who comes will get a _____", "Next week we'll hear the next part of this exciting story", etc.

Session 4: I Can Choose To See Things As God Says They Really Are

Session 5: I Can Make Good Choices With God's Help

Session 5: I Can Make Good Choices With God's Help

Time Plan

Getting Started 30 minutes	Free Play (20 minutes)	
	Welcome (5 minutes)	
	Announcements (5 minutes)	
Worship 20 minutes	Prayer (5 minutes)	
	Game (5 minutes)	Choose one: "Heads or tails"; "Dizzy mummy"; or "Would you rather?"
	Praise (10 minutes)	Orb Of Challenge
Word 45 minutes	Bible Verse (5 minutes)	His divine power has given us everything we need for a Godly life. (2 Peter 1:3)
	Interview (5 minutes)	
	Teaching Time (20 minutes) Reflective Worship (10 minutes) Explore the Bible (5 minutes) Illustration (5 minutes)	1 Kings 3
	Story Time (15 minutes)	*The Adventures Of Lilly Pepper* – Off To Gran's (video: 3.5 minutes) *The Lightbringers* – The Right To Turn the Key (video: 13 minutes)
Response 10 minutes	Prayer (5 minutes)	Remember to give out this week's activity sheet if you haven't already.
	Next Week (5 minutes)	

Overview

Christians have a new heart and a new spirit, but we still struggle with many of the unhelpful ways of thinking and behaving that we grew up with (a primary characteristic of what the Bible calls "the flesh"). However, we don't have to give in to the flesh. We can choose day-by-day and moment-by-moment whether to live according to the flesh's urges or according to the promptings of the Holy Spirit.

THE LIGHTBRINGERS

Getting Started

Free Play (20 minutes)

Welcome (5 minutes)

This is a chance to welcome the children but also an opportunity to have fun with them.

Announcements And Ground Rules (5 minutes)

Remind them of the two simple rules:
1. Nobody leaves their seat. If they need to go to the bathroom then they must put their hand up and ask permission from a leader.
2. When you ask for quiet, everyone sits down, focuses on the front, and makes no sound.

Worship

Prayer (5 minutes)

In two sections:
1. **Giving Thanks:** Children who have prayed for something the week before (or several weeks before) and whose prayers have been answered should be asked to come and tell the others how God answered their prayer.
2. **Bringing Needs:** Some of the children will want to pray for certain things. Allow them to come and mention what they are praying for and ask God together to answer prayer.

Game Choose one (5 minutes)

Game 1 – Heads Or Tails

PREPARATION A coin.

PLAYERS This game can be played with the whole group.

SET-UP The leader has the coin and asks the children to choose heads or tails. To choose heads the children place their hands on their heads and to choose tails the children place their hands on their bottoms.

OBJECT The leader throws the coin in the air. If it lands on tails, then those with their hands on their heads sit down. If it lands on heads, then those with their hands on their bottoms sit down. Watch out for cheaters!

WINNING The last player standing.

Game 2 – Dizzy Mummy

PREPARATION Toilet roll.

PLAYERS Two players per team.

SET-UP One player holds the toilet roll and one player is the spinner. The toilet roll end is tied around the waist of the spinner.

OBJECT The "spinner" spins round and round as the toilet roll is unravelled around their waist. Once the toilet roll breaks, the players must stop.

WINNING The first team to have unravelled all the toilet roll or the one with the most toilet roll around their waist.

Game 3 – Would You Rather?

Ask the children the questions below and get them to go to one side of the room or the other depending on their answer. Ask a couple of them after each round why they chose that particular one.

Alternatives (there must be no sitting on the fence!):
McDonald's or Subway?
Sleep on a big doughnut or in custard?
Have incredibly long fingers or incredibly long toes?
Be able to fly or breathe under water?
Have dinner with Shrek or Homer Simpson?
Go back in time or forward in time?
Eat cheese-flavoured ice cream or banana-flavoured pizza?
Be so small people can't see you or so tall you can see everyone?

Praise — Orb of Challenge (10 minutes)

The song that has been specially written for this lesson is "Orb of Challenge".

This is a fun action game about CHOICES that is put to song. Group members volley a balloon between them and the person caught with the balloon when the music stops must choose between two secret cards. If the person chooses a card marked "Crowd" then everyone else must do the challenge but if the card is marked "Contestant" then the person must do the challenge.

RAP
KEEP IT JUMPIN', KEEP IT HOPPIN' – AIN'T NO QUITTIN', AIN'T NO STOPPIN'
LET'S GET THIS PARTY STARTED HERE – THIS IS OUR TIME, THIS IS THE YEAR
TO GET INFINITY IN GEAR

CHORUS
HEY, MR. DJ, WHAT D'YA SAY – THE CROWD STARTS JUMPIN'
WHEN YOU START TO PLAY THAT MUSIC – PLAY THAT MUSIC

GAME
STOP!
(Pause music while person who last touched the balloon comes forward
and chooses between 2 secret cards labelled Contestant or Crowd)
YOU HAVE BEEN IDENTIFIED – YOU MUST DO AS THE DJ SAYS
(Either the Contestant or the Crowd performs the challenge)

JUMP, I SAY JUMP…
RESUME THE GAME

REPEAT RAP
REPEAT CHORUS
REPEAT GAME

WAVE YOUR HANDS IN THE AIR – WAVE THEM LIKE YOU REALLY CARE…
RESUME THE GAME

REPEAT RAP
REPEAT CHORUS
REPEAT GAME

DO THE ROBOT…

REPEAT CHORUS TWICE
PLAY THAT MUSIC

Words & Music by Wayne Tester, Esther Tester. © 2018 Testricity.com Music (ASCAP) / Fuzzy Socks Music (BMI) (both admin. by Testricity Music Group, www.testricity.com). ℗&© 2018 Testricity Music Group. ALL RIGHTS RESERVED.

Remember, we suggest using a few praise songs each session. As well as the specific song here, you may want to reintroduce some of the songs that have already been used. Enjoy!

Session 5: I Can Make Good Choices With God's Help

Word

I Can Make Good Choices With God's Help

Bible Verse To Memorize (5 minutes)

> His divine power has given us
> everything we need
> for a Godly life.
> 2 Peter 1:3

▶ His divine power has given us everything we need for a Godly life. (2 Peter 1:3)

Interview (5 minutes)

Invite one of the leaders or one of the children to come and tell the group what Jesus has done for them; how He's helped them in work/school; how He cares for them; how they first made their decision to become a Christian. If the person is very nervous, interview them. If they are more confident, allow them to speak freely – taking notice of the timing allowed for this section.

Teaching Time (20 minutes)

1. Reflective Worship (10 minutes)

2. Explore The Bible (5 minutes)

1 Kings 3

▶ Every day we have choices – I bet some of you had a choice of what cereal you would have for breakfast. Did you know, there are over 5,000 different cereals to choose from! Choosing our cereal in the morning is just a small choice but as we get older we may have harder choices to make – what job we'll do, where we will live, etc.

The Bible tells us about a young man who was actually given such a choice by God Himself. The young man's name was Solomon. Solomon had just become king of Israel when one day God appeared to him in a dream. God said to Solomon that he could ask for anything that he wanted!

Solomon could have asked for riches, or for power, or for pleasure, but he asked God to give him wisdom. Solomon said, "But I am only a little child and do not how to carry out my duties……..so give Your servant a discerning heart to govern Your people and to distinguish between right and wrong. For who is able to govern this great people of Yours?" (1 Kings 3:7, 9).

Solomon's choice of wisdom pleased God very much. God said that Solomon would be the wisest man who ever lived. God not only gave him wisdom, but He also gave him wealth, honour, and power such as no other man ever had.

God wants us to be like Solomon and make the right choices too. Making the right choices comes from seeing things as God sees them, which is how they really are, and choosing to believe the truth.

3. Illustration Choose one (5 minutes)

Illustration 1- Changed

Objects Needed: Two clear glass containers, water, dark food colouring, bleach, card, marker pen.

Pour some bleach into one of the clear containers and, using the card and marker pen, label it "God's love". Fill the second container with water and then add the food colouring. When you first add the bleach it won't clear straight away – this is part of the object lesson.

Session 5: I Can Make Good Choices With God's Help

When we accept Jesus into our lives, we are saved and God changes us *(pour a little of the bleach into the water)*. I accepted Jesus into my life when I was 7 *(pour some more bleach in)*. I knew that God loved me but I still made some wrong choices. I would still get into fights and arguments and as I grew up the anger in my life grew. I would ask God to forgive me and God always did but what I needed was to make the right choices *(pour some more bleach)*. Once I realized that God had made me a new creation and I didn't have to live with constant anger and instead act more like Jesus *(pour some more bleach)*, I found I could make better choices. Just like this water has now fully changed I also need to choose to believe the truth that I have been changed by God.

Illustration 2 – Choices

Objects Needed: Small stick, a toy sword.

Imagine you were about to walk into a big fight. Right before the fight someone gave you a choice of which weapon you could use. On your left there's a stick *(hold up the stick)*. On your right, there's a sword *(hold up the sword)*. You can either choose the stick or the sword. Raise your hand if you would choose the stick. Raise your hand if you would choose the sword.

I think the smartest decision is to choose the sword but the truth is most people actually choose the stick. Every time we choose to listen to other people rather than God's Word as written in the Bible we pick up this stick *(pick up stick)* and fight with it. Every time we choose to listen to God's Word we pick up this sword and fight with it.

What fights am I talking about? If our friends tell us that we're rubbish and useless. If we believe what they say rather than what God says about us, then we are choosing the stick not the sword.

Illustration 3 – Don't stop growing

Objects Needed: Seeds (such as tomato seeds), pot of soil, watering can.

God has given us everything that we need to live fully in Him. But just like these seeds *(hold up some tomato seeds)* we need to do certain things to keep us growing.

The first thing the seed needs is soil – without soil this seed will die *(plant the seed in the soil)*. The soil supplies the seed with the nutrients it needs to grow into a healthy tomato plant. It also gives the seed a place to grow its roots. Without a strong root system, the plant cannot grow strong above the ground. Just like the seeds need soil to grow, we need to read God's Word to grow. God's Word, the Bible, helps us know the truth of who we are. By reading the Bible our faith in God becomes strong.

After the seed is planted in the soil it needs to be watered *(hold up the watering can)*. The water provides the moisture and nutrients that the plant needs in order to grow. If this seed doesn't get watered, it will dry up and the seed will die. However, when it is properly watered, it produces juicy, tasty tomatoes. Our "water" for spiritual growth is the Holy Spirit. He will help us, for example, to forgive people when they hurt us.

We've put the seed in the soil and watered it. What else does our seed need in order to grow? *(Allow response)*. Our seed also needs plenty of sunlight. The sun provides the warmth the seed needs to grow. If the plant doesn't receive the right amount of sunlight, it may become weak and possibly die. That is why we don't see very many flowers or plants growing during the autumn and winter! But when spring comes, the sun begins to shine more and we see flowers, plants, and trees grow. Our "sun" for spiritual growth is prayer. Prayer is simply talking to God. It's having a conversation with God.

When we read our Bible, spend time with God, and allow the Holy Spirit to change us, we will grow and make the right choices.

Session 5: I Can Make Good Choices With God's Help

Story Time (15 minutes)

The Story For Younger Children – *The Adventures Of Lilly Pepper*

Chapter 5 – Off To Gran's

The video is 3.5 minutes. Take some time after the story to ask and listen to what the children think. Then go to the response and prayer time.

▶ The summer break has arrived for Lilly and in Chapter 5 she's off to Gran's.

The weekend seemed to last forever. On Sunday morning Lilly went to church. Jason, who had just joined her group a week before, was very annoying and kept pulling faces at her and laughing. Her friend Hannah told her to just ignore him and so she was doing her best. So, she closed her eyes so she couldn't see him. The group leader was talking for a long, long time when Lilly was suddenly somewhere else.

▶ The sun. A beach. She could see the sea rolling up on the shore. And a red bump sticking up. The waves were now reaching the bump and Lilly could hear the bump coughing and then shouting for help. She ran towards the bump. It was a boy. With red hair. She couldn't see much more because somebody had buried him in the sand with just his head sticking out. He was very stuck and the waves were coming in.

She shouted, "Help! Help!"

▶   And with that she jerked awake. She was still sitting in church but everyone was staring at her. "Help who, Lilly?!" Asked a very confused looking leader. "Um, nothing," muttered Lilly, "I was… thinking out loud."

And then her mum had arrived with Jake who was sound asleep and they began the walk home. Lilly was very confused. She had no idea what all that was about. What a strange dream.

▶   Tomorrow, Lilly would set off for Gran's. She usually spent a month of the summer there and then went for a break with mum just before going back to school. She was really excited, but she didn't really show it because all the time she was trying to work out the dream. That night she slept quite lightly thinking about the strange boy at the seaside. Knowing that it couldn't mean anything because, well, Gran lived in the countryside. Lots of wheat fields and cows. So no chance of meeting the boy from the beach. If the boy existed at all. Eventually, she fell asleep. But, the smell of the sea still filled her nose. She didn't feel as if she had slept at all when suddenly she was being woken up by mum saying, "Come on Lilly, let's get up and ready to go to Gran's!"

Her bags were packed. She ate breakfast quickly, gave Mop a big hug, and an hour later they were off. Lilly liked to visit Gran. It was a nice relaxing time in the country. But she was surprised by the way they went.

Session 5: I Can Make Good Choices With God's Help

▶ "Do we normally go this way?"

"No", mum replied, "Gran's staying with her friend this summer to keep her company and wanted you to come stay with her there. We thought you'd love it because well, it's beside the seaside."

"Oh wow!" was all Lilly could say.

But her mind was racing.

Lilly Pepper will soon arrive at the seaside. Will she meet the boy with the red hair? Find out next time. Have fun!

Take some time to ask and listen to what the children think about the story.

The Story For Older Children – *The Lightbringers*

Chapter 5 – THE RIGHT TO TURN THE KEY

The video is 13 minutes. Take some time after the story to ask and listen to what the children think. Then go to the response and prayer time.

▶ "Will it ever stop raining?" were Sophie's first thoughts that morning. The rain continued to hammer on her bedroom window. "Will it ever stop?" She looked at the window. The curtains hadn't been closed.

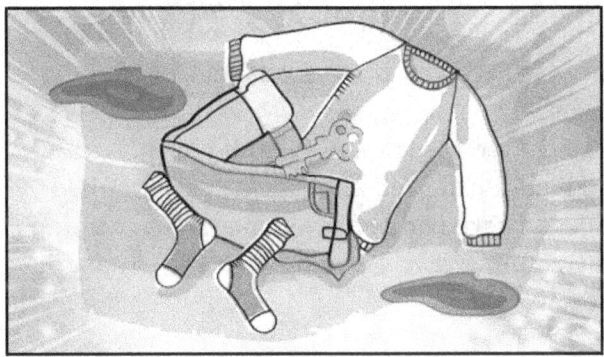

▶ And there she saw the pile of wet clothes on the floor and it all came rushing back. Graveyards, statues that moved, and the most surprising thing, the bravery of Thomas. But there, lying on the floor on top of her clothes was the key. The one Thomas had dislodged. The key. The one that would finally open that box. The crazy, annoying, unbreakable box. And until now the unopenable box.

Well, there was nothing for it. It was time to open the box. She walked over and she picked up the key. Still wearing her PJs, she sat beside the box. And it was then she noticed them. The words on the key. How had she not seen them before?

They read, "ONLY THE SPECIAL ONE CAN USE THE KEY."

And on the other side: "EVERYONE ELSE MUST LET ME BE."

"Oh, what a shame," she thought. "I did so want to open the box. If only I was special…."

Session 5: I Can Make Good Choices With God's Help

▶ And then tears began to well up in her eyes and the overflow ran down her cheeks. It all came rushing back.

The night the policeman had pulled her out of the crashed car. They'd asked so many questions about her mum and dad. Too many questions for a five-year-old girl. And then she was in the police station and everyone just stared at her and whispered that Sophie was all alone and someone needed to be called. And then two ladies arrived and were not very kind and said they would sort it out and then Sophie was taken away from the police station and the women took Sophie to a different office where more conversations were had. She remembered bits of it. They had decided where to take her and then a phone call in the background and an older lady walked in. She smiled, told the other ladies that the plan had changed and that she would deal with this personally. And she had. Within what seemed like minutes they were standing outside the Home, Cook answered the door, a quick conversation took place and Cook responded, "Of course. If that's what Dundenter wants." That bit just came back to her. She was sure that is what was said, but how?

And then she was given some warm food, taken upstairs, given some clean PJs and tucked into bed. It was the following morning that the box had arrived. And it had lived at the bottom of her bed ever since. All that was left of her life before the accident. There had been no funeral. No mention of her parents since. And since she had only found her grandparents' grave by accident – well not exactly by accident, it had come up on a computer search.

She stared at the key and then at the box and then she read the words again:

"ONLY THE SPECIAL ONE CAN USE THE KEY
EVERYONE ELSE MUST LET ME BE."

All that effort last night. All these years of waiting and wondering. But, one thing she knew for sure, she wasn't the special one the key mentioned. She was beginning to understand that God had created her and beginning to understand that God loved her. But she still felt alone, lost and lonely. But most of all she felt abandoned. Unwanted. Unloved.

It happened in the past but she could still feel it now. Unwanted. Unloved. She knew that it was nobody's fault, but she couldn't help feeling that they had all left her. Yes, she had friends, and she had Thomas, who she figured should definitely be counted as a friend since he stood with her last night. But she felt quite the opposite of special.

She remembered the first days in the Home. Sophie was convinced that someone would come to collect her soon. That any moment her mum and dad would walk through the door. But it never happened. She spent a lot of time in her room crying, wondering why nobody came. Her mind eventually began to understand that her parents would never be able to collect her. She concluded they were killed in the accident. But that didn't help. She cried more. She came out of her room only for meal times, and for school. She had to go to school. But this was a different school. This was not the school with her friends. Not the school with Cindy and Clare. She didn't know anybody. She cried in classes. The other children were sometimes mean. They laughed at her tears. Alone, lost, lonely.

Thomas had helped. Not really by looking after Sophie, but more by taking all the attention away. The class soon realized that watching what Thomas would do next was far more entertaining than anything Sophie could do. He often flooded the school toilets, ran away from school with two or three teachers chasing after him – it was amazing how fast a five-year-old could run. And his favourite trick, he would climb onto the school roof and sing very loudly to the whole school. And of course he could never get down, so the fire engine would come, and everyone loved the fire engine, and they would bring him down on a huge ladder.

As time went by, Sophie cried less often, well, certainly less often in public, and she tried to get along with everyone else. She tried to be kind, even to Thomas. And she worked hard and the teachers liked her and she found some new friends to play with. But always in the back of her mind. When it was quiet. When the lights went out. Those nagging words, "What happened? Why did they leave me behind? They must have had a reason."

She stared at the box a bit longer. And then she decided. She would put the key on top of her cupboard. And put the last few days out of her head. And she would do what she did in school. Try and forget about it and carry on.

And that is what she would have done if the rain hadn't suddenly changed its pattern of rapping on her window. The steady hammering became an intense thudding. She didn't think rain could hit that strongly. She turned towards the window, slowly walked across to look out.

What? How? "Oh, nuts," was the only word she could think of.

There, outside her window… how was it possible? This was the second floor. But it must have been possible because there he was. Thomas!

▶   He didn't look any different from last night. He was still wearing the same clothes and water was running down his face. He was still soaking wet. She stared at him through the window. He lifted up his hand, smiled a huge Thomas smile, and waved. What was she to do with him?

He had borrowed the ladder from the shed in the garden and here he was.

She opened the window.

"Thomas, what are you doing?"

"I came to find out what was in the box."

She looked at the floor. Thomas smiled.

"I knew you'd need me for this bit, so here I am."

"For what bit?"

"Well, opening the box of course. I knew you'd find a reason not to do it. Right? Are you frightened?"

"No!" she blurted out.

And then softly she said, "No, not frightened."

"Then what?" he asked. Then added, "Actually, Soph, any chance we can do this conversation inside? I'm like a little damp."

This made her smile. He wasn't damp, he was soaked through. He was soaked through to the skin. She knew it was against the rules. But she knew if she didn't let him in, he would be washed away. So in he came.

"Why are you so wet, Thomas?"

"I got up early, put my clothes back on, they are a bit damp, and I came to find you. There is no way I could come up the stairs. Cook would have spotted me. So I came the alternative route. Up the ladder."

And then he shrugged, "So what's up with the box? Does the key fit? Did we fight the wolf things for no reason?"

She looked down again. "I don't know. I haven't tried it. It's got words on it."

"You're frightened of words?"

"Not words Thomas, what the words say. I can't open the box. I'm not allowed."

All this was delivered a little more aggressively than Sophie had intended and now she thrust the key towards Thomas. He took it carefully – in case it would explode – and he read:

"ONLY THE SPECIAL ONE CAN USE THE KEY
EVERYONE ELSE MUST LET ME BE."

When he was finished, he looked confused and looked at Sophie, he smiled and then he nodded.

"You are such a banana! You thought I was nuts!"

"You don't think you're special, do you?"

She kept looking down. But Thomas continued:

"Sophie, you made the wolf things explode, you are my favourite person in the whole house, and if that wasn't enough, God made you, so you are automatically special. He only makes special. No mistakes, just special."

"Open the box Sophie. You are very special. It will work for you."

He held out the key.

▶   With trembling hands, she took the key. Still not totally convinced. But it had been a strange few days and now it seemed even Thomas was making sense.

She put the key in the keyhole and turned. There was a click and the box began to open.

Want to know what's in the box? I'll let you know next week…

Take some time to ask and listen to what the children think about the story.

Session 5: I Can Make Good Choices With God's Help

Response

Prayer (5 minutes)

Ask the children to stand and have some worship music in the background. Ask them to think of any wrong choices that they have made – you could show the stick from the earlier illustration.

Maybe you have believed what your friends have told you... that you are rubbish or useless. See what lies He shows you now.

Let's pray together and choose not to believe the lies anymore.

> **Pray together**
>
> Dear God,
> I am sorry for not always believing the truth. I choose not to believe the lie that _____ but say yes to the truth that You are always with me and have made me a new creation. Please help me to make good choices. Amen.

▶ Dear God, I am sorry for not always believing the truth. I choose not to believe the lie that……. but say yes to the truth that You are always with me and have made me a new creation. Please help me to make good choices. Amen.

You could read together the "What I Can Do" list from Session 3 in small groups or remind them to look at it at home this week.

Hand out the activity sheet and as time allows spend some time together completing the activity sheet. The children can also take it home to complete.

Next Week (5 minutes)

Highlight next week's course. Keep it exciting:
"Next week everyone who comes will get a _____", "Next week we'll hear the next part of this exciting story", etc.

Session 6: I Can Choose To Have Good Thoughts That Come From God

Session 6: I Can Choose To Have Good Thoughts That Come From God

Time Plan

Getting Started 30 minutes	Free Play (20 minutes)	
	Welcome (5 minutes)	
	Announcements (5 minutes)	
Worship 20 minutes	Prayer (5 minutes)	
	Game (5 minutes)	Choose one: "Tissue toss" or "Roll up"
	Praise (10 minutes)	Absolutely Fabulous
Word 45 minutes	Bible Verse (5 minutes)	We capture every thought and make it give up and obey Christ. (2 Corinthians 10:5b NCV)
	Interview (5 minutes)	
	Teaching Time (20 minutes) Reflective Worship (10 minutes) Explore the Bible (5 minutes) Illustration (5 minutes)	Joshua 6:1-26
	Story Time (15 minutes)	*The Adventures Of Lilly Pepper* – Felix (video: 6.5 minutes) *The Lightbringers* – Two Sophies! (video: 10.5 minutes)
Response 10 minutes	Prayer (5 minutes)	Remember to give out this week's activity sheet if you haven't already.
	Next Week (5 minutes)	

Overview

The environment in which we grew up, traumatic experiences in the past, and giving in to temptation have led to the development of "strongholds" in our minds, which prevent us from living according to the truth. Becoming a Christian does not instantly change the way we have learned to think, but we can demolish strongholds by choosing actively to renew our minds to the truth of God's Word.

Getting Started

Free Play (20 minutes)

Welcome (5 minutes)

This is a chance to welcome the children but also an opportunity to have fun with them.

Announcements And Ground Rules (5 minutes)

Remind them of the two simple rules:
1. Nobody leaves their seat. If they need to go to the bathroom then they must put their hand up and ask permission from a leader.
2. When you ask for quiet, everyone sits down, focuses on the front, and makes no sound.

Worship

Prayer (5 minutes)

In two sections:
1. **Giving Thanks:** Children who have prayed for something the week before (or several weeks before) and whose prayers have been answered should be asked to come and tell the others how God answered their prayer.
2. **Bringing Needs:** Some of the children will want to pray for certain things. Allow them to come and mention what they are praying for and ask God together to answer prayer.

Session 6: I Can Choose To Have Good Thoughts That Come From God

Game Choose one (5 minutes)

Game 1 – Tissue Toss

PREPARATION One box of tissues per team.

PLAYERS One/two players per team.

SET-UP None.

OBJECT Empty the box of tissues using both hands.

WINNING The first team to empty the box of tissues.

Game 2 – Roll Up

PREPARATION Toilet roll.

PLAYERS Six to eight players per team.

SET-UP Line the players up so that they are standing in front of each other facing the same direction. Hand the first player in the line the toilet roll.

OBJECT The first player loosens paper from the roll and carefully passes it to the person behind them. Each player passes it alternately either over their heads or under their bodies. When the roll gets to the end of the line, the person on the end wraps it around his waist and passes it back.

WINNING The first team to have used the whole roll or a predetermined number of times.

Praise Absolutely Fabulous (10 minutes)

The song that has been specially written for this lesson is "Absolutely Fabulous", a celebration of our VICTORY in Jesus!

ALL GLORY, ALL HONOR – WE ASCRIBE TO YOU O LORD
ONE FAMILY, ALL NATIONS – WE UNITE IN ONE ACCORD
THE HEAVENS REJOICE, THE WORLD IS GLAD
LET THE SEA ROAR, LET THE SKY LAUGH
THE PEOPLE OF EARTH WILL STAND AMAZED
SING A NEW SONG, SING PRAISE

CHORUS
YOU'RE ABSOLUTELY FABULOUS
YOU'RE ABSOLUTELY GLORIOUS
PRAISE HIM WITH THE THUNDER OF DANCING
WE LIFT HIM UP WITH A SONG EVERLASTING
REJOICE! SING THE CHORUS OF ANGELS
LET'S RAVE IN TRUTH FOR THE ONE WHO IS FAITHFUL
AND FABULOUS

NEW MERCIES EACH MORNING – LORD, YOUR GRACE AWAKES THE DAWN
WE BLESS YOU WITH DANCING – IN OUR WEAKNESS YOU ARE STRONG
THE HEAVENS REJOICE, THE WORLD IS GLAD
LET THE SEA ROAR, LET THE SKY LAUGH
THE PEOPLE OF EARTH WILL STAND AMAZED
SING A NEW SONG, SING PRAISE

REPEAT CHORUS

AND ABSOLUTELY FABULOUS – YESHUA, YESHUA
ABSOLUTELY MARVELOUS – WE LIFT YOU UP
ABSOLUTELY FABULOUS – YESHUA, YESHUA
ABSOLUTELY GLORIOUS – WE SING YOUR PRAISE

FAMOUS, YOU'RE SO FAMOUS
IN EVERY TRIBE, EVERY NATION
IN EVERY GENERATION
WORTHY, YOU'RE SO WORTHY
IN EVERY TONGUE WE EXALT YOU
WE LIFT ONE VOICE TO CELEBRATE

REPEAT CHORUS

Words & amp; Music by Wayne Tester, Esther Tester. T.J. Ino. © 2018 Testricity.com Music (ASCAP) / Fuzzy Socks Music (BMI) (both admin. by Testricity Music Group, www.testricity.com). ℗&© 2018 Testricity Music Group. ALL RIGHTS RESERVED.

Remember, we suggest using a few praise songs for each session. As well as the specific song here, you may want to reintroduce some of the songs that have already been used. Enjoy!

Session 6: I Can Choose To Have Good Thoughts That Come From God

Word

I Can Choose to Have Good Thoughts That Come From God

Bible Verse To Memorize (5 minutes)

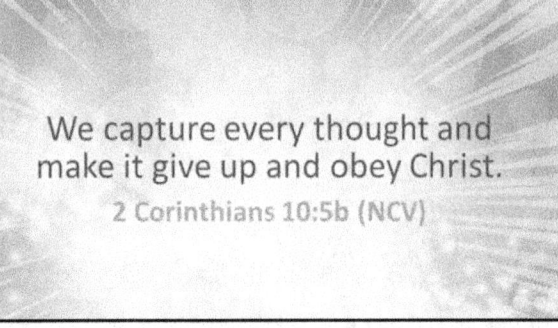

▶ We capture every thought and make it give up and obey Christ. (2 Corinthians 10:5b NCV)

Interview (5 minutes)

Invite one of the leaders or one of the children to come and tell the group what Jesus has done for them; how He's helped them in work/school; how He cares for them; how they first made their decision to become a Christian. If the person is very nervous, interview them. If they are more confident, allow them to speak freely – taking notice of the timing allowed for this section.

Teaching Time (20 minutes)

1. Reflective Worship (10 minutes)

2. Explore The Bible (5 minutes)

Joshua 6:1-26

▶ God wants us to believe HIS word and tear down any lies in our minds that stop us from believing God's truth about ourselves.

In today's lesson we are going to look at a man called Joshua. After the death of Moses, God spoke to Joshua and commissioned him to be the new leader. He told him that every place the sole of his foot touched would belong to the children of Israel! He assured Joshua that as long as He was with him, no man could stand against him. God promised to be with him all the days of his life: "As I was with Moses, so I will be with you. I will not leave you nor forsake you." What an awesome promise!

Joshua was then called into battle (just like we are) and told to go into the city of Jericho. It was a strong fortress, shut up so nobody could go out or come in. But God gave Joshua His plan. The men of war were to march around the city of Jericho for six days, with seven priests, carrying seven trumpets made from rams' horns before the Ark of the Covenant. On the seventh day, they were to march around the city seven times, and the priests were to blow the trumpets. When the people heard a long blast with the ram's horn and the sound of the trumpet, all the people were to shout. Can you imagine what the people of Jericho must have thought? They could look out from the wall and see this strange parade, day after day, silent except for the blowing of the priests' trumpets. What was going to happen? Exactly what God had promised!

God promised "the wall of the city will fall down flat" and the people could go in and conquer the city.

Just like the battle of Jericho there is no object too great when God is for us and with us. God has given us everything we will ever need for our battle!

3. Illustration Choose one (5 minutes)

Illustration 1 – Strongholds

Objects Needed: Lego building plate and Lego.

Build a tower as you are speaking, making it as solid as you can to avoid it falling over!

When we start our lives we are a bit like a blank canvas *(hold up Lego building plate)*. But gradually over time, our experiences can cause us to believe things which aren't true. Maybe we've been bullied or someone says something negative about us (you're useless; you're rubbish; you're ugly). We start to believe it. Perhaps we've believed it for so long it becomes part of our lives and we can't imagine ever getting over it.

We call these beliefs that are very deep but wrong "strongholds", they have a 'strong' hold on us and are hard to get rid of. It's like this tower, it needs a lot of bashing rather than just one push to make it tumble down.

So how do you know if you have a stronghold? Try this:
Is there something you know is right but you can't do? Or
Is there something you know is wrong but you can't stop doing?

When we become Christians we are new creations. Yet, we still believe things that aren't true. Things that make us act in a certain way. But, by knowing what God says about us we can break these walls down.

Illustration 2 – Real Truth

Objects Needed: Glass of fruit juice, jug of water, large plastic bowl.

God wants us to think the way that He thinks. He wants us to be renewing our mind. Now imagine that this glass of juice represents your mind *(show the glass and place it upright in the bowl)*. All those thoughts that are false, God wants us to change the way we think. So, everyone, look really hard at this glass and let's make it change into something else just by looking at it. Ready? Go! *(Stare very intently at the juice)*.

Nothing happened! How can we change what's in the glass? How do we change the way that we think? By filling it up with something else! *(Show the jug full of water)*.

This jug of water will represent God's Word, the Bible. *(Slowly start pouring the water into the glass of juice, letting it overflow into the bowl.)* Instead of thinking about and believing things which aren't true we need to fill our lives with God's Word.

(The juice should be overflowing, and now it should be noticeably diluted.)

Do you see what's happening? The water is replacing the juice. The same way that when we pour

God's Word into our lives it begins to change the way that we think by replacing those false thoughts with God's thoughts. *(Continue to pour the water)*. The more we let the truth of God's Word into our life, the more it will help us to think the way that God wants us to. (The glass should be mostly clear.)

Illustration 3 – Brand New

Object Needed: Picture of deer antlers (or the real thing!)

Have you ever had a bad habit that you have tried to get rid of? When I was younger I didn't think that anyone would like me. So I kept to myself and didn't like talking to people. I didn't trust anyone. It's not easy to get over it. Sometimes there are things that happen in our past that we just need to leave behind. Maybe it's a bad habit, maybe it's someone who hurt us, maybe it's something else.

(Show the deer antlers.)

Do you know what these are? They are deer antlers. Did you know that deer get a brand new set of antlers every year? Each year they grow a set of antlers and then eventually they fall off and a new set begins to grow. That's pretty cool.

That's what God wants us to be like! There are certain things that we need to drop and leave behind like deer leave their antlers behind. We need to leave some bad habits behind. Maybe we need to forgive someone for hurting us and leave that behind.

Session 6: I Can Choose To Have Good Thoughts That Come From God

Story Time (15 minutes)

The Story For Younger Children – *The Adventures Of Lilly Pepper*

Chapter 6 – Felix

The video is 6.5 minutes. Take some time after the story to ask and listen to what the children think. Then go to the response and prayer time.

▶ It's the summer and Lilly's on her way to the seaside… Welcome to Chapter 6, which is called Felix.

▶ They drove for quite some time, but eventually Lilly could see the sea in the distance. Soon they reached the coast road. A long winding road that ran almost beside the sea. They drove past the longest beach and then over the top of a largish mountain and as they began to descend down the other side she saw it. Cliffs on either side. Sea smashing against the rocks. The tide, much further in than when she saw it last time. But it was definitely "IT". The beach she had seen in her dream. The very same beach.

She asked her mum, "Have we been here before?" She thought maybe she was remembering it from a previous visit that she'd forgotten about. But mum assured her that they had never been here before. Lilly didn't understand it, but could think of no other answer than God wanted her here.

Gran was staying just five minutes from the beach with a friend who wasn't well. It was the most amazing place to stay. From the front windows of the house they could see the waves rolling up onto the beach, from the back of the house they could see fields, with the odd dotted tree and fluffy sheep and then in the distance a forest of pine trees. It was amazing. Mum brought Lilly's bags in.

▶ Gran showed her to her room. It looked out onto the beach, it was incredible. It had a huge bed, her own bathroom, a desk and loads and loads of space. She unpacked quickly, tucking her teddy and PJs into the bed, and went back down to join everyone else for dinner.

Gran's friend, whose name was Ethel, was very old, but she didn't look particularly unwell. In fact she looked quite sparkly, wearing very bright clothes and singing in the background every time she left the table to pop into the kitchen. Lilly began to suspect that she wasn't unwell, she just needed company. And she certainly liked company. Fussing over everyone, feeding them with so much food Lilly thought she would burst … although she still found space for extra ice cream. And after dinner it was time to hug mum goodbye and give baby Jake a kiss and then they were gone.

▶ And then it got very strange indeed. Lilly had wandered into the garden when she heard it… shouting from the field at the back. She saw a gang of boys running off in various directions and then a boy left behind shouting, "Help! Someone help!" Lilly climbed over the fence and walked over to the tree and there he was. The same boy with the same red hair. The boy from her dream. She took one look at him and said what's your name. "Felix" the boy mumbled, "Can you untie me?" So she did. But, before she could say any more, Felix began to run. She thought about following him but she didn't know her way around. Feeling very confused she walked back to the house.

Session 6: I Can Choose To Have Good Thoughts That Come From God

▶ Granny and Ethel were settling down to watch some television when Lilly burst into the room and asked:

"Can dreams come true, Gran?"

Gran looked confused. But Ethel burst in as quick as a flash, "I knew it. You're special. My sister was right. God has given you a dream." And she kept looking at Lilly. Lilly was sure old ladies weren't supposed to look so mischievous, but Ethel certainly did and continued, "Well, it happens in the Bible a lot. God gave dreams to Joseph in the Old Testament that got him in to no end of trouble. And Daniel has dreams in the Old Testament too. The Wise Men had a dream telling them not to go back to Herod at the time of Jesus' birth and Peter had a dream in the book of Acts involving animals. He saw lots of animals."

"I don't understand why God would give me a dream?" responded Lilly. She certainly wasn't in the Bible. There were definitely no Lillys in the Bible anywhere.

Gran smiled. "There are lots of things we don't understand Lilly but, if God has shown you something in a dream, there's probably a reason. What was the dream about?"

Lilly wasn't ready to explain quite yet, "Just stuff," she answered. And then walked out … but then she turned and went back in, "What sister, Ethel? Why would your sister tell you I was special?" But it was Gran who answered:

"This is Ethel Stevens. Her 'little' sister is Mrs Stevens, your Principal!"

That night Lilly didn't sleep for a while. She lay in her bed thinking about her busy week. "Well", she thought, "God hasn't just made me in an amazing way, he also tells me things. Wow! Mrs Stevens and Ethel think I'm special! I must be very special indeed."

And with that she turned over and went to sleep, sure that tomorrow she would see Felix again. And she had a pretty good idea of where.

But that's for next time…. Bye!

Take some time to ask and listen to what the children think about the story.

The Story For Older Children – *The Lightbringers*

Chapter 6 – Two Sophies!

The video is 10.5 minutes. Take some time after the story to ask and listen to what the children think. Then go to the response and prayer time.

▶   The lid began to open.

The box was like a large suitcase. It wasn't much smaller than Sophie. It was made of metal. Super tough metal that could not be opened or broken into at any angle. And Sophie knew this because she'd tried. She'd tried with hammers and drills but with no effect.

The lid rose higher still, gently opening as Sophie stared.

The box was the only thing that she truly owned. It had come with her, well arrived shortly after her anyway, and she never really knew how or why, But there it was. At the end of her bed where it had been for nearly five years.

The lid was nearly fully open.

Sophie had to admit that she was very surprised. She understood that she was special. Well, sort of. She got the idea that God made her and God didn't make mistakes, but always her mind was full of words, words that made her feel anything but special.

"They left you Sophie, you were abandoned. Nobody came to find you. Nobody…."

Always those negative thoughts. Always the sad feelings.

But it had worked. The box was opening. And the key made it clear:

"ONLY THE SPECIAL ONE CAN USE THE KEY
EVERYONE ELSE MUST LET ME BE."

Session 6: I Can Choose To Have Good Thoughts That Come From God

▶   She must be special. It had worked. She figured that she would always have to keep reminding herself that she was special. Those voices would always whisper in her head that she wasn't. But she would just have to keep telling them that she was. God made her special, that was the truth of it.

She was still saying the words, "God made me special, I must remember who I am in God, God made me special, I must remember who I am in God…" When she felt the nudge in her ribs. Quite a damp nudge. She'd almost forgotten what she was doing.

"It's open Soph. Look!"

And it was. The box had opened to reveal shiny red material inside and sitting on the top of the cloth was the one single solitary item. The item that Sophie and Thomas had fought the wolf creatures for. There it was, the reason they had been through all this. The reason Thomas was still so damp. There lying on top of the shiny material was an envelope. Nothing more than an envelope. Sophie had no idea what she was expecting, but she was definitely expecting more than an envelope.

Her hands were shaking as she reached into the box and carefully took out the envelope. She opened it slowly. What could be worth all this fuss? It's a piece of paper, a piece of paper with words on it. A letter. She began to read:

> Sophie, if you have opened the box, then you have retrieved the key,
> and if you have the key, then it is nearly time.
> They, 'The Gloom', will soon come looking for you.
> Dundenter has protected you,
> but now they will know that you have opened the box and they will
> come to collect what they believe is theirs.
>
> We have missed you so much
> and love you always,
>
> Mum & Dad xx

Sophie didn't understand. The letter seemed to say that her parents were alive. But if they were alive, then why hadn't they come to get her? It was bad enough when she thought her parents were dead, but now she felt something even worse. Her parents were alive and still hadn't come to get her. She really had been abandoned. But why? Because her parents didn't love her? No, that

142   THE LIGHTBRINGERS

couldn't be true. It couldn't be. There it was at the bottom of the letter, "Love you always." No, she was going to win that battle that was going on in her mind. Right now. She wasn't going to listen to those negative thoughts. She was loved. She was loved by God, she was loved by her parents, and…

"I AM SPECIAL," she proclaimed to a rather startled Thomas. For his part, Thomas smiled, nodded and said, "I never doubted it."

Thomas took the letter and he too began to read. His face looking confused. But Sophie didn't stay long. She was going to find Mr Dundenter and find out what on earth was going on. And with that she stomped out of the room.

▶   She stormed into the kitchen, but Cook simply shook her head. "He's away. Said it was important." Sophie began to walk away. Then she stopped. She turned and looked at Cook.

"You know, don't you? You know something about Mr Dundenter, don't you?"

Cook looked guilty. She stared down at her feet. And then, when she looked up, she had a resigned look on her face.

"I don't know much Sophie. Not much. I just cook you see. But I do know who pays me. Mr Dundenter pays me, Sophie, he owns the Home. He doesn't come and stay often, only once or twice every ten years or so, and then he always fits into the team to work here, and when he does it's always for a reason, usually something is about to happen. And not only does he own the Home, he chooses who gets to stay here. And I do know that the children who live here are very special children and are chosen.

"What, all of us are special? Even Thomas?" She didn't mean to ask that, the words came out before she could stop them. But Cook just smiled and said, "Especially Thomas."

Sophie smiled. For the first time in ages she smiled. We're all special. It was beginning to sink in. God had made her and she was beginning to understand that He had made her special, and Thomas. Although she seemed to be hearing Thomas' voice in her head a lot at the moment. No, not in her head.

Session 6: I Can Choose To Have Good Thoughts That Come From God

▶   He was at the top of the stairs shouting loudly, "Sophie, Sophie, Sophie, look! It's the other you." He was running down the stairs. He had a card. How, how, how could that be? Sophie took the card and stared.

"See, said Thomas, "A picture of you standing in the graveyard when you are older."

And then he stopped and looked at the ground. He realized what he'd said.

"Do you think this photo has been sent back from the future?" But he felt silly even asking. He knew that couldn't happen.

"That's not me, Thomas. That's my mother."

"But this is the person I saw at the graveyard last night, Soph. I know I did. The other you…… The other you was, was your mum! We must find her. Let's go Soph."

But Cook was too quick for the both of them, "Nobody is going anywhere. Thomas, you are changing out of those wet clothes now and before you leave this house again today, you are taking my umbrella. And Sophie, you are still wearing your PJs! And I'm not at all sure fluffy PJs are suitable attire to walk in a graveyard!"

Thomas and Sophie looked at each other. But Cook pressed on, "Of course we know where you're going. We wouldn't be very good carers if we didn't, would we? Dundenter told me you were both doing really well, and you'd sorted out those wolf creatures easily."

Thomas and Sophie didn't think it was very easy!

"But listen. If you have opened the box, the real enemy is coming. And before you face them, you're each eating your oatmeal porridge. And you're each finishing your chores. So go and get changed and be back here in ten minutes. You're not going through those doors, or any of the windows, until you've finished breakfast. And Thomas, you're not going anywhere until you've put that ladder back where it belongs!"

Will they find Sophie's parents, and why did they leave Sophie at the Home, and who are the Gloom? All will soon be revealed.

Take some time to ask and listen to what the children think about the story.

Response

Prayer (5 minutes)

Ask them who finds it hard to believe the truth that God says about them. Show the bricks from Illustration 1 and remind them that now we are new creations, God wants to break down walls in our lives, 'strongholds', and help us know the truth of what God says and get rid of thoughts that aren't true.

Pray this prayer together as a group:

> **Pray together**
>
> Dear God,
> Thank You that You want me to have the right thoughts. Please show me any thoughts which are not from You and take them away. Help me to remember that I am a new creation. Thank You that You will help me to keep growing in You. Amen.

▶ Dear God, Thank You that You want me to have the right thoughts. Please show me any thoughts which are not from You and take them away. Help me to remember that I am a new creation. Thank You that You will help me to keep growing in You. Amen.

Ask them if anything came to mind as they prayed and explain that there's something very simple they can do with those thoughts. They can say:

▶ "I say 'no' to the thought that…… and I say 'yes' to the truth that I am now God's child and I don't have to believe that lie."

Encourage them that this is something they can do any time, any place. You may want to offer to talk/pray with any child who has questions.

Hand out the activity sheet and as time allows spend some time together completing the activity sheet. The children can also take it home to complete.

Next Week (5 minutes)

Highlight next week's course. Keep it exciting:
"Next week everyone who comes will get a _____", "Next week we'll hear the next part of this exciting story", etc.

Session 6: I Can Choose To Have Good Thoughts That Come From God

Session 7: I Am Protected Because God Is Stronger Than Anything

Session 7: I Am Protected Because God Is Stronger Than Anything

Time Plan

Getting Started 30 minutes	**Free Play (20 minutes)**	
	Welcome (5 minutes)	
	Announcements (5 minutes)	
Worship 20 minutes	**Prayer (5 minutes)**	
	Game (5 minutes)	Choose one: "Stack attack" or "Bouncer"
	Praise (10 minutes)	Champion
Word 45 minutes	**Bible Verse (5 minutes)**	Put on the full armour of God, so that you can take your stand against the devil's schemes. (Ephesians 6:11)
	Interview (5 minutes)	
	Teaching Time (20 minutes) Reflective Worship (10 minutes) Explore the Bible (5 minutes) Illustration (5 minutes)	1 Samuel 17
	Story Time (15 minutes)	*The Adventures Of Lilly Pepper* – The Beach (video: 7.5 minutes) *The Lightbringers* – The Battle For The Graveyard (video: 13 minutes)
Response 10 minutes	**Prayer (5 minutes)**	Remember to give out this week's activity sheet if you haven't already.
	Next Week (5 minutes)	

Overview

It's important to understand that we are in a spiritual battle, which makes dismantling strongholds less straightforward than if it were simply a question of learning to think differently. Every day children face a battle for their minds – often our very education system undermines a biblical worldview. However, understanding this, knowing that we have a spiritual enemy, and recognizing that we have an amazing position in Christ will equip us to win.

Getting Started

Free Play (20 minutes)

Welcome (5 minutes)

This is a chance to welcome the children but also an opportunity to have fun with them.

Announcements And Ground Rules (5 minutes)

Remind them of the two simple rules:
1. Nobody leaves their seat. If they need to go to the bathroom then they must put their hand up and ask permission from a leader.
2. When you ask for quiet, everyone sits down, focuses on the front, and makes no sound.

Worship

Prayer (5 minutes)

In two sections:
1. **Giving Thanks:** Children who have prayed for something the week before (or several weeks before) and whose prayers have been answered should be asked to come and tell the others how God answered their prayer.
2. **Bringing Needs:** Some of the children will want to pray for certain things. Allow them to come and mention what they are praying for and ask God together to answer prayer.

Game Choose one (5 minutes)

Game 1 – Stack Attack

PREPARATION 36 plastic cups per team.

PLAYERS One player per team.

SET-UP None.

OBJECT Stack 36 cups in a pyramid and then back down into a single stack.

WINNING The team to do it in the quickest time.

Game 2 – Bouncer

PREPARATION Waste paper basket (enough for one per team) and ping pong balls.

PLAYERS Six players per team.

SET-UP Place the wastepaper basket on a chair and then draw a line with masking tape about 6 feet away.

OBJECT Each player has three ping-pong balls and must bounce them into the basket.

Praise Champion (10 minutes)

The song that has been specially written for this lesson is "Champion" which proclaims that Jesus is our HERO! We are FREE because He has won the fight against sin.

CHORUS
JESUS, THE CHAMPION OF THE WORLD
YOU'RE THE CHAMPION

VERSE
YOU CAME DOWN FROM HEAVEN
AND NOW I'M FORGIVEN
YOUR BLOOD PAID THE PRICE
WHEN YOU RANSOMED MY LIFE
ONCE I WAS BLINDED
BUT NOW I CAN SEE CLEARLY
I AM REMINDED
THAT NOW I AM FREE

YOU CAME AND YOU SAW
AND YOU CONQUERED IT ALL
SATAN'S PLAN WAS A FAIL
AND YOUR GLORY PREVAILS
BY LOVE YOU ARE KNOWN
YOU HAVE MADE ME YOUR OWN
WHEN YOU ROSE FROM THE GRAVE
NOW I GIVE YOU MY RAVE

REPEAT CHORUS

YAHWEH, YAHWEH, YESHUA
YAHWEH, YAHWEH, YESHUA

REPEAT CHORUS 2 TIMES

REPEAT VERSE

REPEAT CHORUS

YAHWEH, YAHWEH, YESHUA
YAHWEH, YAHWEH, YESHUA
YAHWEH, YAHWEH, YESHUA
YAHWEH, YAHWEH, YESHUA

Words & Music by Wayne Tester, Esther Tester. © 2018 Testricity.com Music (ASCAP) / Fuzzy Socks Music (BMI) (both admin. by Testricity Music Group, www.testricity.com). ℗&© 2018 Testricity Music Group. ALL RIGHTS RESERVED.

Remember, we suggest using a few praise songs for each session. As well as the specific song here, you may want to reintroduce some of the songs that have already been used. Enjoy!

Word

I Am Protected Because God Is Stronger Than Anything

Bible Verse To Memorize (5 minutes)

> Put on the full armour of
> God, so that you can
> take your stand
> against the devil's schemes.
> Ephesians 6:11

▶ Put on the full armour of God, so that you can take your stand against the devil's schemes. (Ephesians 6:11)

Interview (5 minutes)

Invite one of the leaders or one of the children to come and tell the group what Jesus has done for them; how He's helped them in work/school; how He cares for them; how they first made their decision to become a Christian. If the person is very nervous, interview them. If they are more confident, allow them to speak freely – taking notice of the timing allowed for this section.

Teaching Time (20 minutes)

1. Reflective Worship (10 minutes)

2. Explore The Bible (5 minutes)

1 Samuel 17

▶ In our lesson today, we are looking at one of the most popular stories in the entire Bible. It is a story about a young man by the name of David who stood before a mighty and scary giant by the name of Goliath. Now, to get an idea of just how tall Goliath was I need some help. Goliath was about 3 metres tall *(mark that out on the floor using masking task)*. Now I need someone who thinks they're tall. *(Pick a child and ask them to lay on the floor and mark the child's height using a piece of masking tape.)* Look how tall Goliath was!

We are told that Goliath had a helmet of brass upon his head and was armed with a coat of mail; that he had brass upon his legs and between his shoulders; that the staff of his spear was like a weaver's beam; that his iron spear's head weighed six hundred shekels (about 7kg or 15lbs); and a shield-bearer went before him. On the other hand, when David agreed to meet Goliath he took only his staff and chose five smooth stones out of the brook and put them in his shepherd's bag.

When David went out to the valley to meet Goliath's challenge, Goliath was not impressed with David at all. He looked at the ruddy young boy and despised him with a great hatred. Goliath felt insulted that the great nation of Israel would send out a young boy to fight against him.

David responded confidently to Goliath that Goliath was no match—though he came with a sword, spear, and javelin and David only had his five small stones; for David came "in the name of the LORD". Without any hesitation, David slung a stone; the stone embedded itself into the forehead of Goliath. Goliath fell to the ground, on his face. You see, kids, David might not have been wearing physical armour but he was clothed with the armour of God and knew that God would protect him.

3. Illustration Choose one (5 minutes)

Illustration 1 – Our Enemy. Our Hero.

Object Needed: Show a clip from *The Incredibles* (or another movie where there is a clear hero and villain).

Ask the kids who was the good guy in this movie and who was the bad guy. There are lots of movies which have good guys and bad guys – the good guys are always the hero and the bad guy is the enemy. Kids, we also have an enemy in real life.

In real life, our enemy is the devil. If our enemy is the devil, who is our hero? Our hero is God, Jesus. The devil hates God and is always fighting Him and trying to ruin things, just like the bad guys in movies. God and the devil are at war. Do you know what they are fighting for? They are fighting for us!

The devil tries to get us to turn away from God by getting us to believe lies or tempting us to sin. But, God doesn't want that! He loves us and wants us to know the truth and be with Him. If we love God and want to be with Him too, then we are in a fight too. We are in a fight against sin, because sin takes us away from God. Does it sound scary to be in a war? But, we don't have to worry, because God is on our side. God is fighting for us. The Bible says that God is our Protector and that He won't let any harm come to us (Psalm 121). In fact, He has greater power than our enemy. God is stronger than anything that will come against us.

Illustration 2 – Armour

Object Needed: Picture of Roman soldier or a costume would be even better. Use a volunteer to go through each piece of the armour.

Have any of you seen pictures of a Roman soldier? *(Show picture of a Roman soldier in armour.)* Why do they wear all that armour? It keeps them from getting hurt when they are attacked by their enemy. When we face battles we need to be protected from something stronger than we are. This is why God has given us all special armour to protect every part of us – you can't see it as it's invisible, but it works in the same way as the armour that the Roman soldiers wore:

   1. The Belt of Truth: The belt worn by a Roman soldier was important because it firmly secured the soldier's weapons needed to fight. If we are to stand up to evil, we must be firmly secured by the truth that is found only in Jesus. Reading our Bibles will help us know the truth about God.

   2. The Breastplate of Righteousness: A Roman soldier wore a protective covering to cover his vital organs, like the heart. We can protect our heart by saying sorry to God for things we've done wrong.

3. Feet wearing the Gospel of Peace: To do battle, a soldier must be prepared to go, and good strong sandals were a must! Imagine walking around without shoes! Our feet would get really sore and damaged. We need to avoid places we know we shouldn't go and keep our protective sandals on. Just like the soldier we need to protect our feet and go where God would want us to go, telling others about Jesus.

4. The Shield of Faith: The shield protected the Roman soldier from arrows and sword blows. We can use the shield in the same way when bad things, like temptations or doubt, come our way. Sometimes the devil will try and make us think that God doesn't love us because of the bad stuff we might have done or that He isn't real. We need to hold our shield and stop these thoughts when they happen and remember that God loves us no matter what.

5. The Helmet of Salvation: This is an essential item for a soldier's survival. The helmet protects the head of the soldier. By putting on our helmet of salvation we can protect our minds, remembering our salvation comes from Jesus, and it is a lasting protection until the day we are with Him in heaven.

6. The Sword of the Spirit: The Roman sword was short and lightweight so they could use it easily. At close range, it was a deadly weapon. The sword of the Spirit represents the Word of God which is the Bible. We can fight the devil with the Word of God, the Bible! That's why it's important to memorize Scripture. Why not start with the Bible verses in this course. You could choose one of the 'I am' statements and try to learn the verse that goes with it.

Illustration 3 – Be Prepared

Objects Needed: Two oranges, a glass bowl full of water (large enough for two oranges to be completely submerged, knife.

If we don't have our spiritual armour on, we will sink. *(Hold up an orange.)* Now, this orange represents us and the peel around it represents our armour. Now, when we have our armour on *(place the orange into the bowl)* we can stand firm *(the orange will float on top of the water)*. But, without our armour *(start peeling the second orange and then place it in the water)*, we will sink. For example, if we forget to put on our belt of truth, when someone says something unkind we might believe what they say rather than the truth that we are wonderfully made.

Session 7: I Am Protected Because God Is Stronger Than Anything

Story Time (15 minutes)

The Story For Younger Children – *The Adventures Of Lilly Pepper*

Chapter 7 – The Beach

The video is 7.5 minutes. Take some time after the story to ask and listen to what the children think. Then go to the response and prayer time.

▶ Hello! Last time Lilly met Felix but he ran off. Will they meet again? Let's find out in Chapter 7, The Beach,

▶ She woke up early the next morning but the sun was already shining brightly. She looked at the beach in the distance, smiled to herself, washed, dressed and wandered down for breakfast.

Gran had made the tastiest breakfast ever, which she ate slowly to savour every mouthful.

"What do you want to do today, Lilly?" Gran asked.

Lilly knew exactly what she wanted to do. "Can we go to the beach?"

Gran nodded, "Of course we can. I'll pack us some lunch."

An hour later as the sun climbed higher and higher they made their way to the beach. The sea was a long way out so the morning was spent making sand castles, drinking orange juice and eating sandwiches. The sea was coming in quickly and just after lunch when the water looked exactly like it did in her dream, she asked if she could go for a little walk up the beach and around the large rocks. Gran took a look at the sea and told Lilly that she could go, but she needed to be back soon because the tide came in quickly and she could end up trapped in the next cove.

▶   It took Lilly no time at all to walk around the rocks and she wasn't the slightest bit surprised to see a red bump sticking up out of the sand. This beach was deserted. Lilly figured that everyone else must have known that the sea would come in soon and it would be dangerous. She could see some boys running off into the distance, the same boys as yesterday, she guessed. She ran over to the head sticking out of the sand. But this time she was going to do it differently. She leaned over the head,

"Hello again Felix… since you didn't ask yesterday, my name is Lilly Pepper. Well, it isn't really Lilly Pepper, but you can call me Lilly Pepper. God showed me all this in a dream. Now I could dig you out, but I know if I do you will only run away again. So instead, I am going to leave you buried and ask you a few questions. If you agree, then nod. But if you don't agree, I am leaving and the sea is now very close. What's it to be?"

Well, Felix's head started going up and down frantically. He could see the sea getting closer.

"Ok. Why do these boys keeping doing mean things to you? And why do you let them?"

Felix went silent and looked like he was about to cry. But he made an attempt at answering.

"Those boys are my friends."

Lilly almost laughed, "I don't think so. But carry on."

"Well, they are my friends, and they do mean things to me because I deserve it. I'm ugly and horrible and not very smart and if the sea does wash over me, well, it wouldn't matter anyway."

Lilly was taken by surprise and wasn't quite sure how to respond. She tried, "You are not ugly. And I'm sure you are not horrible. And you're probably very smart. But what I know for sure is that they are not your friends."

Session 7: I Am Protected Because God Is Stronger Than Anything

He didn't look convinced. But, when one big wave came in and soaked Lilly and covered Felix, there was no more time for talking. Lilly dug frantically until Felix was free. But the moment he was free he started to run away. This time Lilly was having none of it. She began to chase after him.

▶ They were half way up the beach when both of them realized that there was no way out this way, only a sheer rock face that they certainly weren't going to be able to climb. They turned back, but they had left it far too late. The sea was rapidly approaching. They managed to clamber up a short way and scramble into a cave in the rock where they hoped the water wouldn't reach them.

They sat. And Lilly stared. She was just a little bit angry with Felix. She had rescued him twice and both times he had tried to run away. They sat on a rock in the cave. The light from outside was enough to allow them to see each other. When they had caught their breath, Lilly was determined to get to the bottom of the unanswered questions:

"Now, Felix, you are going nowhere and neither am I. So, why do you think you are ugly? And why do you think you aren't smart? Did your parents tell you that or your teachers?"

Felix stared at his feet, "Nope. My mum only says nice things about me. My dad lives a long way away with his new wife, but he always says nice things too. My teachers give me smiley faces and stars because they say I work hard, and I do. But, my friends say I'm ugly and stupid and that is why they need to tie me up, or bury me in the sand, or throw me in the river. And so I let them because they all say it."

And now Lilly Pepper was very angry.

"How dare they?" she began.

And that same talk that she had given in school about God making us and us being wonderful came pouring out. Felix felt like a train had hit him such was the strength of Lilly's words.

"You are loved by God Felix. He thinks you are amazing. And he doesn't make mistakes and He did make you. And those bullies need a good punch on the nose."

She knew the last bit wasn't quite what God would want her to do, but she was very cross, and she wasn't done yet.

"So who are you going to believe Felix? Silly boys who do mean things or God who made the universe? Who do you think tells the truth?"

It was like a war in Felix's mind. He'd never heard words like this before. And he had to say, this Lilly Pepper was very convincing.

▶ He was about to respond when he suddenly felt his toes go cold and wet. He looked down.

"Um, Lilly, we could be in real trouble."

Lilly looked down. The water had made it up as high as the cave and was rising quickly.

Will Lilly and Felix escape the cave? We'll find out next time.

Take some time to ask and listen to what the children think about the story.

Session 7: I Am Protected Because God Is Stronger Than Anything

The Story For Older Children – *The Lightbringers*

Chapter 7 – The Battle For The Graveyard

The video is 13 minutes. Take some time after the story to ask and listen to what the children think. Then go to the response and prayer time.

▶   It was several hours later before Thomas and Sophie were standing in the street ready for another visit to the graveyard. But, at least they had an umbrella and more importantly, at least it was daytime…

There were levels of strange and given the last few weeks, they had experienced a lot of strange. But, this seemed the strangest thing of all. Thomas and Sophie walking together in the daylight towards an old and unused graveyard. Sophie looked at Thomas. He looked almost presentable now. She'd been used to seeing him dripping wet. But the umbrella was doing its job well. She was beginning to think that he always looked wet. But today, he looked, well, normal. She stopped, she looked at him.

"Thomas, thank you."

He shrugged his shoulders, "What for?"

"Well, we could start with keeping me company last night when we walked through the rain, or helping when the wolf things showed up, and finding the picture of my mum. But most of all, I want to thank you for being my friend."

His face showed his embarrassment, he looked at the ground and then he looked worried, he lifted his head and spoke with panic in his voice.

"Sophie, you're, you're not going to kiss me are you?"

She laughed out loud: "No way!" Thomas smiled, they walked on and in no time at all they were at the entrance to the graveyard.

▶   But something was obviously wrong. The graveyard gates were open and there standing in the middle of the graveyard was Sophie's mum and beside her a man… "Dad!" Sophie exclaimed. They were standing so very still and there was something on their mouths. Sophie ran so quickly Thomas didn't have time to stop her.

They were still some distance away when they saw what was wrong. Her parents' hands were tied and there was tape over their mouths.

And now they were there. Sophie pulled the tape from her mum's mouth and then her dad's. There were tears running down her face as she hugged them both. Yet, again she was getting wet. The umbrella had been abandoned at the gates as they had run to meet them. Mum was crying too. But dad spoke first, his voice low and sad:
"Sophie we've missed you so much. And Dundenter has kept you so safe. But, it seems that in our escape and in our rush to come and find you, we have led The Gloom straight to you. They are here."

Dad looked at Thomas. "Thomas, right? Thomas the brave warrior." He tried to smile, but through the smile he said again, "Sorry".

"Sorry for what? But, who's tied you up? Where, where have you been?"

▶   But, Sophie's dad had stopped talking. Her parents were staring at something behind Sophie and Thomas. Sophie turned. There was a line of them. About a dozen men and women. Their faces were grey. They looked so very sad. But at the same time, so very mean. If "angry" could look like something, it would look like these 'people'. And she didn't understand how or why really, but she could almost feel the evil wolf things looking out through these people's eyes, like they were being controlled by the wolf things themselves.

"Who are they, Sophie's mum?" whispered Thomas. Clearly not feeling like a brave warrior now. "They're not going to change into wolf things are they?"

Sophie's mum looked at him. "The wolf things are just a shape that the darkness takes on when it wants to frighten us. They are evil. The Gloom are the servants of the darkness and all that is evil and all that is bad. They know about God but they have chosen to give themselves to the darkness, becoming servants of evil and full of evil themselves and they hate *The Lightbringers* and they hate those who pray. The wolf things are all darkness, they are the creators of nightmares, the bringers of sadness. These are The Gloom, Thomas. They serve the stealers of hope. And then she turned and said, "I am so glad to see you, Sophie. I have missed you so much. But, I am so sorry to bring you into this."

"Why are they our enemies? What have we done to them? And what do they plan to do to us?" asked Thomas, who was glad Sophie and her parents were back together, but was a little more interested in how exactly he was going to get out of this situation. "They don't seem to have any weapons."

"The Gloom serve the darkness, Thomas, and the creatures of darkness will try to gain control of your mind," answered Sophie's mum. They will bring to mind every negative thought about yourself that you have ever had, every lie you've believed about yourself. They will steal hope and love. And without hope and love, we are nothing better than The Gloom."

Thomas was now shaking. He knew what she meant. His mind was already beginning to go dark. The Gloom simply stood and stared, but he could feel the darkness beginning to push into his mind. Whispered words. Horrible words. He sat on the ground, not knowing how to fight this enemy. He began to pray, "God help me". But, it wasn't Thomas they focused on. They would deal with him soon. He was not the priority. They had come for Sophie. It had all been about Sophie. They had to destroy Sophie. The Gloom had been on the earth for a long time, serving the darkness, new people filling the gaps of those who died, but they knew that their numbers were not large anymore and they knew that Sophie's family had been followers of God for a very long time. Praying generation after generation, talking to God. Letting God's light shine through them. They were Lightbringers.

The Gloom hated all God's people. But, *The Lightbringers* were the worst of them all. This was the gift God gave to his followers to be able to tell others about him. To bring light into places of darkness. And The Gloom were not going to allow more Lightbringers. Many of their number had already themselves become followers of God because of these persistent, relentless Lightbringers. They hated Lightbringers. So, they would have loved to see Sophie give up. At such a young age she had been through so much and The Gloom were sure she would give up. Just a few more bad words whispered in her ears, or maybe her friend Thomas giving up would stop this new Lightbringer from fully recognizing what God had made her.

▶ Sophie's face looked suddenly sad. Her eyes were losing their sparkle. She fell to her knees, tears filling her eyes. Her mind felt that a battle was taking place inside it. She was trying to be strong, but it was no good. All this bad had forced its way in and was winning. Words toppled around her mind,

"Nobody loves you, nobody cares for you, you were left, they abandoned you because nobody wanted you. They hate you Sophie. Nobody likes you Sophie. Nobody will ever care for you."

Thomas could see his friend in such pain. He could hear Sophie's mum shouting, "Stop, please stop." He continued his prayer, "God help Sophie. God help Sophie."

The Gloom stared. Their cruel, mean, angry stare. As the darkness worked at destroying love, destroying hope. Making everything dark.

And then suddenly and without warning, the rain stopped. And for the first time in what felt like weeks the sun shone from behind a dark grey cloud. The beam of light from the sun landed directly on Sophie. She stared at the sunshine. Her face screwed up in pain. Her eyes looking dark. And then it happened. Thomas didn't know what, but it was as if a spark went on inside Sophie.

▶ She remembered who God made her to be. Who she was in Him. Her eyes sparkled. He was sure they had actually sparkled. And now they were bright again. And she stood. How was it even possible? She stood and she looked so strong and proclaimed in a voice that was suddenly powerful:

"This ends now! I reject the lies I've been believing that I'm alone and abandoned because the truth is I am loved by my Father God who, by the way, is always with me. You do not get to control me. Go away! I belong to Jesus!"

Session 7: I Am Protected Because God Is Stronger Than Anything

That last word was delivered with such passion that several of The Gloom toppled over. The ropes around mum actually snapped. Now the whole graveyard was flooded with light. Sophie's mum's hand was on her shoulder. Thomas stood too. His mind suddenly clear. No, not clear. Flooded with light. He felt, he felt amazing.

"Enough. This ends…." That was Sophie's dad's voice.

"No", the voice of The Gloom. Even their voices sounded like sadness, "No, not yet. If we cannot harm you, then we will destroy the Home. And all those special people will have no home, nowhere to live and it will be because of you, you will know it was your fault and you will be guilty and you will not bring any more light Sophie Stanmore because the sadness will cover you."

▶   And now they were moving quickly. They were soon out of the graveyard and getting into dark cars. And they were gone.

"Quick" said dad, "Well done Sophie. You are indeed a Lightbringer. But, equally well done Thomas. You both made this possible, you stood firm in the truth. But now, we must be quick. This is far from over."

Hurriedly, all four of them piled into a car. A very small green car and within minutes they were outside the Home. Dark cars filled the street. But The Gloom were nowhere to be seen. The fight for the Home had begun….

But not until next week will we find out who wins the battle!

Take some time to ask and listen to what the children think about the story.

Response

Prayer (5 minutes)

Ask the children to stand and show them how to put on their spiritual armour. Pretend to put on each item using actions. If you have already used Illustration 2 to explain the armour you may prefer just to say the prayers and omit the descriptions.

Pause and say each prayer together after they have put the item on.

Let's start with the BELT OF TRUTH *(pretend to put a belt on)*. The belt worn by a Roman soldier was important because it firmly secured the soldier's weapons. We need to put this on first to be secured by the truth we know about God.

> **BELT OF TRUTH**
>
> **Pray together**
>
> Lord, help me to remember what You say in Your Word is true about me.

▶ Lord, help me to remember what You say in Your Word is true about me.

Next is the BREASTPLATE OF RIGHTEOUSNESS *(pretend to put a breastplate on)*. Every Roman soldier wore a protective covering to protect their vital organs, like the heart. We can protect our hearts by saying sorry when we've done something wrong.

> **BREASTPLATE OF RIGHTEOUSNESS**
>
> **Pray together**
>
> Lord, help me to keep my heart clean, I'm sorry for the wrong things I've done.

▶ Lord, help me to keep my heart clean, I'm sorry for the wrong things I've done.

Then the SHOES OF PEACE *(put on shoes)*. To do battle a Roman soldier had to have good, strong sandals. Imagine walking around with no shoes. Our feet would get really sore and damaged. Just like the soldier we need to protect our feet and go where God would want us to go, telling others about Jesus.

Session 7: I Am Protected Because God Is Stronger Than Anything

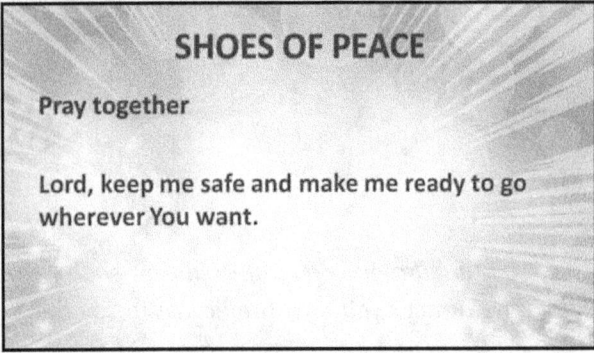

SHOES OF PEACE

Pray together

Lord, keep me safe and make me ready to go wherever You want.

▶ Lord, keep me safe and make me ready to go wherever You want.

SHIELD OF FAITH *(pretend to hold up a shield)*. A Roman soldier would use his shield to protect against arrows and swords. We can use the shield in the same way when bad things come our way. We hold it up and stop those thoughts and remember that God loves us no matter what.

SHIELD OF FAITH

Pray together

God, thank You for the protection You give me and that I can say no to things that aren't helpful or good for me.

▶ God, thank You for the protection You give me and that I can say no to things that aren't helpful or good for me.

HELMET OF SALVATION *(put your hand on your head)*. This is an essential item for a soldier's survival. By putting on our helmet of salvation we can protect our minds – remembering we belong to Jesus.

HELMET OF SALVATION

Pray together

Lord, protect me from believing lies rather than Your truth.

▶ Lord, protect me from believing lies rather than Your truth.

Lastly the SWORD OF THE SPIRIT *(pretend to hold a sword)*. A Roman soldier's sword was short and light so they could use it easily. It was a deadly weapon. The sword of the Spirit represents the Word of God which is the Bible. We can fight the things that try to take us away from God by speaking out God's truth. Just like we did when we spoke out the truths from the lists.

166 THE LIGHTBRINGERS

> **SWORD OF THE SPIRIT**
>
> Pray together
>
> Thank You, Lord, for Your Word, which helps me to know what is true. Help me to read it and understand it more and more!

▶   Thank You, Lord, for Your Word, which helps me to know what is true. Help me to read it and understand it more and more!

A great way to help you remember the armour is to put it on each day when you get out of bed, or before you go to school. Let's pray that God will help you remember that the armour is there and what it's used for!

Hand out the activity sheet and as time allows spend some time together completing the activity sheet. The children can also take it home to complete.

Next Week (5 minutes)

Highlight next week's course. Keep it exciting:
"Next week everyone who comes will get a _____", "Next week we'll hear the next part of this exciting story", etc.

Session 7: I Am Protected Because God Is Stronger Than Anything

Session 8: I Can Have Peace Because God Helps Me Whatever I'm Feeling

Session 8: I Can Have Peace Because God Helps Me Whatever I'm Feeling

Time Plan

Getting Started 30 minutes	Free Play (20 minutes)	
	Welcome (5 minutes)	
	Announcements (5 minutes)	
Worship 20 minutes	Prayer (5 minutes)	
	Game (5 minutes)	Choose one: "Bean face" or "Snow ball fight"
	Praise (10 minutes)	When I Get To Heaven
Word 45 minutes	Bible Verse (5 minutes)	Let the peace of Christ rule in your hearts. (Colossians 3:15)
	Interview (5 minutes)	
	Teaching Time (20 minutes) Reflective Worship (10 minutes) Explore the Bible (5 minutes) Illustration (5 minutes)	Exodus 16
	Story Time (15 minutes)	*The Adventures Of Lilly Pepper* – The Cave (video: 6 minutes) *The Lightbringers* – The Battle At The Home (video: 13.5 minutes)
Response 10 minutes	Prayer (5 minutes)	Remember to give out this week's activity sheet if you haven't already.
	Next Week (5 minutes)	

Overview

There are *feelings* and then there is *truth*. They don't always tell us the same thing. In this lesson we will look at how we commit ourselves to the truth and choose to believe that what God says is true, then the less our feelings will run away with us.

Getting Started

Free Play (20 minutes)

Welcome (5 minutes)

This is a chance to welcome the children but also an opportunity to have fun with them.

Announcements And Ground Rules (5 minutes)

Remind them of the two simple rules:
1. Nobody leaves their seat. If they need to go to the bathroom then they must put their hand up and ask permission from a leader.
2. When you ask for quiet, everyone sits down, focuses on the front, and makes no sound.

Worship

Prayer (5 minutes)

In two sections:
1. **Giving Thanks:** Children who have prayed for something the week before (or several weeks before) and whose prayers have been answered should be asked to come and tell the others how God answered their prayer.
2. **Bringing Needs:** Some of the children will want to pray for certain things. Allow them to come and mention what they are praying for and ask God together to answer prayer.

Game Choose one (5 minutes)

Game 1 – Bean Face

PREPARATION   Each team will need – two tins of baked beans and two packets of Haribo's, a bowl or tray.

PLAYERS   One player per team.

SET-UP   Empty the tins of beans into the bowl or tray. Place the Haribo's on top of the beans.

OBJECT   Player needs to remove the Haribo's from the tray of beans using their mouth.

WINNING   The team to do it in the quickest time.

Game 2 – Snow Ball Fight

PREPARATION   Screw up 100 sheets of paper so that they look like snowballs.

PLAYERS   Four players per team (if possible have girls versus boys).

SET-UP   Using masking tape, tape a line down the middle of the game area. Place the four girls one side of the line in front of the boys' team (so the kids at the front can't help them) and scatter the snowballs at the front of the stage.

OBJECT   The teams have to throw the snowballs at the other side.

WINNING   The team to have the least snowballs on their side.

Praise   When I Get to Heaven (10 minutes)

The song that has been specially written for this lesson is "When I Get to Heaven". God has promised us that we will enter the Promised Land. The journey may be difficult but it will be worth it in the end!

FOREVER YOUNG, I WILL NEVER GROW OLD
I'LL DANCE IN STREETS PAVED WITH SOLID GOLD
I'LL SING WITH ANGELS "HOLY IS THE ONE"
"WHO WAS AND IS AND IS TO COME"
IT'S GONNA BE THE BEST DAY EVER
WHEN I SEE PARADISE

CHORUS
WHEN I GET TO HEAVEN, OH, OH, OH
I'M GONNA DANCE!
WHEN I GET TO HEAVEN, OH, OH, OH
I'M GONNA DANCE!
I'M GONNA DANCE!
I'M GONNA DANCE!

I'M GONNA DANCE THROUGH THE GATES OF PEARL
OUT OF THE DARK, "HELLO", LIGHT OF THE WORLD
I'LL SING WITH ANGELS "WORTHY IS THE LAMB"
"ALPHA AND OMEGA, THE GREAT I AM"
GONNA BE WITH JESUS FOREVER
TEARS GONE FROM MY EYES

REPEAT CHORUS

WHEN I SEE JESUS' FACE
WHEN I BEHOLD HIS MERCY AND GRACE
THERE WON'T BE NO HOLDIN' ME BACK
NO, NO, NO

I'M GONNA DANCE!
I'M GONNA DANCE!
I'M GONNA DANCE!
I'M GONNA DANCE! DANCE! DANCE!

REPEAT CHORUS

Words & Music by Wayne Tester, Esther Tester. © 2018 Testricity.com Music (ASCAP) / Fuzzy Socks Music (BMI) (both admin. by Testricity Music Group, www.testricity.com). ℗&© 2018 Testricity Music Group. ALL RIGHTS RESERVED.

Remember, we suggest using a few praise songs for each session. As well as the specific song here, you may want to reintroduce some of the songs that have already been used. Enjoy!

Session 8: I Can Have Peace Because God Helps Me Whatever I'm Feeling

Word

I Can Have Peace Because God Helps Me Whatever I'm Feeling

Bible Verse To Memorize (5 minutes)

> Let the peace of Christ rule in your hearts.
> Colossians 3:15

▶ Let the peace of Christ rule in your hearts. (Colossians 3:15)

Interview (5 minutes)

Invite one of the leaders or one of the children to come and tell the group what Jesus has done for them; how He's helped them in work/school; how He cares for them; how they first made their decision to become a Christian. If the person is very nervous, interview them. If they are more confident, allow them to speak freely – taking notice of the timing allowed for this section.

Teaching Time (20 minutes)

1. Reflective Worship (10 minutes)

174 THE LIGHTBRINGERS

2. Explore The Bible (5 minutes)

Exodus 16

▶ If we feel overwhelmed by negative emotions, like being angry or sad, what can we do about it?

Moses led the Israelites through the desert on a journey to the Promised Land. It was not easy to travel through a vast desert. Sadly, the people forgot the amazing miracles God had performed in delivering them from Egypt, even the parting of the Red Sea! Instead their emotions started to run away with them. They began to murmur and complain. They longed to return to Egypt and eat meat and bread like they used to have in Egypt. Not only did they forget God's miracles and fail to trust Him with their present situation, they forgot how painful their time in Egypt actually was.

Because of their constant grumbling and not putting their faith in God, no one over 20 years old, except two faithful men named Joshua and Caleb, saw the Promised Land. Not even Moses. Of the people alive during the time they crossed the Red Sea, only children would make it to the Promised Land.

If we feel overwhelmed by negative emotions, what can we do about it? Have faith in God and believe what God's Word tells us is true rather than what our feelings/experiences want us to believe.

3. Illustration Choose one (5 minutes)

Illustration 1 – Our Emotions

Object Needed: Thermometer.

Can you tell me what this is? It takes your temperature. It is called a thermometer. When would your mother or a doctor use a real thermometer with you? When they think you are sick. If your temperature is too high, you have a fever. How can this thermometer tell if you have a fever? There are numbers on the side that say what your temperature is measured in degrees Centigrade/

Fahrenheit. Does anyone know what your body temperature should be? About 37° C/98.6°F is normal. If you have a fever, you might run a slight temperature of 37.2°C/99°F or 37.7°C/100°F. If it gets to 38.3°C/101°F, 38.8°C/102°F, or 39.4°C/103°F, it gets more serious, and something needs to be done about it. If it gets over 40°C/104°F, it is serious. You are very sick! You have an emotional temperature also. Emotions are your feelings. If you are feeling calm and happy, you do not have an emotional fever. You might get a slight case of irritation or get mad about something for a minute or two and then get over it. You might cry about something and then it is all right again.

If, however, you get very angry, and your emotional temperature continues to build, that's not good. You don't want to let your emotional temperature climb and climb. You need to do something to get it lowered. You need to talk about what's making you feel bad. You need help to solve the problem. You need to get your feelings under control. If you let your emotions get hotter and hotter, you might explode and do or say something you will regret. Just like a fever of 40°C/104°F or more, an emotional fever is dangerous.

So what should you do if this happens? When you get sick you would go and see a doctor. When you get angry, speak to someone. I find the best person to speak to is God as He is my best friend and can handle how I am feeling.

Illustration 2 – Explode!

Object Needed: Can of fizzy drink.

Our Bible Verse tells us that we need to let the peace that comes from Christ control our thoughts. If we don't have peace but instead let anger build up, then what happens is we eventually let out our anger by hurting those around us.

Have you ever been really mad at someone? *(Take out can of fizzy drink.)*

When we get angry it is like shaking this can of drink. *(Shake the can hard then act like you are going to open it.)*

What would happen if I opened this can? It would explode everywhere! *(Set the can down and make sure you give it at least a minute or two before picking it up again.)*

So, if you are all angry, like this can, and you sin by getting in a fight or calling someone bad names it would be like opening this can and it spraying everywhere! Sometimes, what we need to do is walk away and pray and ask God to help us to calm down and not respond in sin.

(Take the can and open it. It should open normally now. Make this dramatic so the kids think it will spray everywhere.)

See all this can needed was a few moments of quiet and it calmed down and it could be opened without exploding. When we are angry we only need a few moments so that we can react without sinning.

Illustration 3 – Self-Control

Object Needed: Dog leash.

(Take out the dog leash and show it to everyone.)
Does anyone know what this is? That's right, it's a dog leash. Do you know what it's used for? *(Wait for responses.)* You clip it to a dog's collar so it can't get away from you.

Have you ever walked a dog before? Most of the time they don't just walk calmly by your side. They are running around and sniffing different things. That's why you need to use a leash. If you didn't have a leash your dog might be running all over the place and it might get in all kinds of trouble. The leash helps you to control the dog and not let it get too far from you.

The Bible tells us that God wants us to have self-control so that we don't just act on whatever emotion we happen to feel but we act on what God says is true. Self-control is kind of like this leash that you would put on a dog, except it's putting a leash on yourself. Have you ever worn a leash before? When we have self-control we don't let ourselves be overwhelmed by our emotions. Just like a dog would like to run wild, our emotions want to run wild and do whatever they want. But God wants us to have self-control.

It's not always easy to control ourselves when we are tempted, or when we are angry, but this is what God wants us to do. The more we read the Bible the more we can learn the truth. So, don't just let yourself run wild!

Don't act on how you feel but act on what God says is truth. If you feel overwhelmed by negative emotions start looking at your situation in a way that reflects what Gods say is actually true.

Session 8: I Can Have Peace Because God Helps Me Whatever I'm Feeling

Story Time (15 minutes)

The Story For Younger Children – *The Adventures Of Lilly Pepper*

Chapter 8 – The Cave

The video is 6 minutes. Take some time after the story to ask and listen to what the children think. Then go to the response and prayer time.

▶   Welcome back! We left Lilly and Felix stuck in a cave filling with water. Will they escape? Let's find out in Chapter 8, The Cave.

▶   The water was now up as far as their knees. They crawled a little further up the side of the cave. But it was clear now that the tide would come in and completely fill this cave and they'd drown.

"See, Lilly," Felix began, "I really am stupid. I told you to come into this cave and now we will die. I am probably the stupidest person in the entire world."

Well Lilly was pretty sure that Felix was a whole lot smarter than most of the boys in her school and she thought he was better looking as well, but she definitely wasn't going to tell him that. She'd had enough of listening to Felix moan, so she decided that some direct talking was needed:

"Felix, you are very smart. God made you. And if you didn't suggest we come into this cave, then we would have been washed out to sea a long time ago. But, Felix, you can spend all your time feeling sorry for yourself or you can decide to believe the truth. God made you, Felix, and He made you special. And He loves you very much Felix. So stop moaning or I'll throw you into the sea!"

He looked at her in alarm. But her little wink told him that she wasn't really going to throw him into the sea. Well, he thought she wouldn't. He looked at her for a few minutes. He was thinking about how to respond to her.

"Nobody ever talked to me like you." he began.

Lilly smiled, "That's because there is only one Lilly Pepper and she is awesome."

He laughed out loud and suddenly felt altogether better about … well everything.

And then he remembered. "Lilly there is no point in me recognizing who God made me to be if I'm about to drown."

"Well," Lilly began. "At least if you agree that you have become a follower of Jesus, when you drown you'll go straight to heaven."

Felix was about to scream. But Lilly winked again. "Take a breath Felix. God isn't going to let us die. Now pray and ask Him for help and we'll see what happens next." Felix really hadn't met anyone like Lilly Pepper before and he'd not prayed much before either. But, he didn't dare disagree with Lilly. So he had a go,

"Hey God. I think we need Your help. The sea is about to cover us and we're going to die. So, can You help? Oh, and if You can help us quickly that would be really good. Amen."

"Lilly. I'm not sure it worked."

▶   "Really?" Lilly responded, "Then what's that light coming towards us?"

And it was true. There was a light making its way across the cave. Felix thought it must be an angel. But as it got closer, a voice shouted from just behind the light.

"How are you doing? Fancy a ride in our boat??"

Lilly was astonished. It was Gran and Ethel in a rowing boat. Ethel, who was supposed to be unwell, was rowing and Gran held a flashlight at the front.

"Anyone for a lift on the Gran and Ethel ferry?" shouted Gran.

Well Lilly couldn't believe her eyes, but she was delighted. God really did answer prayers in the most remarkable ways. But she wasn't going to show Felix her surprise. She simply turned to him and said, "Told you so!"

And so into the boat they got and they all rowed back to the shore and walked back to the cottage. Two very wet children and two very bouncy old people.

▶ Lilly had to know. As they sat drinking their hot chocolate, Lilly asked Gran and Ethel,

"So how did you know? How did you know where we were?"

The two ladies just looked at each other and laughed. Eventually Ethel turned to Lilly and said,

"Well little Miss Pepper, I was praying and reading my Bible this morning and every verse I felt God wanted me to read was about water. Which is strange because that's not where I was with my usual Bible reading today. And then when I asked God why, I felt that I should read 1 Samuel 22. It's a bit of the Old Testament, but it wasn't about water, but about a cave. I had no idea what it all meant until your Gran called and said you were missing. And then I knew what it all meant and I had that special peace that God brings when you've understood what He is saying, so I was ready with my rowing boat when your Gran arrived. Old people can be special too, Lilly.

And of that Lilly had no doubt.

They sat and finished their hot chocolate. But there was another important thing God wanted Felix to do. We'll find out what next time. Bye!

Take some time to ask and listen to what the children think about the story.

The Story For Older Children – *The Lightbringers*

Chapter 8 – The Battle At The Home

The video is 13.5 minutes. Take some time after the story to ask and listen to what the children think. Then go to the response and prayer time.

▶   They reached the house just in time to see The Gloom breaking open the door and pouring in. But to the astonishment of Sophie, Thomas, and Sophie's parents, they soon came pouring back out. Covered in the thickest, squelchiest, special mix oatmeal porridge. Even from outside, Sophie could hear Stacey shouting, "Are they dead?"

But they weren't dead. Despite their comical appearance, looking more creamy than grey, they nevertheless looked really, really angry. Mum drove around the back and seconds later they jumped over the fence and in through the patio doors to see all the inhabitants of the Home behind the kitchen counter. There were several huge saucepans of oatmeal porridge in front of them and Cook giving orders.

"Not until you see their eyes. Don't waste your ammunition. Get ready."

And The Gloom were back. Stood in a line, staring, all twelve of them.

"Wait!" shouted Sophie as she, Mum, and Thomas rushed behind the counter.

"Good. Reinforcements," said Cook, "Help yourself to oatmeal porridge."

And they did. Great big handfuls of sticky, squelchy oatmeal porridge. And they waited for Cook's command.

"Fire."

And they threw as hard as they could. Great big dollops of oatmeal porridge covering The Gloom. Everywhere. In their noses, in their ears, down their backs. They were covered.

"Hooray!", shouted Stacey. "Now they must be dead."

Session 8: I Can Have Peace Because God Helps Me Whatever I'm Feeling

Sophie made a mental note to remember to talk to Stacey about her obsession with things dying at some point. But not right now. And anyway, The Gloom were far from dead. They stood and stared and wiped oatmeal porridge from their eyes and stared some more. It was clear they would not retreat this time.

"Ok," Cook declared, "let's get ready again. There's still plenty of oatmeal porridge." And they filled their hands full of oatmeal porridge.

But then it began. Sophie felt it almost immediately. The darkness invading her mind. Those whispered lies. "Nobody wants you, your parents left you, nobody cares." Sophie began to fight. Sophie was doing her best not to listen. But, it was hard. She was using all her energy just to stop herself from running away."

Cook, Mum and Dad had clearly faced this before. But, twelve of The Gloom, all being controlled by the evil darkness whispering in their minds, was hard for even the strongest follower of Jesus to resist. And Sophie didn't understand why, but it always seemed easier to believe the bad stuff.

▶ Cook and Sophie's parents stood in complete concentration. Sophie could see they were whispering. Probably praying.

Stacey began to cry. But not just cry, she was wailing, howling, sobbing, heart rending sobs.

Kevin was on the floor, his face all twisted. Thomas had dropped to his knees at the first sign that The Gloom would not be defeated by oatmeal porridge and was praying once more, but his prayers were struggling to come out. It was like an invisible grey fog was choking back his words.

The Gloom had now entered the room and were getting the darkness to fill everything, especially those they thought were the strongest. Sophie's mum was surrounded by four of The Gloom, her dad by another four and whatever was going on was clearly causing them pain. Her eyes were closed, her hands over her ears, desperately trying to stop those voices in her mind.

In her mind, Mum remembered the last time she felt like this. The night they were driving with Sophie. And how from nowhere The Gloom had appeared on the side of the road. And such cruel lies. Lies filling her head. And she remembered she had lost control of the car and it had crashed and then she remembered being dragged out of the car, her and her husband, by The Gloom.

But they hadn't seen Sophie. Maybe God had hidden her from them, but whatever the reason, Sophie would be safe, she knew Dundenter would find her and protect her. But she and her husband were captured. The Gloom had taken them and kept them in that room of despair, feeling worthless, feeling they had failed. Locked up for years until they finally recognized who God had made them to be. Recognized who they were in Jesus.

The Gloom were so sure they had defeated them, so convinced that their prisoners had believed the lies that they started leaving them with just one guard. And then after many years it was Sophie's dad whose eyes seemed to change. It was as if a dark cloud had been taken away. He had stood up taking The Gloom guard by surprise. The guard had commanded him to sit down, but he had looked at him and proclaimed,

"God has shown me that Jesus is much stronger than you are. And I am in Jesus so I am much stronger too. You have no authority over us. Release us in the name of Jesus!"

Well, the Gloom Guard didn't release them. Instead he ran out of the house in terror, leaving them simply to walk out.

▶   And now Sophie's mum could see that same understanding in Sophie. She was amazed at how someone so young could know who she was in God when it had taken her and Dad so long. Such an understanding of who God had made her already.

Sophie was winning, she was sure she was winning, but for how much longer? Every time she pushed those horrible voices away, new ones came. Nasty voices. Cruel voices. Whispering lies. Of course. That was it. How do you get rid of lies? Not by telling them that they are wrong. No, by telling the truth. That was it….

She knew the truth. She spoke truth to herself. "I am not alone. God is with me. I know He loves me. It says so in His Word. And Mum and Dad, they love me. And I can do everything with God's help."

But still the whispers. Still the lies. Mum was now on the floor. Cook had tears in her eyes. Stacey was crying loudly. Kevin was lying on the ground as if he had been hit. The Gloom filled the room. There were only twelve but they seemed to be everywhere. The darkness descended. Sophie continued to fight the lies. She knew who she was. She knew who God had made her. But she was beginning to understand, this isn't always easy. The room looked even darker. She could hear Thomas' whispering prayers, Stacey's sobs, Kevin's pain. And then:

Session 8: I Can Have Peace Because God Helps Me Whatever I'm Feeling

▶ "ENOUGH!" The voice was like thunder.

The Gloom turned and stared and there in the doorway he stood. His eyes were the same, kind and sparkling, but everything else about Mr Dundenter looked different. Had he suddenly grown? Whatever it was, her mind was free, the room was silent. Sobs had stopped. All attention was on this one man who looked like he was filling the door.

"This ends."

Clearly The Gloom hadn't quite got the message. They had no intention of ending. All twelve turned and faced Dundenter. Who smiled! Sophie couldn't believe it. He actually smiled.

"You really want to do this?" he asked gently.

But, clearly they did. And now their full attention was on him. Intense concentration. Everything focused on this one man, all The Gloom asking darkness to attack Dundenter. The darkness didn't need to be asked, they hated this man with an intense hatred.

Sophie's mum leaned on the counter next to Sophie. Sophie was understandably concerned.

"Mum, will they hurt him?"

Sophie's mum shook her head gently. "No darling. That is Dundenter. He has learned to hear the voice of God so clearly. All he is hearing right now is truth. God is whispering truth. It's not about power Sophie, it's about knowing the truth of who you are in Jesus. Look!"

And Sophie looked. And Dundenter stood. Smiling. Almost laughing.

And Dundenter spoke:

"And now take your negative words, your cruel lies and go. And, Darkness, know that you have lost. So leave, before I get really annoyed."

And the strangest thing happened. Shapes like the wolf things came out of some of the people and disappeared. These people fell to the ground crying. The others turned and ran away. And Dundenter shouted after them,

"And when you return to your base you'll discover there's not so many of you out there telling lies because I've had to deal with lots of you over the last few months and many of you have realized how wrong you are and many of you have become followers of God. But whatever you decide, the followers of Jesus will keep speaking the truth and believing God's truth and we will stand and the darkness will fail."

Those who were left went to Dundenter who prayed for them, and Sophie was sure that they went from a greyish colour to a normal colour almost immediately. They all looked embarrassed, but Dundenter gave them a card with an address on and shortly afterwards they left.

And when the room was clear they stood and looked at each other, sighed and then gave the loudest cheer, "We've won. They've gone. Hoorah!"

"Are they dead?" Asked Stacey.

They all burst out laughing. It was done.

▶ And that night many cakes were consumed and there was so much laughter. Sophie sat close to her mum and dad and finally got to know where they had been. They told her how The Gloom had kept them prisoner, making them feel useless and worthless until one day they understood who they are in God and were able to break free. And then they explained how they had come straight to find her and discovered her in the graveyard the previous night. They had hidden ready to help her but instead they'd watched with pride as Sophie and Thomas dealt with the wolf things so well. But, as they tried to leave to follow Sophie and Thomas they walked out of the gate and straight back into a whole squad of The Gloom who recaptured them and tied them up.

Sophie felt so angry with The Gloom for taking her mum and dad away for all those years. But, they were here now and she was so exhausted that she sank into a deep sleep with her head resting on her mum's shoulder.

Dad carried her up to her room and tucked her into bed.

Eventually the house was quiet. All slept. A strange day indeed.

Sophie's parents have returned. What will happen to Sophie now? And what about Thomas? That's for next time...

Take some time to ask and listen to what the children think about the story.

Session 8: I Can Have Peace Because God Helps Me Whatever I'm Feeling

Response

Prayer (5 minutes)

Ask the children to stand.

We are going to spend a few minutes just telling God how we are feeling right now.

If you know that you struggle with anger, tell God now. Allow some time for the children to chat to God.

Offer the children the chance to have a leader pray with them by asking them to raise their hand.

Once the children have been prayed for, gather everyone together.

Whatever you are feeling, God wants to fill you with His peace. So hold out your hands and allow God to fill you with His peace. Allow His peace to wash over you.

Finish the response time by saying the following prayer:

> **Pray together**
>
> Lord,
> We thank You that You want us to have joy not sadness, love instead of anger, and peace instead of anxiety. Thank You that as Your children we can know the truth of who we are and handle our feelings well. Amen.

▶ Lord, we thank You that You want us to have joy not sadness, love instead of anger and peace instead of anxiety. Thank You that as Your children we can know the truth of who we are and handle our feelings well. Amen.

Hand out the activity sheet and as time allows spend some time together completing the activity sheet. The children can also take it home to complete.

Next Week (5 minutes)

Highlight next week's course. Keep it exciting:
"Next week everyone who comes will get a _____", "Next week we'll hear the next part of this exciting story", etc.

Session 9: I Can Forgive Others

THE LIGHTBRINGERS | 87

Session 9: I Can Forgive Others

Time Plan

Getting Started 30 minutes	Free Play (20 minutes)	
	Welcome (5 minutes)	
	Announcements (5 minutes)	
Worship 20 minutes	Prayer (5 minutes)	
	Game (5 minutes)	Choose one: "Elephant march" or "Defy gravity"
	Praise (10 minutes)	I Love You Like
Word 40 minutes	Bible Verse (5 minutes)	Be kind and compassionate to one another, forgiving each other, just as in Christ God forgave you. (Ephesians 4:32)
	Teaching Time (20 minutes) Explore the Bible (10 minutes) Illustration (10 minutes)	Matthew 18:21-35
	Story Time (15 minutes)	*The Adventures Of Lilly Pepper* – Forgive (video: 7.5 minutes) *The Lightbringers* – Forgive Them? (video: 12 minutes)
Response 15 minutes	Prayer (10 minutes)	Remember to give out this week's activity sheet if you haven't already.
	Next Week (5 minutes)	

Overview

Learning to forgive from the heart sets us free from our past and heals our emotional pain. It's not easy. But it is essential. This lesson will take some time exploring this and giving children opportunity to truly forgive.

Getting Started

Free Play (20 minutes)

Welcome (5 minutes)

This is a chance to welcome the children but also an opportunity to have fun with them.

Announcements And Ground Rules (5 minutes)

Remind them of the two simple rules:
1. Nobody leaves their seat. If they need to go to the bathroom then they must put their hand up and ask permission from a leader.
2. When you ask for quiet, everyone sits down, focuses on the front, and makes no sound.

Worship

Prayer (5 minutes)

In two sections:
1. **Giving Thanks:** Children who have prayed for something the week before (or several weeks before) and whose prayers have been answered should be asked to come and tell the others how God answered their prayer.
2. **Bringing Needs:** Some of the children will want to pray for certain things. Allow them to come and mention what they are praying for and ask God together to answer prayer.

Session 9: I Can Forgive Others

Game Choose one (5 minutes)

Game 1 – Elephant March

PREPARATION   Each team will need a pair of tights and a tennis ball; 8 cones or water bottles per team.

PLAYERS   One player per team.

SET-UP   Put the tennis ball in the foot of one leg of the tights. Put the tights over the player's head with the empty leg tucked into their shirt and the leg containing the tennis ball swinging in front of them. Place the cones or water bottles in two parallel rows about 8 feet apart.

OBJECT   Players need to knock over the cones or water bottles with the tennis ball.

WINNING   The team to do it in the quickest time.

Game 2 – Defy Gravity

PREPARATION   Three balloons per person.

PLAYERS   Two or three players per team.

SET-UP   No set-up required.

OBJECT   The teams have to keep their three balloons in the air.

WINNING   The team to keep them in the air the longest.

Praise I Love You Like (10 minutes)

The song that has been specially written for this lesson is "I Love You Like". God showed His love by FORGIVING our sin. This is our song of love back to Him. We love God because He loved us first. We FORGIVE others because God forgave us first.

RAP
I LOVE YOU LIKE A SYMPHONY
LOVE YOU LIKE A RHAPSODY
LOVE YOU LIKE A HARMONY LOVES A MELODY
I LOVE YOU LIKE A STARRY NIGHT
LOVE YOU LIKE A KISS GOODNIGHT
LOVE YOU LIKE A FIREFLY LOVES A HOT JULY

YOU'RE LIKE THE WINTER SUN
THAT'S WARMING ME INSIDE OUT
SUDDENLY MY WORLD'S NOT SO COLD
YOUR LOVE IS ENDLESS AND I'M DEFENSELESS
I GIVE YOU ALL OF ME, I GIVE YOU EVERYTHING

CHORUS
LOVE YOU, LOVE YOU, LOVE YOU – LORD, I REALLY LOVE YOU
MORE THAN THE DESERT LOVES THE RAIN
LOVE YOU, LOVE YOU, LOVE YOU – LORD, I REALLY LOVE YOU
I'LL NEVER EVER BE THE SAME
LOVE YOU, LOVE YOU, LOVE YOU – LORD, I REALLY LOVE YOU
MORE THAN A ROCKSTAR LOVES THE FAME
LOVE YOU, LOVE YOU, LOVE YOU – LORD, I REALLY LOVE YOU
MORE AND MORE AND MORE EACH DAY

I COULD GET LOST IN YOU
'CAUSE YOUR LOVE'S A GALAXY
MY HEART IS SPINNING ROUND YOUR LIGHT
YOU DRAW ME NEARER AND NOW IT'S CLEARER
YOU ARE MY DESTINY, YOU ARE MY EVERYTHING

REPEAT CHORUS

REPEAT RAP

REPEAT CHORUS

I LOVE YOU LIKE

Words & Music by Wayne Tester, Esther Tester. © 2018 Testricity.com Music (ASCAP) / Fuzzy Socks Music (BMI) (both admin. by Testricity Music Group, www.testricity.com). ℗&© 2018 Testricity Music Group. ALL RIGHTS RESERVED.

Remember, we suggest using a few praise songs for each session. As well as the specific song here, you may want to reintroduce some of the songs that have already been used. Enjoy!

Word

I Can Forgive Others

Bible Verse To Memorize (5 minutes)

> Be kind and compassionate to one another, forgiving each other, just as in Christ God forgave you.
> Ephesians 4:32

▶ Be kind and compassionate to one another, forgiving each other, just as in Christ God forgave you. (Ephesians 4:32)

Teaching Time (20 minutes)

Note: For this session there is no worship time before the lesson to allow more time for the response in prayer at the end.

1. Explore The Bible (10 minutes)

Matthew 18:21-35

▶ Jesus told a simple story so that people could understand a very important lesson about forgiveness. Peter, one of Jesus' disciples, came to Him and asked Him a question, "Lord, how many times should I forgive someone when they do something wrong to me?"

Jesus knew that we should always forgive so that we can stop hurting. But instead of saying, "Always," Jesus said, "Peter, you should forgive someone seventy-seven times!" Some versions of the Bible even say "seventy times seven".

Then Jesus decided to tell Peter a parable to help him understand how important it is to forgive someone. A parable is a simple story that has a very important meaning. This is Jesus' parable:

Once there was a king who was very rich. He had many servants who worked for him. Some servants were in charge of lots of the king's money. They were also in charge of other servants.

The king decided to check to see if one of his servants was taking care of the money. When the king checked on the money he found out that his servant had not paid the bills but had borrowed the money for himself. It was not just a little money. The servant had borrowed thousands and thousands of pounds/dollars! He had borrowed so much money that he could never pay it back. This man had a huge debt.

At first the king decided the only way to get his money back was to sell the servant and all of his family as slaves. The servant was very upset. His wife and children would all have to go and live in different places. They might never see each other again. The servant begged the king to forgive him for what he had done. He begged and begged him to not sell his family as slaves.

The king felt sorry for the servant. He decided to forgive the servant for borrowing all those thousands of pounds/dollars. He even told him that he would not have to pay the money back.

Do you think the servant was happy? Do you think that he was so happy that he treated everyone nicely that day? No he did not.

As soon as the servant left the king he found another servant who owed him money. The servant only owed this man a few pounds/dollars. His debt was very small. Even though the king had been nice to him, the servant grabbed this man and began to choke him. He told him that he would throw him in prison until he paid back the few pounds/dollars.

Some of the other servants heard what had happened and went and told the king. What do you think the king thought? He had forgiven the servant a huge debt but the servant could not forgive another even a small debt. The king was very angry and threw the man in prison where he was tortured. He would have to stay in prison until the debt was paid.

Do you think Peter understood the parable that Jesus told him about forgiveness? The parable means that God has forgiven us for everything we have ever done wrong to Him. He has forgiven us a huge debt! Now he wants us to forgive people who have hurt us.

God forgave us a huge debt like the king in the parable did and we should forgive others for their small debts against us.

Jesus knew that when we don't forgive other people, it is bad for us. It's like being tortured. When we forgive others, it feels like we are letting them off the hook but all we are doing is handing them over to God who promises that He will make sure that they have to answer to Him for what they have done (Romans 12:19)

Meanwhile we can walk free!

2. Illustration In Three Parts (10 minutes)

Illustration Part 1 – Carrying Alone

Object Needed: A sports bag.
You will either need to load the bag with heavy objects, or pretend it is heavy.

Person 1: *(Dragging the bag.)* This is so heavy.
Person 2: That looks heavy.
Person 1: *(Still dragging.)* It is very heavy.
Person 2: How far do you have to go?
Person 1: To the other side of the stage.
Person 2: That far. That's quite a long way. Do you want some help?
Person 1: *(Still dragging.)* Oh no! I like to carry my own baggage thank you.
Person 2: Why?
Person 1: I think it's good for me to carry this bag myself.
Person 2: Why?
Person 1: Stop asking me these silly questions.

(Eventually person 1 falls down and shouts.)
Person 1: Ok! Help me then.
Person 2: *(Dragging together now.)* See it's easier with two.
(The two people remain for the next illustration.)

Illustration Part 2 – What's In The Bag?

Objects Needed: The words: "Hurts", "Revenge", "Unforgiveness" must be in the bag written on flash paper.

Person 3: What are you two doing?
Persons 1&2: We're carrying this bag.
Person 1: It's easier with two.
Person 3: Are you sure you should be carrying it?
Person 1: Of course! It's my bag.
Person 3: But what's in it?
Person 1 Just things.
Person 3: What things?
Person 1: Oh, just things!
Person 3: Show me.

Person 1 opens the bag and takes out the first piece of paper.

Person 3: It says: "Unforgiveness".
Person 1: Yes! I got it when Ashley broke my bike and I promised I'd never forgive him.
Person 2: I didn't know you had that stuff in there. This is nothing to do with me, I'm out of here.

Person 2 walks off. Person 1 takes out the next item.

Person 3: It says: "Hurts".
Person 1: Yes! I got it when Tina next door was really horrible to me.
Person 3: When was that?
Person 1: Oh, about five years ago.
Person 3: Takes out the final item.
Person 3: It says: "Revenge".
Person 1: Yes! Mr Harold across the road, burst my ball when it went over his fence for the fiftieth time last year. So, when I'm a bit bigger I'm going to smash all his windows.
Person 3: But that's terrible.
Person 1: I know, that ball cost me £1.99.
Person 3: No not that! You wanting to smash his windows. In fact, you shouldn't be carrying any of these things. You're supposed to give them all to God. You have to forgive people and let things go. You have to give all your hurts to God.
Person 1: I know! But it's really hard to let go.
Person 3: But you have to. Let me show you why!

(They both stand still as another person comes on dressed as a runner. If you're short of people, Person 3 needs to dash off and return in a tracksuit).

Illustration Part 3 – Running The Race

Object Needed: A runner looking as if he's about to start a race.

Person 2: Look, he's ready to start his race. On your marks, get set, go, BANG!
(The runner begins to run frantically – on the spot of course – Person 2 commentates.)

Person 2: *(In commentator voice.)* And our runner is off to an amazing start, leaving everyone else miles behind. He is clearly the fastest and the best. No one can catch him, surely he will win…
Person 2: *(To person 1)* But watch this….
(Person 2 picks up the bag and hands it to the runner.)

Person 2: Just hold this for me please.
(The runner takes the bag and collapses under its weight.)

Person 2: *(In commentator voice again.)* Oh dear. It's all gone terribly wrong. Everyone is overtaking him. He'll never finish the race now.
(The runner remains on the ground.)

Person 2: You see! With all those bad things, he could never finish the race. We too have a race to run. Not an actual race, more something we have to do in our lives for God. But, if we keep holding on to all these bad things we'll never do anything for God.
Person 1: So how do I get rid of all this stuff?
Person 2: You make a choice to give them to God.
Person 1: *(Praying.)* God, there's a lot of bad things here. I choose to give them to You. I forgive Ashley for breaking my bike.

(Person 2 sets fire to flash paper 'Unforgiveness'.)

Person 1: And I forgive Tina for being horrible to me.

(Person 2 sets fire to flash paper "Hurts".)

Person 1: *(Stops Praying.)* Do I have to forgive Mr Harold too?!
Person 2: Yes!
Person 1: Oh well! *(Prays)* And I forgive Mr Harold and I won't smash his windows.
(Person 2 sets fire to flash paper "Revenge"..)

Person 2: Feels better doesn't it?
Person 1: Yes, I guess it does.

Story Time (15 minutes)

The Story For Younger Children – *The Adventures Of Lilly Pepper*

Chapter 9 – Forgive

The video is 7.5 minutes. Take some time after the story to ask and listen to what the children think. Then go to the response and prayer time.

▶ Hello again! Lilly and Felix escaped from the cave last time but God has more for them to do. Welcome to Chapter 9, Forgive.

▶ It was already getting dark when Ethel remembered to phone Felix's mum. Everyone knew Ethel and it didn't take her long to reassure Felix's mum that all was well. She told her that Felix was having something to eat with her and her best friend's granddaughter. In fact, Ethel went one stage further and arranged for Felix to stay over. She had plenty of old clothes upstairs, and found a pair of PJs for Felix so his clothes could dry out before he'd have to explain to his mum that he nearly drowned.

So both in their PJs, and now enjoying several slices of Gran's special cake, they sat down to watch a movie. It was a very old movie called "The Neverending Story" but they enjoyed it. It told the story of Bastian, a boy who saved a land called Fantasia from The Nothing and in so doing became brave and was able to fight the bullies who were being mean to him in the real world.

Lilly was only seven but she was smart and she could tell exactly what Felix was thinking as the movie came to an end. "You'd like to do that to the bullies who are mean to you wouldn't you?"

▶ "Yes," Felix muttered, but as he spoke tears ran down his cheeks. "They never really hurt me, and I know I could have drowned on the beach but I never did and I know I could have been in real trouble being tied to the tree and I was definitely scared when they dangled me over the river by my legs." Lilly just stared with her mouth wide open as Felix described the mean things the bullies had done. But it was the last line that made her feel very sad, when Felix added,

"But it wasn't the things they did to me that hurt. It was how it made me feel inside. I think I hate them Lilly."

Lilly shook her head. "Felix you mustn't. If you carry things like hate inside you it will stop you being who God created you to be. We have to get rid of bad stuff from our hearts."

He looked at her, tears now pouring down his cheeks. "I can't help it," he sobbed. They made me feel terrible. You're asking me to do something impossible. You'll be asking me to forgive them next."

Lilly simply sat there and looked at him and nodded.

"You can't be serious," he almost shouted, "forgive them, after what they did?"

Lilly nodded again, "God can help you."

But, Felix didn't know what to do. He was sure that he should be angry with the bullies, they were mean. And he didn't feel like forgiving them. But he really did want to be all that God had created him to be. And he was fed up with that horrible feeling in his tummy every time he thought about those bullies.

He sat and stared. He wiped the tears away with his thumb. "How will God help me?"

Lilly thought quickly, "God can only help if you'll make the choice to forgive them Felix. But if you will, I'm sure God will help you and take all the hurt and pain away. Or definitely start to take it away. Sometimes it takes a little longer to heal inside." Felix shrugged his shoulders. He looked down and almost whispered, "Ok, let's do this."

▶ Lilly placed her hand on his shoulder. She'd seen it in church enough times and began to wonder what to pray. She didn't see Gran and Ethel watching from the kitchen, but they closed their eyes and began to pray as well.

Lilly prayed, "Dear God. Please help Felix. He wants to forgive the bullies. Can You help him and take away the hurt inside. Please help him, Jesus."

She kept watching Felix. First, Felix prayed, "God, I forgive those bullies for calling me names and leaving me out of their fun which made me feel so lonely and ugly. I give all my hurt over to You." Then he sobbed uncontrollably. Lilly watched. He cried for some time and then Felix felt it. A warm feeling in his tummy. Getting bigger and bigger and bigger. Like someone was rubbing his tummy. And then he felt really calm. And really peaceful like he was being wrapped in a lovely warm duvet made out of love. And then the tears stopped and he opened his eyes and he felt…. well, amazing… he felt amazing.

▶ He smiled. And then he began to laugh and Lilly stared. Felix was now laughing uncontrollably. Although Lilly didn't understand what was going on she started to laugh as well. And through the laughter Felix said, "I've forgiven them Lilly. I really have. I know what they said about me was lies. The truth is God made me special and loves me just as I am." And now they were both laughing so much that tears were running down their faces. In the kitchen Gran and Ethel were holding their hands over their mouths so that their giggles could not be heard.

They laughed. And Felix forgave. And God began to heal Felix's hurt. And Felix laughed some more.

But Felix and Lilly will meet the bullies again… Find out more next time. See you then!

Take some time to ask and listen to what the children think about the story.

Session 9: I Can Forgive Others

The Story For Older Children – *The Lightbringers*

Chapter 9 – Forgive Them?

The video is 12 minutes. Take some time after the story to ask and listen to what the children think. Then go to the response and prayer time.

▶ Sophie woke early, the sun bursting in as soon as she opened the curtains. The sky above was the deepest blue; the sun was shining brightly. After all the excitement of 'the battle' Sophie went down to breakfast wondering what would happen next and when!

▶ Sophie sat opposite Dundenter. Thomas sat at the end of the table. He looked so sad. Sophie said nothing, but deep down she knew why. She was leaving and her parents were coming for her, and nobody was coming for Thomas. But, Sophie tried not to dwell on that for too long, she was more concerned about when she was leaving, and anyway, where were her parents?

She asked Mr Dundenter. He smiled, "They just found out that God has given you a new home, really close to here. They're getting it ready for you to move into. They'll be back later this morning. Don't worry."

"Well", said Sophie, "I am packed. Everything is packed. I am ready. But I will miss you."

Dundenter smiled, his eyes still kind. He looked so different from the fierce man who had confronted The Gloom only the day before. He continued, "They'll be here by lunch time, but do you realize that you have packed something that you have to leave behind, Sophie?"

Sophie looked confused. "I'm not sure I have Mr Dundenter. I know I arrived here with nothing at all, but I'm sure it's OK to take my clothes with me now."

He smiled that knowing smile. "The thing you have packed is not in any bag Sophie."

She patted her pockets. But they were empty apart from her tissue. And she was quite sure Mr Dundenter couldn't mean that. She looked confused.

"It's inside you Sophie. Not in your pockets and not in your bag."

Now Sophie was really confused. But Mr Dundenter continued:

"It's an emotion Sophie. A feeling. Remember when I talked with Thomas when he was up the tree? Well Thomas had one of those things too. Something he was carrying inside. His thing was fear. He felt afraid, so he would climb things. School roofs, trees, whatever he could find, to escape. And then of course he would feel frightened of being up so high and he would end up trapped. But he learned to trust and he learned to talk to God, and now he's really awesome at that. And I know he wouldn't mind me telling you because he doesn't have it anymore. You saw him with the wolf things. He's not afraid anymore. He is not carrying fear any longer. He asked God to take it away.

"But I'm not afraid Mr Dundenter. I've felt afraid a few times, but I don't think I have fear inside me, and I certainly have never got stuck up on the school roof!"

"No, not fear Sophie. Yours is different. The Gloom took your parents away from you. All those years thinking your parents were dead. That was so wrong of them and it was so hard for you. But, if you really want to be free you are going to have to forgive them for that. If you hold on to unforgiveness, it will end up hurting you and holding you back.

Sophie wasn't completely sure what this meant, but she did know that she wasn't keen to forgive those who hurt her. Particularly, the nasty Gloom who tried to hurt her and all her friends. And had kept her mum and dad prisoners all those years.

But it was almost as if Mr Dundenter read her mind, "You don't forgive because you feel like it Sophie. It's a choice. You do it for your own good. Your feelings will take time to heal. But, if you forgive, it will set you free from spending all your time thinking about the sad things of the past. And one more thing. God forgave us. We need to let that be our example. And we definitely didn't deserve that. Now pop up to your room and talk to God and ask Him who you need to forgive."

So, Sophie did as Mr Dundenter said and went to her room. She knelt beside her bed because that seemed like a good place to pray and she talked to God. But she didn't really need to pray much. She knew it was The Gloom, she had to forgive The Gloom. And then she had an idea. To show she was forgiving them she would write their name on a piece of paper and to show that she was getting rid of the bad emotion she would crinkle up the paper and throw it away. And that is what she did. Into the waste basket went the words:

I FORGIVE THE GLOOM BECAUSE THEY KEPT MY PARENTS PRISONER AND TRIED TO HURT MY FRIENDS, WHICH MADE ME FEEL ANGRY AND FRIGHTENED AND ALONE.

Session 9: I Can Forgive Others

Content that the job was done, she skipped out of her room, down the stairs and sat opposite Mr Dundenter. "Done!" She proudly announced.

Mr Dundenter shook his head and said, "Sophie, I suspect you've not even begun. Just humour me. Pop back upstairs and ask God if there is anything else."

Sophie was far from convinced but she went and knelt. She waited for a while and felt nothing at all. She decided she would pray out loud, "God, I have forgiven The Gloom even though they were mean and tried to kill me and to kill Thomas and all my friends, but do I need to forgive anyone else?"

Nothing. She was beginning to feel sure that Mr Dundenter was wrong.

▶   But then she felt a name, a thought, not sure what it was, but she began to remember the time when some girls were really mean to her in school and she had said that she would get them for being mean, but that was years ago and … Oh! She prayed quickly,

"God, I choose to forgive the girls who hurt me. Who said mean things. Who made me cry. Which made me feel horrible inside, I choose to forgive them."

And she wrote their names on a piece of paper and she dropped it into the waste basket.

But now lots of things were coming to her. Lots of names coming to her mind. Lots of times she felt hurt. Lots of times when people were unkind. And now there were many names on the next piece of paper… lots of names going into the waste basket. And some of the things made her feel sad all over again, and a tear would run down her cheek as she said, "I forgive them". And then she would pray some more. And then it hit her. She wasn't expecting it. It came from nowhere. Surprising names.

MUM and DAD!

She didn't understand. And then she did. Her parents had left her. And even though she now knew why, she still felt left behind. Abandoned. Unloved. All those words coming back up again. Her mum and dad had left her. Now tears were pouring down her cheeks, she was sobbing, and sobbing, and sobbing.

"But Mum and Dad, you could have escaped sooner. Or I could have been taken prisoner too. I would have been OK. And then we could have been together."

202   THE LIGHTBRINGERS

She knew none of it was true. But she couldn't stop her feelings. She wept and wept, and wept. And then she caught her breath between sobs and understood the truth. She continued to cry, but she managed to whisper the words,

"I choose to forgive Mum and Dad for leaving me behind which made me feel abandoned, which made me feel unloved." She still felt some sadness, but she also felt strange. As if a giant weight was lifting.

And then with trembling hands she wrote the words on a sheet of paper:

MUM AND DAD

▶   She dropped it into the waste basket.

And she stayed in her room for a while longer and then she washed her face and she walked back downstairs. Mr Dundenter didn't look as if he had moved at all. He looked at her.

"That's better", he said. "Travelling a little lighter now?"

And she knew it was true. She felt lighter. She had forgiven them.

"I can't wait to see Mum and Dad", she said to Mr Dundenter.

But Mr Dundenter just smiled, "Eat your lunch quickly then, they're on their way."

One more episode left. Will Sophie's parents return? What about Thomas? Find out next week.

Take some time to ask and listen to what the children think about the story.

Response

Prayer (10 minutes)

This week we are going to encourage the children to follow the example of the characters in the stories. They will need paper, pens, and space. Ask them to think about what Felix (Adventures of Lilly Pepper) or Sophie (Lightbringers) had to do. Even though it was really hard, they chose to forgive and forgiveness allowed that heavy weight of unforgiveness to go and those sad feelings to begin to leave.

Before the children pray, you may find it helpful to explain to them why they need to forgive, and answer any questions they may have.

Forgiving others is always hard to do, it takes courage not just a warm fuzzy feeling, to make the choice to forgive someone. It shows strength not weakness. When you forgive you're not saying what the person did was OKay. You have decided to hand it all over to God and trust Him to deal with it in the right way. You have also decided not to hold it against the person who hurt you, so that you can stop hurting.

So why forgive?
God tells us to because He knows it's the best thing for us.
If we don't it will keep on hurting us.
So the enemy can't use it against us.

What is forgiveness?
It's not a feeling, it's a choice you make to do it!
It's between you and God.
It's not forgetting but it does mean you are no longer 'hooked' to that person.

Pray the opening prayer as a group then get them to find a space and start to write down anyone who comes to mind. Share the simple prayer they can then pray for each person on their list. Once they've done that get them to tear up the paper and drop it into the trash.

The pattern Sophie/Felix followed is not uncommon. The superficial things come to mind first, then more will follow. So, allow time. You could play some worship music while this happens. When you are sure enough time has passed, bring them all together again and sing a song of praise together.

Remember that, although forgiveness is crucial, it can be very difficult for some. So give the children permission to ask for help or to stay around and talk to you at the end. You may need to pray with them a little more. You may also find that younger children need more individual help with this so adapt this prayer time to suit the age of your child/children.

And, of course, an inevitable consequence of being alive is that we will get hurt from time to time. Encourage them to use the forgiveness prayer whenever they need to in the coming weeks and to make forgiving others a way of life.

> **Pray together**
>
> Dear Heavenly Father,
> Help me to remember who the people are that hurt me so that I can forgive them. I know Jesus will heal me from my hurts. In Jesus' name.
> Amen.

Pray together:

▶ Dear Heavenly Father, Help me to remember who the people are that hurt me so that I can forgive them. I know Jesus will heal me from my hurts. In Jesus' name. Amen

Ask them to spread out around the room and write down any names that have come to mind and then pray this prayer on their own for each name.

> **Pray together**
>
> Dear God,
> I forgive [name] for [what they did to hurt you] which made me feel [tell God how it made you feel].
> Amen.

▶ Dear God, I forgive [name] for [what they did to hurt you] which made me feel [tell God how it made you feel].
Amen.

They should then tear the paper up or, even better, you could have them come forward one at a time and put their piece of paper into a shredder or collect all the pieces of paper and burn them all.

It would be good to finish this time with a prayer or song of thanks.

Hand out the activity sheet and as time allows spend some time together completing the activity sheet. The children can also take it home to complete.

Next Week (5 minutes)

Highlight next week's course. Keep it exciting:
"Next week everyone who comes will get a _____", "Next week we'll hear the next part of this exciting story", etc.

Explain when and what *The Steps To Freedom In Christ* is all about (the Steps should ideally be done before Session 10 but can also be done after it).

You could say something like this:

We are going to have the chance to get rid of all the things that are holding us back when we do *The Lightbringers* Trail, *The Steps To Freedom In Christ*. We will ask God to show us what things might be holding us back and then get rid of them so that by the end of our time we will know that there's nothing to stop us running straight for the finishing line in our race to live for Jesus for the rest of our lives.

Session 10: I Can Live Every Day Walking In God's Truths

Session 10: I Can Live Every Day Walking In God's Truths

Time Plan

Getting Started 30 minutes	Free Play (20 minutes)	
	Welcome (5 minutes)	
	Announcements (5 minutes)	
Worship 20 minutes	Prayer (5 minutes)	
	Game (5 minutes)	Choose one: 'Supersize me' or 'Stocking race'
	Praise (10 minutes)	Can't Stop
Word 45 minutes	Bible Verse (5 minutes)	Be strong in the Lord and in His mighty power. (Ephesians 6:10)
	Interview (5 minutes)	
	Teaching Time (20 minutes) Reflective Worship (10 minutes) Explore the Bible (5 minutes) Illustration (5 minutes)	Luke 8:4-15
	Story Time (15 minutes)	*The Adventures Of Lilly Pepper* – The Bullies Return (video: 7 minutes) *The Lightbringers* – Happily Ever After (Hopefully!) (video: 7.5 minutes)
Response 10 minutes	Prayer (5 minutes)	Remember to give out this week's activity sheet if you haven't already.
	Next Week / Commissioning As Lightbringers (5 minutes)	

Overview

Having taken hold of the freedom Christ won for them, we need to look at how we continue to walk in that freedom every day. Growing in maturity depends on the extent to which children continue to renew their minds and learn to distinguish good from evil.

Getting Started

Free Play (20 minutes)

Welcome (5 minutes)

This is a chance to welcome the children but also an opportunity to have fun with them.

Announcements And Ground Rules (5 minutes)

Remind them of the two simple rules:
1. Nobody leaves their seat. If they need to go to the bathroom then they must put their hand up and ask permission from a leader.
2. When you ask for quiet, everyone sits down, focuses on the front, and makes no sound.

Worship

Prayer (5 minutes)

In two sections:
1. **Giving Thanks:** Children who have prayed for something the week before (or several weeks before) and whose prayers have been answered should be asked to come and tell the others how God answered their prayer.
2. **Bringing Needs:** Some of the children will want to pray for certain things. Allow them to come and mention what they are praying for and ask God together to answer prayer.

Game Choose one (5 minutes)

Game 1 – Supersize Me

PREPARATION   A boiler suit; lots of small balloons.

PLAYERS   Five players per team.

SET-UP   One of the players needs to put on the boiler suit (zipped half way). The balloons need to be in one place.

OBJECT   Players need to grab balloons and fill the boiler suit.

WINNING   The team to have put in the most balloons at the end of the dedicated time.

Game 2 – Stocking Race

PREPARATION   A pair of stockings, sack, and heavy work gloves (such as gardening gloves).

PLAYERS   One player per team.

SET-UP   Place the gloves and the stockings in the sack.

OBJECT   The players have to put on the gloves and then the stockings.

WINNING   The player to wear the gloves and the stockings first.

Praise Can't Stop (10 minutes)

The song that has been specially written for this lesson is "Can't Stop" and is about how the TRUTH of what God has done for us keeps us GROWING!

I CAN'T STOP THIS MELODY
I CAN'T STOP YOUR LOVE FOR ME
I CAN'T STOP THIS Praise TO YOU
I CAN'T STOP, THIS IS WHAT I DO
I CAN'T STOP THIS HOLY TRANCE
I CAN'T STOP YOUR MERCY CHANCE
I CAN'T STOP, I JUST GOTTA DANCE
I CAN'T STOP

CHORUS
I JUST CAN'T STOP
(I LOVE YOU LORD, YOU KNOW IT)
I JUST CAN'T STOP
(I'M NOT AFRAID TO SHOW IT)
I JUST CAN'T STOP
(I LOVE YOU LORD, YOU KNOW IT)
I JUST CAN'T STOP
(I'M NOT AFRAID TO SHOW IT)

YOU MAKE ALL THINGS BEAUTIFUL
I CAN'T STOP, I'M IMMORTAL
YOU TURN DUST INTO WONDERFUL
I CAN'T STOP, I'M A MIRACLE
I CAN'T STOP THIS HOLY TRANCE
I CAN'T STOP YOUR MERCY CHANCE
I CAN'T STOP, I JUST GOTTA DANCE
I CAN'T STOP

REPEAT CHORUS 2 TIMES

IN THE IMAGE, IN THE IMAGE, IN THE IMAGE
I'M MADE IN THE IMAGE, IN THE IMAGE, IN THE IMAGE, IN THE IMAGE
I'M MADE IN THE IMAGE OF GOD
IN THE IMAGE, IN THE IMAGE, I'M MADE IN THE IMAGE OF GOD
IN THE IMAGE, IN THE IMAGE, IN THE IM, IN THE IM, IN THE IMAGE

REPEAT CHORUS 4 TIMES

Words & Music by Wayne Tester, Esther Tester. © 2018 Testricity.com Music (ASCAP) / Fuzzy Socks Music (BMI) (both admin. by Testricity Music Group, www.testricity.com). ℗&© 2018 Testricity Music Group. ALL RIGHTS RESERVED.

Remember, we suggest using a few praise songs for each session. As well as the specific song here, you may want to reintroduce some of the songs that have already been used. Enjoy!

Word

I Can Live Every Day Walking In God's Truths

Bible Verse To Memorize (5 minutes)

▶ Be strong in the Lord and in His mighty power. (Ephesians 6:10)

Interview (5 minutes)

Invite one of the leaders or one of the children to come and tell the group what Jesus has done for them; how He's helped them in work/school; how He cares for them; how they first made their decision to become a Christian. If the person is very nervous, interview them. If they are more confident, allow them to speak freely – taking notice of the timing allowed for this section.

Teaching Time (20 minutes)

1. Reflective Worship (10 minutes)

2. Explore The Bible (5 minutes)

Luke 8:4-15

▶ Have any of you ever planted seeds before? Some of you may have planted a garden or watched your parents or grandparents plant a garden. There is a lot of work involved in the planting and caring for a garden. You'll need a shovel to break up the ground and a rake to remove the rocks and keep the soil smooth. You need to chop down the weeds that might try to take over your garden. You will probably need some fertilizer and, unless it rains a lot, you will need a hose to water your garden. Oh, I almost forgot, the most important thing that you will need is... the seed! You can't have a garden without seeds. Now we have everything we need to produce a great crop of fruit and vegetables.

One day Jesus told a story about a farmer who planted some seeds. As he scattered the seed in his field, some of them fell onto the footpath and the birds ate them. Other seeds fell on rocky ground. The seeds sprouted, but they wilted and died under the hot sun because they didn't have deep roots. Some of the seeds fell in areas where there were a lot of weeds and the weeds choked out the young plants. BUT some of the seed fell on good, fertile soil and that seed grew and produced a wonderful crop.

Do you think Jesus was really trying to teach people how to plant a garden? No. The story has a much deeper meaning. In Jesus' story, the seed represents the Word of God and the soil represents the people who hear the word. Many times people hear the Word of God, but they don't understand it. They don't take it in. That is like the seed on the footpath. The devil comes and takes away the seed that has been planted in their heart before it has the opportunity to grow in their life.

The seed that fell on rocky soil represents those who hear the word and receive it with great joy, but when the newness wears off and the excitement fades, they drift away because they don't have deep roots.

The seed that fell among the weeds represents people who hear God's Word and believe what it says, but soon the message is crowded out by the worries of life and the desire to get more stuff. If seed is planted in a bunch of weeds, the weeds will soon take over!

A person who hears God's Word, tries to understand what it says and put it into practice in their daily life is like good soil. In good soil, the seed takes root and grows stronger and stronger. That is the kind of soil that Jesus wants us to be.

3. Illustration Choose one (5 minutes)

Illustration 1 – Growing Up

Object Needed: Baby food.

Is anybody here hungry? I know sometimes it's hard to sit through kids club without a snack, so I thought I'd bring a little something along this evening! Are you guys hungry? All right, who wants some… strained peas? Or maybe mixed vegetables? Or look, broccoli! What's the matter? Is there something wrong with this food? Of course there is! This is baby food, isn't it? And you guys don't want to eat this anymore? Why? Because you're not babies! You're all grown up, and you can eat grown up food.

What food do you like best? Is it pizza? Or maybe hamburgers? I love all that stuff too. I wonder, though, do any of you like mussels? Or how about sushi? Some of you might enjoy that food one day, but right now, you've found your ideal food. This baby food reminds me of when I first became a Christian. The Bible says that, when you accept Jesus as your Lord and Saviour, you are born again. That makes you a baby Christian, doesn't it? And everyone knows a baby needs… baby food.

But, there's something else we can learn from this baby food: we have to grow up some time, don't we? Because you don't see your parents sitting down to a nice jar of strained peas, do you?

That's why it's important that you don't stop learning about Jesus after you accept Him as your Saviour. It's really helpful to read your Bible, chat with Father God wherever you are, go to church, and worship God. This is the spiritual food you'll need to grow up strong in the Lord, just as real food helps your body grow.

I want to challenge you: don't get stuck in the baby food stage but seek God with all your heart.

Illustration 2 – Get Strong

Object Needed: Weights.

Do you know what these are? Has anyone ever used these before? Maybe you have seen your parents using them. Well, weight lifting has never interested me. But if you want to get strong muscles then these will help you. There's a saying "No pain, no gain!" Growing physically strong might not be your thing either, but hopefully you do want to grow strong in God.

Ephesians 6:10 says this: "Be strong in the Lord and in His mighty power". If we get to know God, then we will get strong. So how do we do this? God's Word, the Bible, will help us grow spiritually. Just like picking up these weights will make me physically strong. If I want to get strong in God, then I should read my Bible.

God has chosen us, now it is up to each one of us to say, 'Yes, I believe that I am a Child of God with direct access to my Father God.'

Illustration 3 – Junk Food Faith

Objects Needed: A variety of junk food e.g. chocolate, cake, Coke etc., lunch box *(place all the junk food in the lunch box).*

I didn't have time to eat my lunch today so you don't mind if I eat it now do you? So, let's see... I have some chocolate... oh, and here are some cookies. Let's see what else... here is a candy bar. Hey, do you think my mother would pack me a lunch like this? No way! This is all junk food! Do you know what would happen to me if I ate a steady diet of junk food like this? I would become weak and sickly because this junk food does not have the vitamins and nourishment needed to grow a strong, healthy body. Our bodies need the nourishment we get from meat, bread, fruit, and vegetables. No one can survive for very long on a junk food diet.

No one would think of feeding their body a steady diet of junk food. And yet, many people feed their minds with a steady diet of junk food every day. They feed it with TV, movies, comic books, magazines, and other junk. They never give their minds the real nourishment that it needs to be strong and healthy. They never feed it with the Word of God. The Bible says that our strength comes from the Lord, and that comes to us through His Word.

Illustration 4 – True Or False?

Come up with two true and one false statements about yourself or one of the other leaders/helpers. Ask the children to vote on which one they think is false.

To grow stronger, we need to be a bit like a detective and uncover lies, false things we've been believing. These are things opposite to what God says about you. When you've uncovered a lie, try and find a Bible verse that says the truth. You could use one of the verses from the postcards we gave out or ask someone to help you find one. When you've done that write a simple prayer:

Father God I turn my back on the lie that..........and I speak out the truth that............
Amen.

You can say this every day until you are certain that you know the truth. Sometimes that takes quite a long time, one or even two months, but it's worth it!

Session 10: I Can Live Every Day Walking In God's Truths

Story Time (15 minutes)

The Story For Younger Children – *The Adventures Of Lilly Pepper*

Chapter 10 – The Bullies Return

The video is 7 minutes. Take some time after the story to ask and listen to what the children think. Then go to the response and prayer time.

▶ Welcome to the last episode of *The Adventures Of Lilly Pepper*. Last time Felix learned to forgive the bullies. Let's find out what happens when he meets them again in Chapter 10, The Bullies Return.

Lilly Pepper was awake first. She went downstairs and found some juice and was pouring it into a glass when Felix wandered into the kitchen. Lilly wasn't sure where Ethel had found the PJs that Felix was wearing, but they were odd. They had blue stripes, which was fine, but the bottoms were too short and the top was too big. So the bottoms ended just past Felix's knees, but the top covered his hands.

But, Felix was happy. You didn't need to be a genius to work that out. He had a huge grin on his face as he sat opposite Lilly and poured some milk into a mug and began to drink. The lump in his stomach had gone. He felt … well … happy. He was so excited!

After breakfast they dressed and decided to go for a walk. Gran was a little nervous but told them that as long as they stuck together and didn't go too far they would be OK. So Lilly and Felix headed to the beach. The tide was coming in. The seagulls flew overhead and the sun shone on their backs, making large shadows in front of them. It was the perfect day.

216 THE LIGHTBRINGERS

▶ And then it all went wrong. It was as if a large cloud covered the sun. And from around an outcrop of rocks the bullies appeared. There were five of them and they walked up the beach. As they got closer, Lilly could see that they weren't that old, maybe 10 or 11. But that was three years older than Lilly and Felix and there were a lot of them!

As they got closer, Lilly could see that they were going to cause trouble. The tallest of them walked towards Felix, ready to push him over, when Lilly stepped in between them. The boy was older and much bigger, but the look in Lilly's eyes made him stop and then step back. But, they weren't done. And when Felix stepped forward again they were ready with their mean and unkind words, "Hey Felix, you're so stupid and ugly and now you have to hide behind a little girl."

▶ Felix shrugged his shoulders, smiled and said, "Well, actually that's not true. God didn't make me stupid or ugly. I am wonderfully made by a God who loves me."

"What?" came the voice of a very confused bully. But, before they could say more Felix added, "And I've forgiven you for all the mean things you did to me. I've forgiven you."

"But, we don't want your forgiveness." Came the voice of one of the other bullies.

"Well that's up to you," responded Felix. "If you want to carry a big weight because you don't want to let go of all the bad things, well that really is up to you. But when you're ready, come and find me, and I'll pray with you and God will take away all that stuff and make you brand new from the inside out."

The bullies now just stared. But Felix wasn't finished. "And one more thing. That bit about me hiding behind a girl. You need to know that right now I am standing here to protect you from that girl. She is very cross with you."

And she was. Lilly was looking very cross indeed. They kept hurting her friend and she wanted to punch them on the nose, but she was also amazed at Felix. He had learned so much so quickly. But now Lilly stepped beside Felix and stared at the bullies.

"Now go away." She said. "And leave us alone. Unless that is, you want us to pray for you."

▶   The bullies did the most extraordinary thing. They looked at each other and turned and ran away as quickly as they could.

Lilly and Felix continued their walk along the beach. Lilly was still cross but added, "they won't come near you again." But, Felix was thinking of something else and turned to Lilly, "Lilly, they are probably mean to me because someone was mean to them. Let's say a prayer for them." And to Lilly's amazement Felix did. There on the beach he prayed for the people who had been mean to him. And when he was done, he smiled and they turned and walked home again.

The remaining days of the summer were packed with fun and the sun continued to shine.

▶   Both Lilly and Felix were quite sad the day Lilly's mum and baby Jake came back to take her home. They hugged and looked brave as they packed her bags into the car. Felix knew that Lilly would come and visit again soon. But they both still had a tear in their eyes when they waved goodbye to each other.

Ethel came over and put a hand on Felix's shoulder, "Wonderful isn't she that Lilly Pepper? God will do amazing things through that little girl. And my sister, the Principal, will keep an eye on her."

Felix smiled and nodded. Gran added, "But He's going to do some amazing things through you too Felix. Now that He's got you all cleaned up inside. Best get ready for it."

▶ And that is all Gran would say.

Both Lilly and Felix would meet again and a whole new adventure would begin again soon.

Bye!

Take some time to ask and listen to what the children think about the story.

Session 10: I Can Live Every Day Walking In God's Truths

The Story For Older Children – *The Lightbringers*

Chapter 10 – Happily Ever After – Hopefully...

The video is 7.5 minutes. Take some time after the story to ask and listen to what the children think. Then go to the response and prayer time.

▶ And then shortly after lunch they were there. Her mum and dad were there.

Sophie jumped off her chair, rushed across the room and hugged her parents.

▶ "Where have you been? Last night you said you wouldn't be long."

Mum smiled, "We've only been a few hours, Soph. But we wanted the house to be perfect for you."

Sophie could see the excitement on her parents' faces. Mr Dundenter was looking at her with that big grin.

"And are you ready to go?", asked dad.

"Oh yes", answered Sophie.

"Don't you need to pack?"

"Nope!" responded Sophie. "I've got all that I need and I've left the things I don't need." She smiled at Mr Dundenter.

And with that she bounded up the stairs, picked up her suitcase and the key and ran back down." Dad, please can you get the metal box from my room?" Even Sophie knew when something was rather too big for her to carry!

"Ah the box," Mum exclaimed. "You know, you haven't even begun to see what that box can do."

Sophie looked confused. "Store stuff?" Was all Sophie could manage.

Mum giggled, "Later I'll show you what happens when you turn the key the other way."

And with a big hug for Mr Dundenter, Sophie grabbed her bag and began to walk towards the door.

"See you later, Dundenter," called Dad as he carried the box and followed Sophie and Mum to the car.

It was only when Sophie reached the door that she remembered that she hadn't said goodbye to everyone else. She wasn't going far and didn't want to make too much of it so she shouted, "Bye Stacey, bye Kevin, bye Cook." But she knew she would have to say a special goodbye to one particular person who, for all his bravery and loyalty and friendship, she still thought was a little crazy!

But, he was nowhere to be found. Why wasn't he here to say goodbye? Mum didn't want to wait any longer. She took Sophie's hand.

"But Mum!" began Sophie, but she knew it was no good. He was nowhere to be seen.

And so, a sad Sophie opened the door, and turned once more to the house and shouted, "Bye Thomas, see you very soon."

▶   "Yep. Very, very soon!" came Thomas' voice from behind. She spun around and there he stood. In the street. And he was surrounded by – would you believe it? – suitcases.

"I'm coming too Soph. Your mum and dad said I could come live with you guys. How cool is that!"

Sophie was so excited. She ran and hugged him and wouldn't let go until Thomas with slightly squeezed voice whispered, "You're definitely not going to kiss me, right?"

She stepped back laughing. "Definitely not!"

Session 10: I Can Live Every Day Walking In God's Truths

And later that day after they had been shown their new bedrooms and had unpacked and Sophie had put the box in a special place, Sophie said;

"Isn't this wonderful Thomas?"

He was happy too. She could tell. But then Thomas' face changed and he looked at Sophie and was very serious, "But don't you feel just a little bit sad Soph. Doesn't it mean that our adventures are all over now? It's lovely to have a nice home and your parents are the best, but don't you think it might be…well, well…just a little bit boring?"

Dad overheard and laughed out loud. "Thomas and Sophie, you'd better come with me." Dad walked them outside to what looked like a shed.

But as they got closer Sophie could hear the whirring of… well she didn't know what. It sounded like a hamster running around in his wheel. "Is it a secret pet shop?" thought Sophie, "that would be cool."

▶   But, when they went inside the whirring was not hamsters, it was computers. Computers everywhere. And giant screens and maps covering the walls. And maps marked with Gloom and maps marked with God. There was clearly a lot more God than Gloom. It was very cool.

It's all a bit old this technology now, explained dad. We were prisoners for quite a while – but it still works.

As they looked at the screen more closely, they could see people stood in front of The Gloom in different places all over the world. In some pictures The Gloom were running and in others the places were covered with God with very little darkness.

▶ Mum had joined them as Dad continued, "And this is where you'll work, both of you. For you are Lightbringers. Your job is simple. Wherever you are, whatever you do, you bring light, and you bring light by showing people who they are in God. God didn't set you free and teach you how to be truly who you are in Him for you to sit around getting bored, there's work to do. Others to set free. Others who don't know who God made them to be yet. People of all ages who need to understand that they are created to be amazing. That's what you get to do. All over the world you bring light. And there will be times when you'll face The Gloom again, but you'll grow strong and you'll know the Truth that God made you and you are so, so special. And the darkness will always be afraid of you. And people who are sad, and feel as if they are surrounded by darkness will see the light. Because you will bring light. So what do you think?"

And Thomas and Sophie looked at each other. They looked around the room. They looked at Mum, they looked at Dad. They looked at each other and said the only thing that came to mind… "Wow!"

And there we'll leave Sophie and Thomas for now. But this of course is not the end of the adventure, but simply the beginning. *The Lightbringers* are about to go international!

Take some time to ask and listen to what the children think about the story.

Response

Prayer (5 minutes)

Ask the children to stand and then read together the "Special, Safe, And Accepted" list from Session 1.

> **Special, Safe, And Accepted**
>
> **I am SPECIAL because God says...**
> His Holy Spirit lives inside me (1 Corinthians 3:16)
> He has made me to do good things (Ephesians 2:10)
> I can always come to God and talk with Him (Ephesians 3:12)
> I can do things I find hard because God gives me strength and helps me (Philippians 4:13)

▶   I am **SPECIAL** because God says:
His Holy Spirit lives inside me (1 Corinthians 3:16)
He has made me to do good things (Ephesians 2:10)
I can always come to God and talk with Him (Ephesians 3:12)
I can do things I find hard because God gives me strength and helps me (Philippians 4:13)

> **Special, Safe, And Accepted**
>
> **I am SAFE because God says...**
> I am not guilty or bad because God has forgiven me (Romans 3:31-34)
> Nothing can come between God and me (Romans 8:35-39)
> He will finish the good work He started in me (Philippians 1:6)
> I am safe with Jesus and in God (Colossians 3:3)
> I am a child of God and I am safe from evil (1 John 5:18)

▶   I am **SAFE** because God says:
I am not guilty or bad because God has forgiven me (Romans 3:31-34)
Nothing can come between God and me (Romans 8:35-39)
He will finish the good work He started in me (Philippians 1:6)
I am safe with Jesus and in God (Colossians 3:3)
I am a child of God and I am safe from evil (1 John 5:18)

> **Special, Safe, And Accepted**
>
> **I am ACCEPTED because God says...**
>
> I am His child (John 1:12)
>
> Jesus chose me to be His friend (John 15:15)
>
> I am a saint – a special person set aside by God (Ephesians 1:1)
>
> I have been forgiven for all the things I've done wrong (Colossians 1:14)

▶ I am **ACCEPTED** because God says:
I am His child (John 1:12)
Jesus chose me to be His friend (John 15:15)
I am a saint – a special person set aside by God (Ephesians 1:1)
I have been forgiven for all the things I've done wrong (Colossians 1:14)

God wants all of us to walk in these truths and speak them over our lives EVERY DAY. Like the seeds we read about earlier, we need to allow God's Word to take root in our hearts – for some of us it's easy to do this, but for some of us it's harder, because of the negative words which have been spoken over our lives.

Gather the children into small groups to pray for each other. If they are willing, ask them to share which of the truths they are struggling to believe so that others can pray for them. You could also ask the children to say which one stands out for them and give thanks for each one they share.

> **Closing prayer**
>
> Lord, thank You that now I'm Your child. I really am special, safe, and accepted. Help me to walk in these truths every day. Amen.

Close the session by praying together:

▶ Lord, thank You that now I'm Your child. I really am special, safe, and accepted. Help me to walk in these truths every day. Amen.

Session 10: I Can Live Every Day Walking In God's Truths

Commissioning As Lightbringers

If you have already done *The Steps To Freedom In Christ* and this is the final session of the course, finish by commissioning everyone as Lightbringers and hand out certificates. Refer to the short commissioning section on page 255.

You could close the session by having a praise party as a way of celebrating everything that God has done over *The Lightbringers* course.

Hand out the activity sheet and as time allows spend some time together completing the activity sheet. The children can also take it home to complete.

The Lightbringers Trail: Steps To Freedom In Christ

Introduction

This session is a vital part of *The Lightbringers* course as it gives the children an opportunity to clear out any rubbish from their lives that is holding them back in their relationship with Father God. It should be run between Sessions 9 and 10 or after Session 10. Please read the notes on page 30 which give essential information about the session.

The Steps To Freedom In Christ are on the downloadable worksheet for this session in versions for both the younger and older age groups which are self-explanatory. Simply go through them, having the children say the prayers. Then give them space, just between them and God, to make their response. Note, that no one is expected to share with anyone else the things that come up.

With the younger age group, it is advisable for you to say the prayers a line at a time and get them to repeat after you. They can do this as a group except when they are confessing their individual issues.

There is also a PowerPoint presentation for each age group. In this Leader's Guide, we have included images of the main slides only.

Make It A Way Of Life!

As children go through the Steps they will ask questions or an issue may come up – this is an ideal opportunity to help them understand more of what they've been hearing on the course. You can use content from one of the sessions or remind them about parts of the stories to help them.

Time Plan

Getting Started 20 minutes	Welcome (5 minutes)	
	Announcements (2 minutes)	
	Bible Verse (3 minutes)	Therefore, since we are surrounded by such a great cloud of witnesses, let us throw off everything that hinders and the sin that so easily entangles. And let us run with perseverance the race marked out for us, fixing our eyes on Jesus, the pioneer and perfecter of faith. (Hebrews 12:1-2a)
	Illustration (10 minutes)	Don't be held back.
Steps To Freedom In Christ 2 hours 30 minutes	Introduction (5 minutes) *The Lightbringers* Trail	Explain what they are going to do as they go along *The Lightbringers* Trail and commit the session to God in prayer. Each Step has a brief introduction, a practical illustration, and an activity to complete in their activity sheet before they do the prayers in the Steps.
	Step One (20 minutes)	Saying "No" to things that are wrong
	Step Two (20 minutes)	Choosing truth
	Break (10 minutes)	
	Step Three (20 minutes)	Forgiving others
	Step Four (15 minutes)	Not doing what we should do
	Step Five (15 minutes)	Pride
	Break (10 minutes)	
	Step Six (20 minutes)	Wrong things we do
	Step Seven (15 minutes)	Family ties
Praise 10 minutes	God Made Me Special	
Commission 15 minutes	Commissioning as Lightbringers (15 minutes)	Do the commissioning here if this is the last session of the course. Otherwise do it at the end of Session 10.
Total: 3 hours 15 minutes		

The Lightbringers Trail: Steps To Freedom In Christ

Getting Started (20 minutes)

Welcome (5 minutes)

This is a chance to welcome the children but also an opportunity to have fun with them.

Announcements And Ground Rules (5 minutes)

Remind them of the two simple rules:
1. Nobody leaves their seat. If they need to go to the bathroom then they must put their hand up and ask permission from a leader.
2. When you ask for quiet, everyone sits down, focuses on the front, and makes no sound.

Explain to the children that today is a special session. They're going to ask God to show them things that they need to pray about and then they're going to do some praying. Just like the characters in the story they're going to be able to get rid of things that are holding them back.

Bible Verse

> Therefore, since we are surrounded by such a great cloud of witnesses, let us throw off everything that hinders and the sin that so easily entangles. And let us run with perseverance the race marked out for us, fixing our eyes on Jesus, the pioneer and perfecter of faith.
>
> Hebrews 12:1,2a

Therefore, since we are surrounded by such a great cloud of witnesses, let us throw off everything that hinders and the sin that so easily entangles. And let us run with perseverance the race marked out for us, fixing our eyes on Jesus, the pioneer and perfecter of faith. (Hebrews 12:1-2a)

Illustration – Don't Be Held Back
(10 minutes)

Objects Needed: bungee or rope, prizes.

Form two teams of two people. One from each team holds an object at the other end of the room. While standing next to each other the other members from each team race to retrieve the object. The winner is the one who brings it back to you first.

After the first race; say, "it's the best of three." For the second race, attach the bungee or rope to the winner of the first race and have one or two people hold it [Caution: ensure this is done in a way that will not cause injury to participants if they try to race with it attached.] Then get ready to start the race.

When the inevitable cries of "That's not fair!" come, start a discussion along the following lines....

If you are competing in a race, the last thing you want is something that can hold you back. Well, the rest of our lives is like a race and we're all at the starting line. It's a race to live for Jesus and let Him work through us. Some people won't reach the finishing line. If you want to reach the finishing line, then it's essential to get rid of anything that can hold you back. What sort of things do you think can hold us back from living for Jesus?

Today we're going to learn how to get rid of those things. [At this point you could untie the bungee/rope and have the second and third races].

Both our teams finished the race and both get a prize! Well done!

Today we're going to go through *The Steps To Freedom In Christ*. We will ask God to show us what things might be holding us back and then get rid of them. So, that by the end of our time we will know that there's nothing to stop us running straight for the finishing line in our race to live for Jesus for the rest of our lives.

Steps (2 hours 30 minutes)

Introduction (5 minutes)

Explain what they are going to do and commit this time to God asking Him to show them what they need to bring before Him. Pray for protection over them as they go through the Steps.

Celebrate Each Step

As you work through the Steps, encourage the children to celebrate each one they complete and encourage them to keep going! There's all sorts of ideas you could come up with to do this, here are just a few:

- Stand in a circle and get them to give themselves a clap and say 'Well done!"
- Line up and take turns standing on a paper circle marked with the Step number.
- Make large numbers that can be hung up with a 'fanfare' as they finish each Step.
- Provide a roll of paper and ask the children to draw around their foot to get an outline of their footprint (*make sure that the footprints are close together*). When everyone has done this, the children have to guess whose foot is whose and what size feet they have. Ask the children to write their names in their footprint. Mark a line on the paper so that all the footprints are below the line and write a number 1 in the centre. Repeat this at the end of each step (*without the guessing the feet part*).

Step One – Saying "No" To Things That Are Wrong (20 minutes)

In this first Step, we are going to look at things you need to just say "no" to – put simply there is some stuff that as Christians we just shouldn't do because it's not good for us and will hold us back. God wants us to be safe so He tells us what these things are. If we try to find out about the future or try to use any power that doesn't involve God, then we are dabbling in things that are wrong and are not going to help us!

For example, do you think it's OK to …? (*Use examples from the Step 1 on the activity sheet.*)

Illustration – More And More

Object Needed: Candies

It is natural to want more of a good thing but this could cause us to get addicted! Give out a candy and let everyone take one. Then ask who wants another. It is impossible to have just one; you have two or three and then five or six and then suddenly they are all gone! Are candies good for you? If you have too many – no! Then why do we keep wanting more?

Sometimes when we do things that God says are not good for us, we can want more. God tells us in the Bible that occult things are dangerous and will stop us running that race. We might start reading stories with witches in them, and we enjoy it so we read more scary stories, and then maybe we are so interested that we start trying to do spells, and then we buy a spell book – and before long we are so interested it takes over our life! That is one reason why it is unwise to get involved with any occult things – even things that look like good fun, such as dressing up as a witch to go trick-or-treating. We can become fascinated and it takes our mind away from God and the truth.

Activity 1

In groups complete the activity for Step 1 that is on the activity sheet for this session. Note that the idea here is simply to get them to think generally about things they've seen rather than specifically identify things they have done (which comes a little later). After two or three minutes get them to look at their lists. Which list is longer? And how much longer!

You see we are surrounded by things which are wrong. Consequently the more that we are interested in scary things like witches, the less we are interested in God. And that pleases the enemy and holds us back from running the race for Jesus.

Step One Prayers

Using the PowerPoint and/or the activity sheet, pray the opening prayer together.

Opening Prayer (5-to-8-Year-Olds)

> **Opening Prayer**
>
> Dear God, thank You that You love me and want me to be free. Please fill me with Your Holy Spirit and show me the stuff in my life that I need to stop doing. Thank You that You are here with me and I don't need to be afraid of anyone or anything. Anything that comes between me and Jesus is not welcome here and must go now in Jesus' name. Amen.

Dear God, thank You that You love me and want me to be free. Please fill me with Your Holy Spirit and show me the stuff in my life that I need to stop doing. Thank You that You are here with me and I don't need to be afraid of anyone or anything. Anything that comes between me and Jesus is not welcome here and must go now in Jesus' name. Amen.

Opening Prayer (9-to-11-Year-Olds)

> **Opening Prayer**
>
> Dear God, thank You that You love me and want me to be free. Please fill me with Your Holy Spirit and show me the stuff in my life that I need to stop doing. I decide here and now to believe the truth You tell me. I know that is the only way I will be free. Thank You that You are here with me and I don't need to be afraid of anyone or anything. Amen.

Dear God, thank You that You love me and want me to be free. Please fill me with Your Holy Spirit and show me the stuff in my life that I need to stop doing. I decide here and now to believe the truth You tell me. I know that is the only way I will be free. Thank You that You are here with me and I don't need to be afraid of anyone or anything. Amen.

The declaration for the 5-to-8-Year-Olds is incorporated in their opening prayer.

Declare (9-to-11-Year-Olds)

> **Declare**
>
> I am a child of God. Anything that comes between me and Jesus is not welcome here. You must go now in Jesus' name. You cannot stop me from listening to God and getting rid of the stuff that holds me back. GO AWAY!

I am a child of God. Anything that comes between me and Jesus is not welcome here. You must go now in Jesus' name. You cannot stop me from listening to God and getting rid of the stuff that holds me back. GO AWAY!

Now ask them to pray the first Step 1 prayer together as a group:

Pray (5-to-8-Year-Olds)

> **Pray**
>
> Father God, please show me anything I have done or joined in with that has led me away from You. Amen.

Father God, please show me anything I have done or joined in with that has led me away from You. Amen.

Pray (9-to-11-Year-Olds)

> **Pray**
>
> Father God, please show me the things I have done or joined in with that have led me away from You. I want to be free from the fake stuff so that I can do Your will. Amen.

Father God, please show me the things I have done or joined in with that have led me away from You. I want to be free from the fake stuff so that I can do Your will. Amen.

Now ask them to mark any they have done on the list in their activity sheet. There's space to add anything else they think of. When they are ready, they should pray the second prayer on their own. Before they do that, provide an example which will help them understand what they need to do. Say you had just prayed the opening prayer in Step One, you could suggest that they needed to pray something like:

"Dear God, I have watched some violent movies, had my fortune told, and listened to an imaginary friend. I say 'no' to those things. Thank You that You have already forgiven me. Jesus is my King. Amen."

Pray (5-to-8-Year-Olds)

> **Pray**
>
> Dear Father God, I have _____
> *(name everything you marked on the list or wrote down)*. I say 'no' to these things. Thank You that You have already forgiven me. Jesus is my Lord. Amen.

Dear Father God, I have _____ (name everything you marked on the list or wrote down). I say 'no' to these things. Thank You that You have already forgiven me. Jesus is my Lord. Amen.

Pray (9-to-11-Year-Olds)

> **Pray**
>
> Dear Father God, I am sorry for getting involved with _____ *(name everything you marked on the list or wrote down)* and I turn my back on them. Thank You that You have already forgiven me. Jesus is my Lord. Amen.

Dear Father God, I am sorry for getting involved with _____ *(name everything you marked on the list or wrote down)* and I turn my back on them. Thank You that You have already forgiven me. Jesus is my Lord. Amen.

Celebrate

"You did it!"
Use an activity to celebrate the end of this Step.

Step Two – Choosing Truth (20 minutes)

In this second step we are going to look at choosing the truth. The world and the enemy tell us lots of lies about ourselves and others – and also about God.

Illustration – Carrots Make You See In The Dark

Objects Needed: carrot (ready to eat!); cardboard box.

Has anyone ever told you that carrots will help you see in the dark? Do you think this is true? Well, how about we see if this is true or a lie! So, I need a volunteer to eat this carrot. (Volunteer eats the carrot). Ask the volunteer if their eyes feel brighter! You could even check their eyes. So, we need to see if this has really worked by making it dark. Let's use this cardboard box. (*Place cardboard box over the volunteer's head*). OK can you see?

Of course, carrots aren't going to make you see in the dark. It's just a myth. I wonder if there are some lies that we might find easier to believe, e.g., that having lots of friends will make me happy. Or that it's OK not to tell the truth sometimes.

Activity 2

In groups complete the activity for Step 2 on the activity sheet. For each statement, the children have to decide if it is true or false.

- Snakes have slimy skin (F)
- 213 x 36 = 7668 (T)
- Money and things will make you happy (F)
- Frogs have to drink lots of water (F)
- Rabbits are born blind (T)
- Glass is made out of sand (T)
- Watching bad movies won't harm me (F)
- I can always come to God and talk with him (T)

How can we prove whether the statements are true or a lie? Most answers can be looked up somewhere but some are harder to prove and ones we might believe to be true really aren't.

Step Two Prayers

Using the PowerPoint and/or the activity sheet, pray the opening prayer together. Then get them to mark on the list what they have believed.

Pray (5-to-8-Year-Olds)

> **Pray**
>
> Father God, please show me things I've believed that are not really true. I choose to believe the truth about who You are and who I am as Your child. Amen.

Father God, please show me things I've believed that are not really true. I choose to believe the truth about who You are and who I am as Your child. Amen.

Pray (9-to-11-Year-Olds)

> **Pray**
>
> Father God, I know You want me to know and believe the truth. Thank You that You are my Father God and I am Your special child. You see everything and still love me. Please show me things I've believed that are not really true. In Jesus' name. Amen.

Father God, I know You want me to know and believe the truth. Thank You that You are my Father God and I am Your special child. You see everything and still love me. Please show me things I've believed that are not really true. In Jesus' name. Amen.

When they're ready they can then say the next prayer on their own and include all the things they've marked:

Pray (Both 5-to-8-Year-Olds & 9-to-11-Year-Olds)

> **Pray**
>
> Dear God, I am sorry that I have believed the lies that: *(name everything you marked)*. Thank You that You love me and have already forgiven me. Amen.

Dear God, I am sorry that I have believed the lies that: (name everything you marked). Thank You that You love me and have already forgiven me. Amen.

Declare The Truth (5-to-8-Year-Olds)

Time to declare the truth! Let's stand up and read out loud together.

> **Declare The Truth**
> 1. There is one true God who loves me.
> 2. Jesus is the Son of God who died for me.
> 3. I am a child of God.
> 4. God's truth sets me free.
> 5. I choose to use my body to do only good things.
> 6. I love God with all my heart, soul, and mind.

1. There is one true God who loves me.
2. Jesus is the Son of God who died for me.
3. I am a child of God.
4. God's truth sets me free.
5. I choose to use my body to do only good things.
6. I love God with all my heart, soul, and mind.

Declare The Truth (9-to-11-Year-Olds)

> **I Believe**
> - There is one true God who loves me and wants to know me.
> - Jesus Christ is the Son of God who defeated the enemy.
> - God loves me so much He sent His son to die for me.
> - I have the authority to stand against the enemy because I am God's child.

I believe:
- There is one true God who loves me and wants to know me.
- Jesus Christ is the Son of God who defeated the enemy.
- God loves me so much He sent His son to die for me.
- I have the authority to stand against the enemy because I am God's child.

> **I Believe**
> - God's truth sets me free. I will not pay any attention to bad thoughts and lies from the enemy.
> - I choose to use my body to do only good things.
> - I ask my Father God to fill me with His Holy Spirit, and guide me into all truth.
> - I love God with all my heart, soul, and mind.

- God's truth sets me free. I will not pay any attention to bad thoughts and lies from the enemy.
- I choose to use my body to do only good things.
- I ask my Father God to fill me with His Holy Spirit, and guide me into all truth.
- I love God with all my heart, soul, and mind.

Celebrate

"You did it!"
Celebrate the end of this Step.

Step Three – Forgiving Others (20 minutes)

Start this session already tied up to a volunteer (see Illustration 'Twinned')
In this next Step we are going to think about whether there are still people that we need to forgive. Remind them about what you talked about in Session 9 and the people they forgave. It's something that we can do whenever someone hurts us so that we can be free.

Illustration – Twinned

Objects Needed: volunteer and rope.

Remember when we looked at forgiveness, God tells us that we need to forgive others just like He has forgiven us. What happens if we don't? Well, it's a bit like me being tied to (*insert volunteer's name*). It's a bit tricky to get to where I want to go when I am stuck to another person. And that's what it's like when we don't forgive someone. We remain stuck to them and we find it hard to go where we want to go and hard to run a race.

Step Three Prayers

Using the PowerPoint and/or the activity sheet pray the opening prayer together.

Pray (Both 5-to-8-Year-Olds & 9-to-11-Year-Olds)

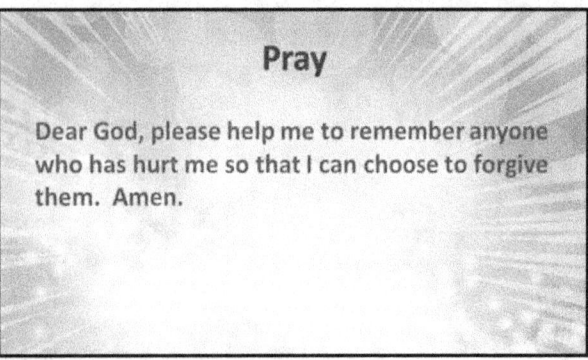

Dear God, Please help me to remember anyone who has hurt me so that I can choose to forgive them. Amen.

Give them time to write down on a separate sheet of paper any names they need to forgive.

Now ask them to say the prayer for each person on their own, saying what they did to them and how it made them feel. Give them an example here: "Lord, I forgive Amy for leaving me out of the game at playtime which made me feel alone and sad."

Pray (Both 5-to-8-Year-Olds & 9-to-11-Year-Olds)

> **Pray**
>
> Lord, I forgive _____ (name the person)
> for _____ (say what they did to hurt you).
> It made me feel _____ (say how you felt).

Lord, I forgive (name the person)
for (say what they did to hurt you).
It made me feel (say how you felt).

When they've finished praying all the names they can finish by praying:

Pray (Both 5-to-8-Year-Olds & 9-to-11-Year-Olds)

> **Pray**
>
> Dear God, please heal me where I've been hurt and bless each of the people I've forgiven.
> Amen.

Dear God, Please heal me where I've been hurt and bless each of the people I've forgiven. Amen

When they've done that, get them to tear up the piece of paper. They can say the next prayer of blessing on their own.

Celebrate

"You did it!"
Use an activity to celebrate the end of this Step.

THE LIGHTBRINGERS 243

Step Four – Not Doing What We Should Do (15 minutes)

In this next Step we are going to be look at times when we have disobeyed others instead of doing what our teachers, parents, or leaders have asked us to.

Now who likes being told what to do? Have you ever thought, "Why should I do that?" But God has put these people in our lives to help us. They want the best for us, but, at times, we don't want to do the things they ask of us.

We don't have to obey them if they are telling us to do something that is wrong. However, when it's just something normal that we don't like or don't feel like doing, saying no to them can give the enemy an opportunity to hurt us and hold us back so we can't run the race.

Illustration – Rules

Objects Needed: a board game (with a set of rules) and a Bible.

Now most of us love playing board games – you may even have a family board game night every week. A very popular game is one called 'Frustration'. Have you ever played it? It's very easy to play, but like most games, before you play – what do you need to do? That's right, you must read the rules. If you don't read the rules you won't know how to play the game.

Who makes up the rules for a game? The person who makes up the game makes the rules, don't they? The one who created the game makes rules for the enjoyment of all who play the game. If someone doesn't follow those rules, it takes away from the enjoyment of the game. Have you ever played a game with someone who won't follow the rules? It gets messy and people get upset!

Activity 4

In groups complete Activity 4 in your activity sheet.

Use the space to write down any rules you have at home or at school.

Why do we have rules? What would happen if we didn't have them? For example, if you ignored the school rule, no running in the corridor, what might happen?

God has also given us guidelines to protect us because He loves us so much. They are here in this book (hold up the Bible) and if we don't follow them we can get hurt.

Step Four Prayers

Using the PowerPoint and/or the activity sheet pray the opening prayer together.

Pray (5-to-8-Year-Olds)

> **Pray**
>
> Dear God, I have disobeyed You, my parents, my teachers and others. Thank You that I am forgiven. I now choose to obey You and others who want the best for me. In Jesus' name I pray, Amen.

Dear God, I have disobeyed You, my parents, my teachers, and others. Thank You that I am forgiven. I now choose to obey You and others who want the best for me. In Jesus' name I pray, Amen.

Pray (9-to-11-Year-Olds)

> **Pray**
>
> Dear God, I am sorry for the times when I have been disobedient to _____ *(list the names you marked on the list)*. I'm sorry for _____ *(say what you've done that was disrespectful or rebellious)*. Thank You that You totally forgive me. I now choose to obey You and others who want the best for me. Amen.

Dear God, I am sorry for the times when I have been disobedient to ....(*list the names you marked on the list*)**. I'm sorry for ....**(*say what you've done that was disrespectful or rebellious*)**. Thank You that You totally forgive me. I now choose to obey You and others who want the best for me. Amen.**

Celebrate

"You did it!"
Use an activity to celebrate the end of this Step.

Step Five – Pride (15 minutes)

Have you ever thought you are better than everyone else? Or thought, "I don't need anyone else"? That's called 'pride' and it's something that God says is not good as no one is better than anyone else. We are all equally loved by Father God.

Now who has seen the movie *The Lion King*?

Illustration – Simba's Pride

Object Needed: Copy of *The Lion King* and means to play it. Start time: 11:40 "I'm gonna be King of Pride Rock". Clip length: 6 minutes

Simba is full of pride – he thinks that being King means always getting his own way and doesn't realize that being King means being responsible and putting others first.

Activity 5

In groups complete Activity 5 in your activity sheet.

Look at the list in your activity sheet of ways we can be proud Have you felt any of these? Fill in the space below each sentence with what God says.

Thinking you are better than someone else.
God says…

Thinking I don't need anyone else.
God says…

Doing what I want instead of helping others.
God says…

Not saying sorry when I do things wrong.
God says…

Step Five Prayers

Using the PowerPoint and/or the activity sheet, pray the opening prayer together.

Pray (5-to-8-Year-Olds)

> **Pray**
>
> Dear God, sometimes I think I am better than others. I want my own way and I have not let others have their way. I need You and I need other people to help me live right. I choose to be like Jesus. In His name I pray. Amen.

Dear God, Sometimes I think I am better than others. I want my own way and I have not let others have their way. I need You and I need other people to help me live right. I choose to be like Jesus. In His name I pray. Amen.

Pray (9-to-11-Year-Olds)

> **Pray**
>
> Dear God, I'm sorry that I've thought only of myself and often thought I'm better than others. I turn my back on doing things my way and ask You to fill me with Your Holy Spirit so I can do Your will. I choose to make others more important that myself and make You, Father God, the most important of all. Amen.

Dear God, I'm sorry that I've thought only of myself and often thought I'm better than others. I turn my back on doing things my way and ask You to fill me with Your Holy Spirit so I can do Your will. I choose to make others more important than myself and make You, Father God, the most important of all. Amen.

Celebrate

"You did it!"
Use an activity to celebrate the end of this Step.

Step Six – Wrong Things We Do (20 minutes)

Start this session with the puppet (see illustration 'What controls you?')

In Step Six we are going to look at sin. Sin is any WORD, THOUGHT, or ACT that goes against God. It's stuff that we do that makes God sad. God wants us to be free from those things that we maybe keep doing that we know are wrong.

Illustration – What Controls You?

Object Needed: Puppet

You see this puppet – do you think this puppet is real? (*Maybe pretend to talk like a bad ventriloquist!*) I think we can tell that this is my hand and this puppet isn't really talking but it's me controlling the puppet. I can control its mouth (*move mouth*) and control what it says. Just like I am controlling this puppet, sin can control us if we let it. But this isn't God's plan for us. He sent Jesus so that we don't have to be controlled by sin anymore.

Step Six Prayers

Using the PowerPoint and/or the activity sheet, pray the opening prayer together.

Pray (5-to-8-Year-Olds)

> **Pray**
>
> Dear Father God, please show me the wrong things that I've done so I can be free. In Jesus' name I pray. Amen.

Dear Father God, please show me the wrong things that I've done so I can be free. In Jesus' name I pray. Amen.

Pray (9-to-11-Year-Olds)

> **Pray**
>
> Dear Father God, I agree with You that I have done some wrong things. Please show me all the things that I've done so I can be free. In Jesus' name I pray. Amen.

Dear Father God, I agree with You that I have done some wrong things. Please show me all the things that I've done so I can be free. In Jesus' name I pray. Amen.

Now have them look at the list in their activity sheet and mark the ones they've done.

Once they've done that, get them to say the next prayer including everything they've marked in their activity sheet.

Pray (Both 5-to-8-Year-Olds & 9-to-11-Year-Olds)

> **Pray**
>
> Father God, I am sorry that I have: *(say each one that you marked on the list).*
>
> Thank You that You forgive me. I turn away from these wrong things. Help me to do what is right. Amen.

Father God, I am sorry that I have: (say each one that you marked on the list). Thank You that You forgive me. I turn away from these wrong things. Help me to do what is right. Amen.

Celebrate

"You did it!"
Use an activity to celebrate the end of this Step.

Step Seven – Family Ties
(15 minutes)

In this last step we are going to look at actions or attitudes in our family that can hold us back from walking with God and finishing the race.

Illustration – Family Ties

Object Needed: A photo of a famous parent who looks like their child – this needs to be someone whom the children would recognize so you could use cartoon characters (e.g. Homer Simpson and Bart Simpson) or it would be fun to use a photo of their leader and leader's parents (if they look similar!); Leader; and some rope.

Have you ever been told that you look like your parents? This is a picture of [*insert name*] and their child [*show photo*]. Do they look the same? We often inherit our parents' looks in some way. Sometimes we might even look like our grandparents or great-grandparents! What can sometimes happen is that we can not only inherit looks but also actions or attitudes from them. And some of these actions and attitudes may not be what God wants.

Ask the leader to stand and, while talking, use the rope to tie them up.

The Bible talks about how sin can pass down from one generation to another and affect us. We can be held back without even knowing it *Ask the leader to try to walk around.* God doesn't want us to live like this, He wants us to be free! *Cut the ropes.*

Activity 7

In groups complete Activity 7 in your activity sheet.

Complete the family tree and ask each child to share some things they like about someone in their family.

Step Seven Prayers

Using the PowerPoint and/or the activity sheet, pray the prayer for this Step.

Pray (5-to-8-Year-Olds)

> **Pray**
>
> Dear God, I say "no" to the wrong things in my family's past that may affect me. I belong to Jesus. I say "yes" to God and "no" to the enemy who must go now. These things can no longer hold me back in my friendship with my Father God. Amen.

Dear God, I say "no" to the wrong things in my family's past that may affect me. I belong to Jesus. I say "yes" to God and "no" to the enemy, who must go now. These things can no longer hold me back in my friendship with my Father God. Amen.

Pray (9-to-11-Year-Olds)

> **Pray**
>
> I turn my back on anything that my family before me might have messed up with or struggled with that affects me now. I belong to Jesus. I say "yes" to God and "no" to the enemy who must go now.

I turn my back on anything that my family before me might have messed up with or struggled with that affects me now. I belong to Jesus. I say "yes" to God and "no" to the enemy who must go now.

> **Pray**
>
> I specifically turn my back on _____ *(include anything that has come to mind)*. These things can no longer hold me back in my friendship with my Father God. Dear God I come to You as Your child. I ask You to fill me with Your Holy Spirit. Help me to live for You and give all that I have to You. You are amazing! Amen.

I specifically turn my back on _____ (include anything that has come to mind). These things can no longer hold me back in my friendship with my Father God. Dear God I come to You as Your child. I ask You to fill me with Your Holy Spirit. Help me to live for You and give all that I have to You. You are amazing! Amen.

Share

Talk about the tips for staying free in the activity sheet.

Celebrate

"You did it!"
Use an activity to celebrate the end of this Step.

The Lightbringers Trail: Steps To Freedom In Christ

Praise God Made Me Special (10 minutes)

The song for the Steps to Freedom is "God Made Me Special" and is about how much we are loved by God.

GOD MADE ME SPECIAL
HE MADE ME DIFFERENT THAN ANYONE ELSE
HE MADE ME SPECIAL
HE GAVE ME FREEDOM TO JUST BE MYSELF
GOD MADE ME JUST THE WAY HE WANTED
HE MADE ME JUST THE WAY HE WANTED ME TO BE
GOD LOVES ME MORE THAN ANYTHING

GOD MADE ME. GOD MADE ME SPECIAL.
GOD MADE ME. GOD MADE ME SPECIAL.
I'M SPECIALLY MADE – SUPER DUPER SPECIALLY MADE.
I'M SPECIALLY MADE – SUPER DUPER SPECIALLY MADE.

GOD MADE ME SPECIAL
HE MADE ME DIFFERENT THAN ANYONE ELSE
HE MADE ME SPECIAL
HE GAVE ME FREEDOM TO JUST BE MYSELF
GOD MADE ME JUST THE WAY HE WANTED
HE MADE ME JUST THE WAY HE WANTED ME TO BE
GOD LOVES ME MORE THAN ANYTHING

GOD MADE ME. GOD MADE ME SPECIAL.
GOD MADE ME. GOD MADE ME SPECIAL.
I'M SPECIALLY MADE – SUPER DUPER SPECIALLY MADE.
I'M SPECIALLY MADE – SUPER DUPER SPECIALLY MADE.

Words & Music by Wayne Tester, Esther Tester. © 2018 Testricity.com Music (ASCAP) / Fuzzy Socks Music (BMI) (both admin. by Testricity Music Group, www.testricity.com). ℗&© 2018 Testricity Music Group. ALL RIGHTS RESERVED.

Use a few praise songs at the end of the Steps to Freedom. As well as the specific song here, sing some of the songs that have already been used. Enjoy!

Commissioning As Lightbringers

If you have already done Session 10 and this is the final session of the course, finish by commissioning everyone as Lightbringers and hand out certificates. Otherwise, wait until after you have done Session 10.

This short additional section is designed to come after the last session of *The Lightbringers*, which will vary according to where you place *The Steps To Freedom In Christ*.

We encourage you to mark the children's completion of the course by giving them an opportunity to tell God they want to follow Him for the rest of their lives and then commission them as Lightbringers by giving them a certificate (children love receiving certificates!). You can download a design for the certificate from the website.

This is the end of *The Lightbringers* course but just the start for them as they walk in their new identity and the freedom they have in Christ.

Commission Outline

Before the session, download the certificate and print off a copy for each child, then complete them with each child's name and the date. You could also get a glow stick or battery operated tea-light ready to give to each child.

Call each child out to the front to hand them their certificate and ideally a glow stick/tea-light. Encourage all the children to clap and cheer as each child collects their certificate. You could play one of their favourite Lightbringers songs in the background.

When every child has received their certificate ask them all to stand and hold up their glow stick/tea-light if they have one.

▶   *Ask them to repeat after you (in the loudest voice that they can!)*

> **Shout it out**
>
> Thank You God that I am a Lightbringer living in freedom.
>
> Thank You for the mission You have for me:
>   *To go into the world and bring the light of Jesus!*
>
> AMEN.

Thank You God that I am a Lightbringer living in freedom.

**Thank You for the mission You have for me:
To go into the world and bring the light of Jesus!**

AMEN!

*At the end give the biggest cheer EVER!
Finish with their favourite Lightbringers song.*

Extra Activities

Prayer Activities

Prayer Walk

Send the children to walk around the building on the outside. Send a leader first and then after she has travelled 5 metres/yards send the first child. The instructions are simple:

1. Walk and talk to God in the same way that they might walk and talk to a friend; they are going to tell God how they feel and what is bothering them etc.
2. Never lose sight of the person in front.
3. Never catch up with the person in front, always leave a 5 metre/yard gap.

When the child has gone 5 metres/yards, send the next until all the children have gone. This calls for close supervision, you need to send adults in between every 5 or 6 children.

Prayer Circles

1. Ask the children to find a space. In the space ask them to talk to God about themselves for one minute.
2. After one minute the children join together with another child and together they pray for each other. They put their hands on each other's shoulders and in turn pray something like, "God, help my friend learn more about You."
3. After one minute the two join with another two and pray in their four that God will give them a good night.
4. After one minute the four join with another four and pray that God will look after their families – or something similar.
5. After one minute the eight join with another eight and pray that God will….
6. And so it continues until you have one very large group. You then pray for the whole group.

Longer Prayer Nights (15 minutes)

Some nights you may wish to hold an extra-long prayer section. You can do this in several ways:

P.R.A.Y.

The four corners of the building are given the letters P, R, A, and Y respectively. If there are more than 40 children, then the centres will also need to be used as follows:

```
P   R   A
Y       Y
A   R   P
```

A leader is placed at each base and the children are split into four groups (or eight for over 40 people). The children start at one of the bases, but will only remain there for two minutes. After two minutes they will move clockwise to the next base. The bases are:

P for Praise

At this base the children will stand in a circle and give thanks for one thing which is good in their lives. "God, thank You for my family", "God, thank You for the children's club", "God, thank You that I'm healthy." If they visit another P base then the leader may simply talk them through all the things we have to be thankful for, for example, salvation, creation, life, eternal life.

R is for Repent

At this base the children will be reminded by the leader that all of us have done things wrong, things that hurt God. This would be a good time to quietly think about those things and ask God to forgive us.

A is for Ask

At this base one or two children might lead in prayer and ask God for a good night, or maybe a safe journey home at the end. Or maybe there are specific requests for people they know who are sick.

Y is for Yourself

At this base the children will be encouraged to ask God for something for themselves. Give them quick guidance on what sort of things, but allow the children to ask God to bless them, or to give them a good night at children's club.

From time to time children will spend their 'Ask' and their 'Yourself' time asking God to let their team win. Don't be worried by this, I'm not sure if God has ever got involved in the scoring system at Children's Club.

Games

Guess The Leader

We reveal an interesting fact regarding one of the leaders, or one of the children. For example, "This leader used to live in Spain." Then four leaders are chosen who all try and convince the children that they used to live in Spain. The children then have to "Guess The Leader", guess who was really telling the truth. A variation on this theme is to show a picture of the leader as a baby and the leaders all have to try and convince the children that they are the person in the picture.

My best "Guess The Leader" is the leader who was at the theatre. In the interval she went to the bathroom and on her return sat in her seat and leaned over to kiss her boyfriend – the children never fail to go ughhh! at this point. The 'boyfriend' then turned around and his wife also leaned over and gave this particular leader a very annoyed look. The leader had sat in the wrong seat and kissed the wrong person. You'd be amazed at what your leaders have done, and also how keen their friends are to tell the stories!

This Or That?

Here is an idea from a TV show that helps with getting to know the children or leaders. Play some background music and then for a minute ask the leader questions about their preferences:
- Awake or asleep?
- Music or reading?
- Chocolate or fruit?
- Celebrity A or Celebrity B?

The children/a leader will then choose further questions.

Here are some other sample questions that can be used:
- Toffee or chocolate?
- Shoes or trainers?
- Bath or shower?
- McDonald's or Burger King?
- Cap or hat?
- Dogs or cats?
- Spring or autumn?
- Pepsi or Coke?
- Cinema or video?

Buy It or Bin It

A chance for music and video reviews. It gives the children a chance to share the videos they watch and the music they listen to. It may not seem overtly Christian, but it is incredibly educational! Form a panel of three which includes one leader and two children and allow them to play three videos/songs for 30 seconds each. Then ask them whether they would "buy it or bin it" and why. Periodically introduce Christian music. It teaches the children critical thought, which is very important for their development. Don't allow the children to get away with "because it's good" or "because I like it". They must at least try and explain why. They need their attention drawn to the lyrics: ask if they know what the song is about.

Who Wants To Be A Chocoholic?

Based on the television game show 'Who Wants To Be A Millionaire?'. A child is chosen from the audience. They are asked questions in increasing degrees of difficulty. They are given four answers to the questions and have to choose the right one. For a right answer they gain more chocolate, for a wrong answer they lose it all. The trick is to know when to quit and take the chocolate. The children have lifelines – they can ask the audience or ask a leader. There are only two lifelines.

Aerobics Workout

A piece of music is played and the children copy the leader at the front performing their aerobic workout.

Double Dare

A child is chosen. The child then chooses a leader. The child will then choose between seven different envelopes. In each envelope there is a question, some easy, some very hard. The child will then make a decision before the envelope is opened: will they answer the question or will the leader? The envelope is opened and the question is asked to whoever the child chose. If the child chose to answer the question but gets it wrong, then she gets a shaving foam pie in the face. If she gets it right, then she gets to place the pie in the leader's face. If the leader answers the question, the same rules apply in reverse.

Extra Activities

Impact Your Community And Grow Your Church

Impact Your Community And Grow Your Church

Can We Help You Make Fruitful Disciples?

A church with growing, fruitful disciples of Jesus is a growing, fruitful church that is making a real difference in the community where God has placed it. A key question for church leaders is: "How can I help our people become mature, fruitful disciples as quickly as possible so that they go out and make a real impact?"

A fundamental part of the answer is to help them understand the principles that underlie all of Freedom In Christ's discipleship resources for churches:
1. **TRUTH** Know who you are in Christ
2. **TURNING** Ruthlessly close any doors you've opened to the enemy through past sin and don't open any more
3. **TRANSFORMATION** Renew your mind to the truth of God's Word (which is how you will be transformed).

Freedom In Christ Ministries has equipped hundreds of thousands of church leaders around the world to use this "identity-based discipleship" approach. As churches base their discipleship around these principles, they report not only changed individual lives but whole changed churches. When churches start to look less like hospitals full of those who are constantly struggling with their own issues and more like part of the Bride of Christ, they make an increasing impact on their community. People no longer stay at the "baby stage" year after year but quickly move to maturity, become outward-looking, and find the place where they can make a difference.

Our mission is to equip the Church to transform the nations. We do this by providing church leaders with transformational discipleship resources that can be used right across their church.

Some are specially tailored to the communication styles of different groups such as young people and millennials. Others build on the Freedom In Christ Course. You can see some of them on the following pages.

If you have a FreedomStream subscription (page 271) – or if you take out a free subscription to FreedomStream – you can browse the video component of the courses at your leisure to get a good feel for how they could work in your situation.

But our heart is not to sell you resources. Our heart is to help church leaders develop a long-term, whole-church discipleship strategy. We do not offer a "one size fits all" approach but love to help each church team identify their specific calling and gifting and select the tools that are appropriate for their own situation.

Our offices and Representatives around the world run training courses and have people on the ground who like nothing better than to discuss discipleship with church leaders. If you think we can help you in any way as you look to make fruitful disciples, please get in touch (page 272).

Freedom In Christ For Young People

"Every young disciple is looking to engage with Jesus in a way that will change lives. This innovative, exciting course will help young people discover the truth of who they are in Christ and be set free to be all that God has made them as a result."
Mike Pilavachi, Founder of Soul Survivor

"Freedom in Christ is a creative and relevant course for teenagers with the potential to produce a generation of fruitful young disciples."
Martin Saunders, Editor of *Youthwork* Magazine

The aim of *Freedom in Christ for Young People* is to set young people firmly on the way to becoming fruitful disciples who are sold out for God and will make a radical difference. Watch them change as they connect with the truth about who they are in Christ, become free from pressures that hold them back and learn to renew their thinking — no matter what their circumstances or background.

The course is based on the main *Freedom In Christ Course* and can be run alongside it. The emphasis is on relevant, interactive, multi-media based material tailored to meet the needs of 11-18-year-olds. It is split into two age ranges, 11-14 and 15-18. Each session is packed full of age-appropriate games, activities, discussion-starters, film clip suggestions and talk slots.

There is also a video teaching component for each session. Presented by Nathan Iles and Kate John from Youth For Christ, the video material was shot entirely on location and is punchy, contemporary and entertaining. It gets the main points across in segments of just two to four minutes (with around three segments per session).

Impact Your Community And Grow Your Church

disciple – FIC's message for the millennial generation

Church leaders report that discipling those in their 20s and 30s is one of their biggest challenges. *disciple* is a powerful tool to help you. It speaks the language of 20s and 30s and invites them to dive into the greatest story ever told, God's story. They will learn how to take hold of their freedom and discover their mandate.

- 10 sessions designed to run for approximately 90 minutes each
- Impactful Starter Films introduce the theme for each session
- Extra films (via the app) on topics including Sex, the Occult, and Fear
- Chat and Reflect times allow teaching to take root
- App with extra teaching films, daily devotional, daily nuggets of extra teaching, and Stronghold–Buster Builder with reminders

"Thank you so much for caring enough to do this. You have no idea how much it means to us that you have taken the time to understand and help us overcome all the stuff that comes at us."

"You really get us and understand us, you don't patronize us and talk down to us."

"God is doing incredible things in the young people at our church and I'm just grateful this course has been able to facilitate that."

"*disciple* is really user-friendly. The young adults really engaged and there were definite light bulb moments. The Freedom In Christ message really comes across but in a different way to the *Freedom In Christ Course*. It's been three months since we did it and everyone still refers to it."

The Freedom In Christ Course

Now in its third edition and translated into well over 30 languages, *The Freedom In Christ Course* can transform the way you help Christians become fruitful disciples. Focused on firstly establishing every Christian in the sure foundation of their identity in Jesus, it gives them the tools to break free and stay free from all that holds them back, and a strategy for ongoing transformation. It has ten teaching sessions presented by Steve Goss, Nancy Maldonado, and Daryl Fitzgerald plus *The Steps To Freedom In Christ* ministry component presented by Steve Goss and Neil Anderson.

With a specially designed app to accompany the course, extra teaching films, a worship album produced by Testricity, Leader's Guide, Participant's Guide, and tons of extras, *The Freedom In Christ Course* offers you everything you need to make disciples who bear fruit that will last!

"Men, women, and middle and high school students have been radically transformed."
Bob Huisman, Pastor, Immanuel Christian Reformed Church, Hudsonville, MI, USA

"I recommend it highly to anyone serious about discipleship in the church."
Chuah Seong Peng, Senior Pastor, Holy Light Presbyterian Church, Johor Baru, Malaysia

"The *Freedom In Christ Course* changed me and put me in a position to minister to people in a much more effective way. It really changes the way Christians think about themselves."
Frikkie Elstadt, Every Nation Patria, Mossel Bay, South Africa

"Our church has changed as a result of this course. Those who come to Christ and who do the course end up with a rock solid start to their faith."
Pastor Sam Scott, Eltham Baptist Church, Australia

"It lays a foundation as a wise master builder on which others can build. It is the pure milk of the Word that everyone needs to grow."
Korush Partovi, Pastor, Iranian Church, Isparta, Turkey

Impact Your Community And Grow Your Church

The Grace Course

"For the first time in the decades that I've been a Christian, I'm suddenly 'getting' grace – it's amazing and it's shocking!"

"I realized that it's not about my performance – He just wants my heart."

"It was AMAZING! During the last session after we had finished nobody moved for what seemed like ages. When the silence eventually did break, people began to spontaneously share all that the course had meant to them. Testimonies to what the Lord had done just flowed out, some were life-changing."

"The *Grace Course* does a marvellous job in introducing the concept of grace in a simple, engaging and, at times, even humorous way. It is short and to the point, taking an incredibly deep theological issue and making it understandable and practical."

If you don't first know God's love for you in your heart – not just your head – it's impossible for your life to be motivated by love for Him. Instead you are likely to end up motivated more by guilt or shame or fear or pride. You may be doing all the "right" things, believing all the right things and saying all the right things but there will be precious little fruit.

- 6 sessions plus *The Steps to Experiencing God's Grace*
- Perfectly complements *The Freedom In Christ Course*
- Ideal for both small groups and Sunday teaching
- Present it yourself or use the DVD presentations
- Video testimonies illustrating the teaching points, practical exercises, times of listening to God and Pause For Thought times
- Works especially well as a course during Lent

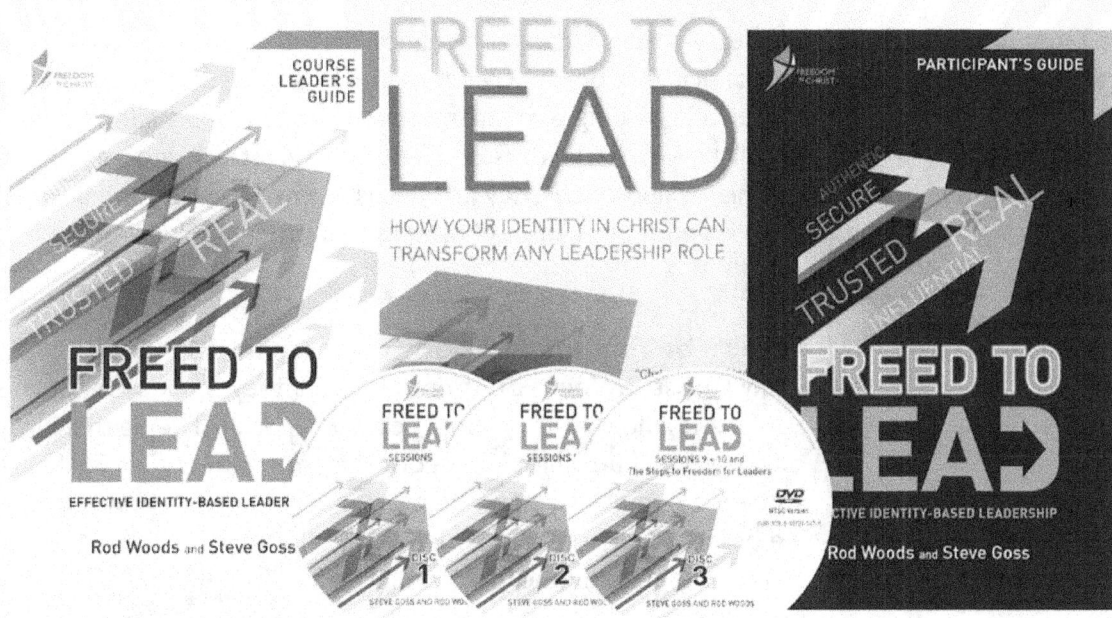

Freed To Lead

"The *Freed To Lead* course has been the most amazing leadership development experience of my career, having been called to both marketplace and church leadership for over 20 years. It dispels worldly leadership myths and practices and provides Biblical foundations for Godly leadership. I wholeheartedly recommend this course for anyone who aspires or is currently called to Godly servant-hearted leadership in any arena."

"An outstanding course – inspirational and motivational, affirming and encouraging."

"It has reinforced my conviction that my identity is first and foremost in Christ, whatever leadership role I may hold."

Freed To Lead is a 10-week discipleship course for Christians who are called to leadership — whether in the marketplace, public service, the Church or any other context. It will transform your leadership, free you from drivenness and burnout, enable you to survive personal attacks, use conflict positively, and overcome other barriers to effective leadership.

Church leadership teams will benefit hugely from going through it together and can then roll it out to others in their church who are in leadership in any sphere or think they may be called to leadership in the future.

- 10–session course or retreat plus *Steps to Freedom for Leaders*
- Excellent follow-up to *The Freedom In Christ Course* and *The Grace Course*, but also stands alone
- Video testimonies and Pause For Thought discussion times
- Ideal for church leadership teams before rolling out across the church

Impact Your Community And Grow Your Church

The Discipleship Series

Steve Goss has written four slim, easy-to-digest books specifically as optional additional reading for participants on the Freedom In Christ course. They prove highly effective in helping participants grasp the principles and are an excellent way for leaders of *The Lightbringers* to understand Freedom In Christ's approach. They are published by Monarch and are available from Freedom In Christ Ministries and other booksellers.

Free to be Yourself — Enjoy your true nature in Christ.
Many Christians focus on trying to act as they think a Christian should act — and find that they simply can't keep it up. They either drop out or burn out. True fruitfulness comes from realizing that we became someone completely new the moment we became Christians. Now we really can be the people God always intended us to be!

Win the Daily Battle — Resist and stand firm in God's strength.
If you are a Christian you are in a raging battle, whether you like it or not. Your only choice is to stand and fight or to become a casualty. Arrayed against you are the world, the devil and the flesh. They seem formidable. However, once you understand just who you are in Christ and how your enemies work, you can expect to emerge victorious from every skirmish with them.

Break Free, Stay Free — Don't let the past hold you back.
Every Christian has a past. It can hold us back big-time. Those of us carrying a lot of "stuff" know that only too well. But even those who have had a relatively trouble-free existence thus far will benefit from understanding how to identify, and resolve, past sin and negative influences that stop us moving on.

The You God Planned — Don't let anything or anyone hold you back.
Once we have claimed our freedom in Christ, how do we remain in it and become the people God is calling us to be? How do we know what God is calling us to be anyway? Are the goals we have for our lives in line with His goals? How can we stop other people getting in the way of our growth to fruitfulness? And how do we avoid getting in their way?

Published by Monarch, they are available from Freedom In Christ or your usual supplier of Christian books.

On-Demand Videos For All Our Courses

You can access all of our video material for small group studies online for one low monthly subscription. Try it for free!

- Access to all the main Freedom In Christ small group courses so you can browse or use the entire range including:
    The *Freedom In Christ Course*
    The *Lightbringers — Freedom In Christ For Children*
    Freedom In Christ For Young People
    disciple (the Freedom In Christ message for 18s to 30s)
    The *Grace Course*
    Freed To Lead
- Free video training courses for course leaders and their teams:
    Making Fruitful Disciples — the Biblical principles of discipleship
    Helping Others Find Freedom In Christ — using *The Steps To Freedom In Christ*
- No need to buy several DVD sets if you have multiple groups running.
- Enable users to catch up if they miss a session.

For further information, pricing, and to start your free trial go to:
FreedomInChrist.org/FreedomStream

Note: features and offer may change from time to time. Please check the website for up-to-date information.

Impact Your Community And Grow Your Church

Can We Help You Make Fruitful Disciples?

Freedom In Christ exists to equip the Church to make fruitful disciples who make a real impact in their community. We have a whole host of resources for you to use but our passion is to help church leaders develop a discipleship strategy right across their church that will be effective for years to come. How can we help *your* church?

We offer:
- A series of introductory and training events for church leaders
- Advice on establishing a discipleship strategy for your church built around our discipleship resources
- Training and equipping for those in your church who will be involved in implementing that strategy.

For contact details of Freedom In Christ in your country, go to
FreedomInChrist.org

Become A Friend Of Freedom In Christ

Have you seen people's lives transformed through our discipleship courses? Would you like to be involved in making the impact even greater? If you are excited about the effect this teaching can have on individuals, churches, and communities, we'd love to have you on the team!

Join our team of international supporters
Freedom In Christ Ministries International exists to equip the Church worldwide to make fruitful disciples who will transform the nations. We rely heavily for financial support on people who have understood how important it is to give leaders the tools that will enable them to help people become fruitful *disciples*, not just *converts*, especially when we are opening in a new country.

Typically your support will be used to:
- help us equip church leaders around the world
- help people overseas establish national Freedom In Christ offices
- translate *The Freedom In Christ Course* and our other material into other languages
- partner with other organisations worldwide to equip leaders
- develop further training and equipping resources

Join the team of supporters in your country
We are passionate about working with those who have themselves been touched by the Biblical message of freedom. Financial support enables us to develop new resources and get them into the hands of more church leaders. As a result many, many people are connecting with this life-changing message. There are always new projects — small and large — that don't happen unless there's funding for them.

To find out more about partnering with us please go to:

FreedomInChrist.org/friends

Credits

We are so grateful to the amazing team who have worked on this resource during the five years it has taken to produce it and to the churches who have tested it for us and given us valuable feedback. Thank you!

Here are some of the people who have made *The Lightbringers* possible:

Project Manager:	Zoë Goss
Publishing Co-ordinator:	Roberto Reed
Executive Producer:	Steve Goss
Film and Editing:	Indy Nottage
Production Assistant:	Linda Mitchell
Audio and Soundscaping:	Chris Mitchell
Music For Story Videos:	Chris Mitchell Wayne and Esther Tester
Lightbringers Songs:	Wayne and Esther Tester
Lyric Videos:	Esther Tester
Layout:	Steve Goss
Illustrations:	Jon Smethurst
Activity Sheets Design:	Jemima Taltavull
Proofreading:	Vic Ford Kristin Hicks Jacky Henderson
Family Version Website:	Gareth Burgess Jacky Henderson
Promotional Video:	Esther Tester Courtney Gibson

www.ingramcontent.com/pod-product-compliance
Lightning Source LLC
Chambersburg PA
CBHW080847010526
44114CB00017B/2387